OSINT for Deep & Dark Web. Techniques for Cybercrime Investigations

Algoryth Ryker

The internet as we know it is just the surface of a vast digital ocean. Beneath the indexed pages of search engines lies the Deep Web—a hidden network of unindexed databases, academic archives, and private networks. But beyond that, shrouded in layers of encryption and anonymity, lurks the Dark Web, a hidden ecosystem that hosts illicit marketplaces, cybercriminal forums, ransomware groups, and other covert activities.

For open-source intelligence (OSINT) analysts, understanding the deep and dark web is essential for tracking cybercriminals, monitoring data breaches, investigating ransomware threats, and identifying emerging cyber risks. However, navigating this clandestine world requires a blend of technical expertise, advanced investigative techniques, and strict operational security (OPSEC) measures to avoid exposing oneself to malicious actors.

This book demystifies the Deep Web and Dark Web, guiding you through the technologies that power them—such as Tor, I2P, and anonymous marketplaces—while equipping you with practical OSINT techniques for cybercrime investigations. You will learn how to track cryptocurrency transactions, analyze leaked data dumps, unmask threat actors, and expose coordinated cybercriminal activities.

From real-world case studies to cutting-edge OSINT tools, this book serves as a practical field manual for analysts, law enforcement officers, cybersecurity professionals, and researchers. Whether you are investigating ransomware gangs, darknet marketplaces, cybercriminal communication networks, or state-sponsored hacking groups, this book will provide the knowledge and tools necessary to conduct effective and ethical investigations in the most hidden corners of the internet.

Welcome to the frontier of Dark Web OSINT.

Chapter Breakdown

1. Understanding the Deep Web vs. Dark Web

Before diving into investigations, it's crucial to separate fact from fiction. This chapter covers:

- What really exists in the Deep Web and how it differs from the Dark Web.
- The legal and illegal uses of the Dark Web.
- How law enforcement and researchers track cyber threats in this hidden space.
- **Case Study**: A high-profile Dark Web operation exposed.

2. Tor, I2P & Other Anonymity Networks

Understanding how criminals stay hidden is key to unmasking them. This chapter explores:

- How Tor, I2P, and other networks work to anonymize users.
- Secure ways to access the Dark Web without compromising OPSEC.
- How intelligence agencies have successfully de-anonymized criminal actors.
- **Case Study**: How law enforcement infiltrated and took down a Tor hidden service.

3. Accessing Dark Web Marketplaces & Forums

Criminal trade thrives in darknet marketplaces. This chapter teaches:

- How illicit goods and services are bought and sold.
- Techniques to monitor and investigate underground cybercrime forums.
- How marketplaces maintain their reputations and evade law enforcement.
- **Case Study**: How an OSINT analyst infiltrated a Dark Web drug market.

4. Investigating Onion Sites & Hidden Services

To track illicit activity, you need to know how hidden services function:

- The structure of Onion sites and how to analyze them.
- OSINT tools for mapping hidden services.
- Techniques to identify mirror sites and market relocations.
- **Case Study**: Exposing a Dark Web administrator's identity.

5. Cryptocurrency & Blockchain Tracking for OSINT

Cryptocurrency fuels the Dark Web economy. This chapter covers:

- How Bitcoin and altcoins are used in illicit transactions.
- Tools for tracking crypto transactions and laundering schemes.
- Blockchain forensics: tracing illegal funds.
- **Case Study**: Following the money trail of a darknet fraudster.

6. Identifying Threat Actors in the Dark Web

OSINT methods for profiling cybercriminals:

- How threat actors build digital personas.
- Patterns in criminal communication and tradecraft.
- Connecting Dark Web activity to real-world identities.
- **Case Study**: Unmasking a fraud ring operating in multiple marketplaces.

7. Monitoring Dark Web Breaches & Leaks

Data breaches fuel identity theft and cybercrime. Learn how to:

- Investigate leaked credentials, databases, and corporate data dumps.
- Use OSINT tools to track compromised information.
- Understand how cybercriminals monetize stolen data.
- **Case Study**: Investigating a massive data breach on the Dark Web.

8. Cybercriminal Communication Channels & OPSEC

Threat actors rely on secure communication. This chapter covers:

- Encrypted messaging apps, private forums, and PGP encryption.
- How law enforcement monitors criminal communication channels.
- The challenges of decrypting messages and tracking conversations.
- **Case Study**: A cybercriminal's OPSEC mistakes lead to their downfall.

9. Investigating Ransomware & Extortion Groups

Ransomware is one of the biggest cyber threats today. Learn to:

- Track ransomware-as-a-service (RaaS) operations.
- Investigate ransomware wallets and payments.
- Understand how extortion groups pressure victims.
- **Case Study**: Analyzing a high-profile ransomware attack.

10. Dark Web Market Shutdowns & Law Enforcement Cases

Major takedowns reveal how darknet markets operate. Topics include:

- The Silk Road, AlphaBay, and Hansa shutdowns.
- How authorities conduct large-scale Dark Web operations.
- Challenges in prosecuting cybercriminals.

- **Case Study**: Inside a law enforcement Dark Web bust.

11. Legal & Ethical Considerations for Dark Web OSINT

Navigating the legal landscape of OSINT investigations:

- Legal risks of accessing Dark Web content.
- The fine line between surveillance and investigation.
- Best practices for ethical OSINT research.
- **Case Study**: When an OSINT investigation crossed ethical boundaries.

12. Case Study: A Dark Web Criminal Investigation

A full real-world investigation, covering:

- How OSINT tools were used to gather intelligence.
- Challenges in tracking anonymous cybercriminals.
- The role of cryptocurrency tracing in identifying suspects.
- Lessons learned for future Dark Web investigations.

Final Thoughts: Mastering Dark Web OSINT

This book will equip you with the knowledge, tools, and strategies to navigate and investigate one of the most secretive parts of the internet. Whether you're an OSINT analyst, cybersecurity expert, journalist, or law enforcement officer, mastering these techniques is critical for tracking cybercriminals, protecting digital assets, and exposing hidden threats in the ever-evolving cyber landscape.

Are you ready to uncover what lies beneath?

1. Understanding the Deep Web vs. Dark Web

In this chapter, we will explore the critical distinction between the Deep Web and the Dark Web, two vast and often misunderstood sections of the internet. While the Deep Web contains all the content that isn't indexed by traditional search engines—such as private databases, password-protected sites, and academic archives—the Dark Web is a hidden part of the Deep Web that requires specialized tools, like Tor, to access. This secluded space is infamous for its association with illicit activities, including cybercrime, but it also hosts anonymous communication platforms and private forums. Understanding the boundaries and interactions between these layers is essential for effective OSINT (Open Source Intelligence) gathering in cybercrime investigations.

1.1 What is the Deep Web? Myths vs. Reality

The internet is often described as a vast ocean of information, and within this ocean, there exists a deep, dark expanse—an area far beneath the surface that most users never encounter. This hidden territory is often referred to as the "Deep Web." While it has become a topic of fascination, the Deep Web is frequently misunderstood, and many myths have emerged about its purpose, structure, and content. In this sub-chapter, we aim to define the Deep Web, dispel common misconceptions, and separate fact from fiction.

What is the Deep Web?

The Deep Web refers to the portion of the internet that is not indexed by traditional search engines such as Google, Bing, or Yahoo. Unlike the "Surface Web," which consists of publicly accessible websites that are indexed by search engines, the Deep Web is made up of sites, databases, and services that are intentionally hidden from the public. This includes anything that is behind a login or paywall, such as:

- **Private databases**: Examples include academic research databases, government archives, and subscription-based services that store sensitive data.
- **Password-protected websites**: Many websites, including email platforms, banking sites, and internal company networks, require authentication to access, making them part of the Deep Web.
- **Online private forums and communities**: These can be encrypted and invite-only spaces where sensitive conversations or activities take place.

- **Medical records, legal documents, and corporate data**: Information stored on private servers, including personal health records and legal proceedings, is often part of the Deep Web.

In short, the Deep Web represents all online content that is not accessible via a simple web search. The majority of the internet is made up of this hidden content, and it is estimated that the Deep Web is far larger than the publicly visible Surface Web.

Myths vs. Reality

While the term "Deep Web" may seem mysterious, it is important to separate it from its more notorious counterpart—the Dark Web. However, confusion surrounding the two has led to a series of myths about the Deep Web. Let's take a closer look at some of these misconceptions and the reality behind them.

Myth 1: The Deep Web is synonymous with the Dark Web.

One of the most common myths is that the Deep Web and the Dark Web are the same. In reality, the Deep Web is simply the part of the internet that isn't indexed by traditional search engines, which includes a wide variety of legitimate, everyday resources. In contrast, the Dark Web is a small, intentionally hidden subset of the Deep Web. It requires specific software, such as Tor (The Onion Router) or I2P (Invisible Internet Project), to access, and is often associated with illegal or illicit activities, including cybercrime, the sale of contraband, and illegal services.

While the Dark Web certainly exists within the larger framework of the Deep Web, it only represents a small, often criminal, portion of it. Most of the Deep Web consists of private data, secure communication systems, and other valuable but legal resources. Thus, the majority of the Deep Web is not a haven for criminals, as many believe.

Myth 2: The Deep Web is only for criminals.

Another widespread myth is that the Deep Web is an online world solely inhabited by criminals and illicit activities. While the Dark Web does contain its share of criminal activity, the Deep Web itself is home to a vast range of legitimate, valuable content. In fact, many organizations, universities, and governments rely on the Deep Web to store sensitive data securely. Examples of legitimate uses of the Deep Web include:

- **Research databases**: Universities and academic institutions often store research papers and studies in private, unindexed databases that can only be accessed by those with proper credentials. These repositories are part of the Deep Web but are not inherently illegal or dangerous.

- **Private financial services**: Online banking systems, investment platforms, and insurance portals are also housed in the Deep Web to protect the privacy of users and their sensitive financial data.
- **Medical records**: Hospitals, clinics, and healthcare organizations often use private portals to store patient records. These portals are not accessible via regular search engines but are crucial for safeguarding personal health information.

While it's true that the Dark Web can be a space for illicit activity, the Deep Web, in its entirety, is an essential part of modern society's digital infrastructure. Many aspects of online security, privacy, and professional communication depend on the Deep Web to ensure confidentiality.

Myth 3: Anyone can access the Deep Web easily.

There's a pervasive belief that the Deep Web is an exclusive or secretive realm, only accessible to tech-savvy individuals or those with special knowledge. While it's true that parts of the Deep Web require specific credentials (such as a username and password) to access, the vast majority of it is simply "hidden" behind the structure of the internet, not intentionally restricted. As a result, anyone can access the Deep Web, but it's important to note that many of its resources are not intended for general public use.

For example, academic databases require a university login or subscription to access, while online banking portals require account credentials. Access to many sections of the Deep Web, therefore, is restricted to specific groups or individuals based on the nature of the content.

However, accessing certain parts of the Dark Web, such as hidden websites using the Tor network, is more complicated and often requires specialized software or knowledge. This is where a clear distinction must be made: while anyone with a legitimate reason to access private data or databases can do so, engaging with the Dark Web requires intentional actions that often involve anonymity tools and may expose users to legal and security risks.

Myth 4: The Deep Web is only dangerous.

Many people believe that the Deep Web is inherently dangerous, teeming with hackers, scammers, and malware. While there is some truth to the fact that the Dark Web hosts illegal activities, the Deep Web itself is not inherently dangerous. It's important to distinguish between the two areas.

The Deep Web houses critical services for the functioning of many institutions, including government operations, corporate infrastructure, and private communication channels. When used appropriately, the Deep Web allows users to conduct research, manage sensitive information, and access secure services. These activities are integral to the modern digital landscape and do not pose a direct threat to users unless they intentionally engage with malicious or illegal content.

However, just like any other part of the internet, the Deep Web requires caution. Unregulated spaces, especially in the Dark Web, can host malicious actors, phishing scams, and other digital threats. But for the majority of users, the Deep Web is simply a tool to maintain privacy and security online, rather than a "dangerous" environment.

The Deep Web is an essential and often misunderstood part of the internet. While it's frequently confused with the Dark Web, the reality is that the Deep Web encompasses a wide variety of hidden resources that serve legal, private, and institutional needs. The myths surrounding the Deep Web often stem from its association with the Dark Web and its general inaccessibility, but it is crucial to recognize the importance of this space for personal privacy, secure data storage, and research.

Understanding the difference between myths and reality about the Deep Web helps demystify it, allowing us to appreciate its value in today's digital ecosystem. As we continue to explore the digital age, understanding the Deep Web's role in information security, privacy, and research will only become more vital for OSINT analysts, cybersecurity experts, and everyday internet users alike.

1.2 How the Dark Web Differs from the Deep Web

The terms Deep Web and Dark Web are often used interchangeably, but they represent vastly different parts of the internet. While both are hidden from traditional search engines, their purpose, structure, and accessibility differ significantly. The Deep Web encompasses a broad range of legitimate, everyday online content that requires authentication or is otherwise not indexed by search engines. The Dark Web, on the other hand, is a small, intentionally concealed portion of the Deep Web that requires specialized tools, such as Tor or I2P, to access. This chapter will clarify the distinctions between the two, examine their respective uses, and debunk common misconceptions.

1. The Deep Web: A Hidden But Essential Part of the Internet

The Deep Web refers to all content that is not indexed by search engines like Google, Bing, or Yahoo. This includes password-protected websites, internal company databases, medical records, financial data, and private academic research repositories. Essentially, anything that requires a login or specific permissions to access falls under the Deep Web.

Key Features of the Deep Web:

- **Not Indexed by Search Engines**: Deep Web pages cannot be found via traditional search engine queries because they are behind login portals or private databases.
- **Legitimate and Secure**: The vast majority of Deep Web content consists of everyday online activities like checking emails, accessing online banking, or viewing subscription-based content.
- **Private and Restricted Access**: Unlike public websites, Deep Web content is accessible only to specific users with the right credentials.

Examples of Deep Web Content:

- **Email accounts (Gmail, Outlook, etc.)** – Your inbox is not indexed or searchable via Google.
- **Online banking and financial services** – Transactions, statements, and account details remain private.
- **Corporate intranets** – Internal company portals for employees.
- **Medical records and academic databases** – Hospitals, universities, and research institutions keep sensitive data on private servers.
- **Government databases** – Tax records, legal documents, and classified reports stored in secure systems.

The Deep Web makes up the majority of the internet—some estimates suggest that over 90% of all web content exists in the Deep Web. It is not illegal or secretive; rather, it is a necessary part of modern digital infrastructure.

2. The Dark Web: A Hidden Network with Anonymity

The Dark Web is a small subset of the Deep Web that is intentionally hidden and requires specialized software to access. Unlike the Deep Web, which primarily consists of private but legal information, the Dark Web is often associated with anonymity, privacy, and illicit activities. Websites on the Dark Web are not accessible through standard browsers like

Chrome or Firefox. Instead, users must use anonymity-focused networks such as Tor (The Onion Router) or I2P (Invisible Internet Project) to gain access.

Key Features of the Dark Web:

- **Requires Special Software to Access**: Unlike the Deep Web, which includes password-protected sites accessible through normal browsers, Dark Web sites require anonymization tools like Tor or I2P.
- **.onion and .i2p Domains**: Instead of traditional domain extensions like .com or .org, Dark Web sites use domains like .onion (Tor network) and .i2p (I2P network) that are not recognized by normal search engines.
- **High Anonymity**: Users and website operators take extensive measures to remain anonymous by using encryption, VPNs, and cryptocurrency transactions.
- **Contains Both Legal and Illegal Activities**: While some use the Dark Web for privacy-focused purposes, such as whistleblowing or circumvention of censorship, others exploit its anonymity for criminal activities, including the sale of illegal goods, hacking services, and drug trafficking.

Examples of Dark Web Content:

- **Darknet Marketplaces** – Websites selling illicit goods such as drugs, counterfeit documents, and hacking tools.
- **Cybercriminal Forums** – Communities where hackers exchange stolen data, malware, and hacking techniques.
- **Whistleblowing Platforms** – Secure, anonymous platforms where individuals share sensitive information (e.g., WikiLeaks).
- **Censored News and Activism** – Journalists and political activists use the Dark Web to report sensitive information in countries with heavy censorship.

The Dark Web is often portrayed as entirely criminal, but this is misleading. While illegal marketplaces exist, the Dark Web also serves legitimate purposes, including providing secure communication for journalists, human rights activists, and individuals living under oppressive regimes.

3. Key Differences Between the Deep Web and the Dark Web

Feature	Deep Web	Dark Web
Accessibility	Accessible with login credentials or paywalls.	Requires special software (Tor, I2P) to access.
Search Engine Indexing	Not indexed but accessible via normal browsers.	Not indexed and requires direct URLs or directories.
Legality	Completely legal. Contains private but legitimate data.	Contains both legal and illegal content.
Use Cases	Banking, email, subscription sites, government databases.	Anonymous browsing, illicit marketplaces, activism.
Security & Privacy	Secure, but standard web tracking applies.	High anonymity, often encrypted transactions.

4. Myths About the Dark Web and Deep Web

Myth #1: The Dark Web and the Deep Web Are the Same Thing

Reality: The Deep Web is much larger and includes ordinary private content like emails, banking portals, and academic journals. The Dark Web is a much smaller, intentionally hidden portion requiring special software to access.

Myth #2: The Deep Web and Dark Web Are Illegal

Reality: The Deep Web is entirely legal and essential for internet functionality. The Dark Web contains both legal and illegal activities—not everything there is criminal.

Myth #3: The Dark Web Is Impossible to Track

Reality: While users attempt to remain anonymous, law enforcement agencies use OSINT (Open Source Intelligence), blockchain tracking, and infiltration tactics to monitor and shut down illegal Dark Web activities.

Myth #4: Accessing the Dark Web Will Get You in Trouble

Reality: Simply accessing the Dark Web is not illegal in most countries. However, engaging in criminal activities (e.g., buying illegal goods, hacking) is illegal and can lead to severe legal consequences.

5. Why OSINT Investigators Need to Understand Both

For OSINT (Open Source Intelligence) analysts and cybercrime investigators, understanding the differences between the Deep Web and the Dark Web is critical. While much of the useful intelligence can be found on the Deep Web (such as private forums, leaked documents, and databases), serious cybercriminal activities often originate from the Dark Web.

- Investigators use Deep Web resources to gather intelligence on individuals, financial transactions, and corporate activities.
- Dark Web investigations focus on cybercrime, including tracking ransomware gangs, darknet marketplaces, and underground hacking forums.
- Blockchain analysis is often used to trace cryptocurrency transactions linked to illegal Dark Web activities.

By distinguishing between these two layers of the internet, OSINT professionals can leverage different investigative techniques to track down threat actors, gather intelligence, and assist law enforcement efforts.

The Deep Web and Dark Web serve very different purposes, yet they are frequently confused. While the Deep Web is a fundamental part of the internet that houses private but lawful content, the Dark Web is a hidden, anonymous network that contains both legitimate and illicit activities. Understanding the distinction between the two is crucial for cybercrime investigators, researchers, and security professionals.

By shedding light on these often-misunderstood areas of the internet, we can navigate them more effectively, conduct ethical OSINT investigations, and use intelligence-gathering techniques to track criminal activities while protecting privacy and security.

1.3 Common Uses of the Dark Web: Legal & Illegal

The Dark Web is one of the most misunderstood areas of the internet. It is often portrayed in the media as a lawless digital underworld where cybercriminals conduct illicit activities beyond the reach of law enforcement. While this portrayal is not entirely inaccurate, it does not tell the full story. The Dark Web is also used for legal and ethical purposes, including secure communication, protecting privacy, and circumventing government censorship.

This chapter explores the common uses of the Dark Web, both legal and illegal, providing a balanced understanding of its role in cybersecurity, digital privacy, and cybercrime investigations.

1. Legal Uses of the Dark Web

Despite its reputation, not all activity on the Dark Web is illegal. Many individuals, organizations, and even governments use it for privacy-focused and ethical purposes. Below are some of the legitimate ways the Dark Web is used.

1.1 Anonymous Browsing for Privacy Protection

Many people use the Dark Web to browse the internet anonymously, protecting themselves from surveillance, censorship, or tracking by corporations and governments. This is particularly useful in countries with strict internet censorship or where freedom of speech is restricted.

- **Whistleblowers and Journalists** – Secure platforms like SecureDrop and ProPublica's Dark Web site allow journalists to communicate with anonymous sources safely.
- **Political Dissidents** – Activists and individuals living under oppressive regimes use the Dark Web to access information and organize without fear of government retaliation.
- **Privacy Advocates** – Individuals concerned about corporate surveillance and data collection use the Dark Web to keep their activities hidden from third parties.

1.2 Circumventing Censorship & Accessing Restricted Content

Many countries heavily restrict or monitor internet access, limiting access to certain websites and online services. The Dark Web provides a workaround for those seeking uncensored information.

- Citizens in China, Iran, North Korea, and Russia use the Dark Web to access banned websites like Google, Facebook, or independent news outlets.
- The Tor network enables users to bypass government-imposed firewalls and access blocked content anonymously.

1.3 Secure Communication & Confidentiality

The Dark Web provides a safe environment for encrypted communication, reducing the risk of interception. Secure messaging platforms are often used by:

- Military and intelligence agencies for secure operations.
- Human rights activists to discuss sensitive topics without being tracked.
- Business professionals and researchers who need secure channels for communication in high-risk industries.

1.4 Legitimate Marketplaces and Services

While Dark Web marketplaces are often associated with illegal goods, there are also legal marketplaces that cater to privacy-conscious consumers. Some examples include:

- Privacy-focused email providers (e.g., ProtonMail's Dark Web service).
- Legal e-books, academic papers, and open-source software.
- Cybersecurity tools and services that are used for legitimate penetration testing and security research.

Example: Facebook launched a .onion site to provide access to users in regions where it is blocked.

2. Illegal Uses of the Dark Web

While there are legal and ethical uses of the Dark Web, a significant portion of its activity involves illegal and criminal activities. The anonymity and lack of regulation make it an attractive hub for cybercriminals, hackers, and organized crime networks.

2.1 Darknet Marketplaces: Illegal Goods & Services

Darknet marketplaces are one of the most well-known illegal uses of the Dark Web. These hidden sites facilitate the sale of:

- **Drugs** – Darknet markets such as Silk Road, AlphaBay, and Hydra have facilitated large-scale drug transactions.
- **Weapons** – Firearms, explosives, and other weapons are sold through black market vendors.
- **Fake Documents & Identity Theft** – Criminals sell counterfeit passports, driver's licenses, and stolen personal data for identity fraud.
- **Stolen Credit Card Information** – Carding forums provide access to stolen financial data for fraud.

Example: The shutdown of Silk Road in 2013 led to the arrest of its creator, Ross Ulbricht, but many alternative markets emerged to take its place.

2.2 Cybercrime & Hacking Services

The Dark Web is a hub for hackers, cybercriminals, and cyber warfare operations. The anonymity it provides allows for the buying and selling of hacking services, malware, and exploits.

- **Ransomware-as-a-Service (RaaS)** – Cybercriminals rent ransomware kits to carry out attacks on businesses and individuals.
- **DDoS-for-Hire Services** – Dark Web sites offer Distributed Denial of Service (DDoS) attacks to take down websites for a fee.
- **Zero-Day Exploits** – Hackers sell vulnerabilities in software before they are patched.
- **Botnets & Malware** – Cybercriminals use botnets to carry out attacks and spread malware like keyloggers and banking Trojans.

Example: The REvil ransomware gang used the Dark Web to communicate with victims, sell stolen data, and demand cryptocurrency payments.

2.3 Human Trafficking & Exploitation

One of the most disturbing aspects of the Dark Web is its use for human trafficking, child exploitation, and illegal pornography. Law enforcement agencies around the world work to identify and shut down these sites, but they frequently reappear under new names.

- Illegal pornography and abuse forums.
- Child exploitation networks like Playpen (shut down by the FBI in 2015).
- Human trafficking rings that sell people for forced labor or other crimes.

2.4 Dark Web Hitmen & Assassination Services (Mostly a Myth)

The idea of hiring a hitman on the Dark Web has been sensationalized in pop culture, but in reality, most of these sites are scams. Many so-called assassination services take payment but never deliver on their "service."

Example: The infamous "Besa Mafia" site claimed to offer contract killings but was later exposed as a scam.

2.5 Terrorist Organizations & Extremist Networks

Terrorist organizations use the Dark Web for recruitment, communication, and propaganda. Some extremist groups use hidden forums to plan attacks, recruit members, and distribute illegal materials.

- Encrypted messaging services allow terrorist cells to communicate without being traced.
- ISIS and other extremist groups have used the Dark Web for funding and propaganda.

3. The Role of Law Enforcement in Dark Web Investigations

Given the scale of illegal activity on the Dark Web, law enforcement agencies worldwide have developed sophisticated techniques to track criminals operating within it.

- **Undercover Operations** – Agents infiltrate marketplaces and forums to gather intelligence.
- **Blockchain Analysis** – Cryptocurrencies like Bitcoin and Monero are commonly used on the Dark Web, but investigators use blockchain tracking tools to trace transactions.
- **Seizures & Takedowns** – Governments regularly shut down illegal Dark Web sites (e.g., Operation Onymous, which took down multiple marketplaces).

Example: In 2021, Operation Dark HunTor led to the arrest of 150 individuals involved in Dark Web drug trafficking.

The Dark Web is not inherently illegal, but it is often misused by criminals due to its anonymity. While it serves legitimate purposes for privacy, free speech, and cybersecurity, it also harbors cybercriminals, drug traffickers, hackers, and terrorist networks. Understanding both the legal and illegal uses of the Dark Web is critical for OSINT analysts, cybersecurity professionals, and law enforcement working to track cyber threats and criminal activities.

As we dive deeper into Dark Web investigations, it's essential to stay informed, cautious, and ethical in our approach, ensuring that intelligence-gathering is used for lawful and constructive purposes.

1.4 Key Threats & Risks in the Dark Web

The Dark Web is a double-edged sword—while it provides a space for anonymity, free speech, and privacy, it also presents significant threats and risks. This hidden layer of the internet is home to cybercriminals, illicit marketplaces, hacking forums, and underground networks that pose dangers not just to individuals but also to businesses, governments, and law enforcement.

In this chapter, we will explore the major threats and risks associated with the Dark Web, ranging from cybercrime and data breaches to financial fraud and personal security risks. Understanding these dangers is crucial for OSINT investigators, cybersecurity professionals, and law enforcement officers involved in Dark Web intelligence gathering and cybercrime investigations.

1. Cybercrime & Financial Fraud

The Dark Web is a breeding ground for cybercriminal activity, where stolen data, hacking tools, and illegal financial services are openly traded. Below are some of the most common threats:

1.1 Stolen Data & Identity Theft

Dark Web marketplaces and forums frequently sell stolen credentials, personal information, and identity documents. This includes:

- Leaked usernames and passwords from data breaches.
- Credit card and banking information used for financial fraud.
- Social Security numbers (SSNs), passports, and driver's licenses for identity theft.
- Medical records and insurance details, which can be exploited for fraudulent claims.

Example: After a major corporate breach, cybercriminals often list stolen data on Dark Web forums, allowing fraudsters to purchase and exploit personal and financial information.

1.2 Dark Web Financial Fraud & Money Laundering

The Dark Web facilitates money laundering, financial fraud, and untraceable transactions through various methods, including:

- Cryptocurrency laundering using services like mixing/tumbling to obscure transaction origins.
- Fake investment schemes promising high returns.
- Carding forums, where cybercriminals buy and sell stolen credit card details.

Example: The Hydra darknet marketplace specialized in money laundering services before it was taken down by law enforcement in 2022.

2. Malware, Ransomware & Hacking Threats

2.1 Ransomware-as-a-Service (RaaS)

Ransomware gangs use the Dark Web to sell and distribute ransomware kits, allowing cybercriminals to launch attacks without technical expertise. These services are known as Ransomware-as-a-Service (RaaS) and include:

- Pre-configured ransomware tools that encrypt victims' data.
- Payment and negotiation portals where victims can pay ransoms in cryptocurrency.
- Affiliate programs, where criminals share profits with ransomware developers.

Example: The REvil ransomware group operated via the Dark Web, selling ransomware to affiliates who launched attacks on businesses and critical infrastructure.

2.2 Hacking Services & Exploit Markets

The Dark Web is home to hacking forums where cybercriminals buy and sell:

- Zero-day exploits for vulnerabilities in software.
- Phishing kits to steal credentials.
- DDoS-for-hire services, which can take down websites and networks.
- Remote Access Trojans (RATs), allowing attackers to control infected computers.

Example: The Exploit.in forum was a well-known Dark Web hub where hackers traded stolen credentials and hacking tools before being shut down.

2.3 Malware Distribution & Botnets

- Malware developers sell keyloggers, Trojans, and spyware to cybercriminals.

- Botnets, which are networks of infected computers, are rented out for large-scale cyberattacks.
- Dark Web forums provide malware tutorials and hacking guides to aspiring cybercriminals.

Example: The Emotet botnet, one of the most dangerous malware networks, was partially controlled through Dark Web communications before being dismantled by law enforcement.

3. Dark Web Marketplaces & Illegal Trade

3.1 Illicit Goods & Services

Dark Web marketplaces operate like Amazon or eBay but sell illegal goods, including:

- Drugs & counterfeit pharmaceuticals (e.g., fentanyl, LSD, counterfeit medications).
- Weapons & explosives for criminal organizations.
- Counterfeit money and forged documents.

Example: The infamous Silk Road marketplace facilitated billions of dollars in drug transactions before being shut down by the FBI.

3.2 Human Trafficking & Exploitation

One of the most disturbing threats on the Dark Web is human trafficking and child exploitation, including:

- Illegal pornography and abuse forums.
- Sex trafficking networks operating in underground communities.
- Online black markets selling kidnapped individuals for forced labor or organ trafficking.

Law enforcement agencies worldwide work aggressively to track and dismantle these networks using OSINT techniques and undercover operations.

4. Terrorism, Extremism & Organized Crime

4.1 Terrorist Recruitment & Propaganda

Terrorist organizations use the Dark Web for:

- Recruitment & training of extremists.
- Propaganda distribution, including violent materials.
- Encrypted communications for planning attacks.

Example: ISIS used the Dark Web to communicate securely and distribute propaganda materials, making it difficult for intelligence agencies to track their activities.

4.2 Organized Crime Networks

Organized crime syndicates use the Dark Web to:

- Launder money through cryptocurrency transactions.
- Buy and sell illegal weapons, drugs, and fake IDs.
- Operate fraud rings, including scams, extortion, and blackmail schemes.

5. Personal Security & Privacy Risks

Even legitimate users who access the Dark Web face risks. Journalists, researchers, and law enforcement officials must take extreme precautions to avoid being exposed.

5.1 Deanonymization & Tracking Risks

Despite its anonymity, the Dark Web is not completely private:

- Law enforcement agencies monitor illegal activity.
- Cybercriminals track users and attempt to dox (expose their identity).
- Malicious websites deploy tracking scripts to collect user information.

Example: FBI operations like Operation Onymous successfully infiltrated and shut down multiple Dark Web sites by tracking administrator activities.

5.2 Scams & Fraudulent Services

Many Dark Web services are scams, including:

- Fake hitman services that take payments but never deliver.
- Bitcoin investment schemes that steal funds from unsuspecting buyers.
- Phishing attacks that steal Dark Web users' credentials.

Example: The "Besa Mafia" hitman-for-hire service was exposed as a scam designed to steal Bitcoin from users.

6. Law Enforcement Strategies & OSINT Investigations

Governments and law enforcement agencies worldwide actively monitor and investigate the Dark Web using advanced OSINT techniques:

- Blockchain analysis to trace cryptocurrency transactions.
- Undercover infiltration of Dark Web forums and markets.
- Automated scraping tools to collect intelligence on illicit activities.

Example: The takedown of the AlphaBay marketplace in 2017 was one of the largest Dark Web investigations, led by the FBI and Europol.

The Dark Web presents significant risks, from financial fraud and cybercrime to terrorism and human trafficking. While it serves as a tool for privacy advocates, whistleblowers, and journalists, it is also exploited by criminals for illegal activities.

For OSINT analysts, cybersecurity experts, and law enforcement, understanding these threats is essential for tracking cybercriminals, identifying threats, and securing digital intelligence. As Dark Web activity evolves, so must investigative strategies and ethical considerations in combating its dangers.

1.5 How Law Enforcement & Researchers Monitor the Dark Web

The Dark Web is often perceived as a lawless digital underground, but in reality, law enforcement agencies and cybersecurity researchers have developed sophisticated techniques to monitor, infiltrate, and investigate its hidden corners. Despite the anonymity provided by networks like Tor and I2P, cybercriminals leave digital footprints that can be tracked using Open-Source Intelligence (OSINT), blockchain analysis, undercover operations, and advanced monitoring tools.

In this chapter, we explore how law enforcement and cybersecurity researchers monitor the Dark Web, the methods they use to track illicit activities, and the challenges they face in their investigations.

1. Key Challenges in Monitoring the Dark Web

Before diving into monitoring techniques, it's important to understand the challenges law enforcement and researchers face when investigating the Dark Web:

1.1 Anonymity & Encryption

- Dark Web users hide their identities using Tor, I2P, and VPNs.
- Communications and transactions are encrypted, making it difficult to track participants.
- Cryptocurrencies like Monero provide an additional layer of financial anonymity.

1.2 Constant Evolution & Market Shifts

- When a Dark Web marketplace or forum is shut down, new ones quickly emerge.
- Admins & sellers migrate to new platforms, requiring constant adaptation in investigations.

1.3 Jurisdiction & Legal Barriers

- Many Dark Web servers are hosted in different countries, complicating jurisdictional enforcement.
- Some governments have limited legal frameworks to prosecute cybercrimes originating on the Dark Web.

Despite these challenges, law enforcement and cybersecurity professionals employ a variety of advanced techniques to track, infiltrate, and dismantle Dark Web criminal networks.

2. Law Enforcement Monitoring Techniques

Law enforcement agencies worldwide, including the FBI, Europol, Interpol, and local cybercrime units, use multiple strategies to monitor and disrupt illegal activities on the Dark Web.

2.1 Undercover Operations & Human Intelligence (HUMINT)

- Agents infiltrate Dark Web marketplaces & forums by posing as buyers, sellers, or hackers.

- Undercover officers engage with cybercriminals to gather intelligence and track transactions.
- Covert communication with informants provides insider information.

Example: The FBI infiltrated Silk Road by posing as drug buyers, eventually leading to the arrest of its founder, Ross Ulbricht.

2.2 Blockchain & Cryptocurrency Tracking

- Cryptocurrency transactions leave digital trails, even when using privacy coins like Monero.
- Law enforcement agencies use blockchain analysis tools (e.g., Chainalysis, CipherTrace, Elliptic) to trace illicit transactions.
- Investigators track crypto wallets linked to Dark Web markets and link them to real-world identities.

Example: The AlphaBay marketplace was shut down in 2017 after investigators followed Bitcoin transactions tied to the site's administrator.

2.3 Dark Web Crawler Bots & Automated Scraping

- Law enforcement agencies use automated web crawlers to index hidden websites, marketplaces, and forums.
- Web scraping tools collect intelligence from Dark Web discussions, user profiles, and advertisements.
- AI-powered tools detect suspicious activities such as the sale of stolen data, drugs, or weapons.

Example: Europol's Dark Web monitoring unit continuously scans and tracks emerging criminal marketplaces.

2.4 Seizing & Taking Down Dark Web Marketplaces

- Law enforcement targets Dark Web servers, domain providers, and administrators to dismantle criminal operations.
- Joint international operations seize and shut down illegal sites.
- Tracking forum administrators through operational security (OPSEC) mistakes can lead to arrests.

Example:

- **Operation Onymous (2014):** FBI and Europol seized multiple Dark Web marketplaces.
- **Dark HunTor (2021):** Led to 150 arrests and the seizure of 500+ darknet market accounts.

3. Cybersecurity Researchers & OSINT Monitoring Techniques

Cybersecurity researchers and OSINT (Open-Source Intelligence) analysts play a crucial role in monitoring the Dark Web to track cyber threats, data breaches, and emerging security risks.

3.1 Dark Web Threat Intelligence Platforms

Cybersecurity firms use specialized tools to monitor, index, and analyze Dark Web activity. Popular platforms include:

- **DarkOwl** – Provides real-time tracking of Dark Web marketplaces and forums.
- **Recorded Future** – Uses AI to analyze cybercrime threats.
- **Flashpoint** – Tracks extremist content and cybercriminal activities.

3.2 Monitoring Data Breaches & Leaked Credentials

- Researchers scan Dark Web forums & leak sites for stolen credentials, financial data, and sensitive information.
- Security teams notify organizations & individuals when their data appears in breaches.

Example: The Have I Been Pwned database allows users to check if their credentials have been leaked in a breach.

3.3 Forum & Chatroom Infiltration

- Researchers join hacker forums & Telegram channels to track cybercriminal discussions.
- Social engineering tactics are used to gather intelligence on threat actors.

3.4 Tracking Ransomware Groups & Extortionists

- Cybersecurity analysts track ransomware negotiations on Dark Web forums.

- Intelligence reports identify new ransomware variants & attack strategies.

Example: The REvil ransomware gang used a Dark Web payment portal for victims to pay ransoms.

4. Case Studies: Successful Dark Web Investigations

Case Study 1: Silk Road (2013)

- The FBI infiltrated the Silk Road marketplace and identified Ross Ulbricht as its operator.
- Investigators tracked Bitcoin transactions and linked them to Ulbricht's personal accounts.
- **Result**: Silk Road was shut down, and Ulbricht was sentenced to life in prison.

Case Study 2: AlphaBay & Hansa (2017)

- The FBI and Europol coordinated a takedown of AlphaBay, the largest Dark Web market at the time.
- Authorities secretly took control of Hansa, another marketplace, tricking users into exposing their information.
- **Result**: Thousands of arrests & marketplace shutdowns.

Case Study 3: Welcome To Video (2019)

- A Dark Web child exploitation site was dismantled by global law enforcement.
- Investigators traced Bitcoin transactions to the site's administrator.
- **Result**: Over 300 arrests worldwide & rescue of victims.

5. Ethical & Legal Considerations in Dark Web Monitoring

Monitoring the Dark Web raises ethical and legal concerns, including:

- **Privacy violations** – Researchers must follow legal guidelines to avoid unlawful surveillance.
- **Entrapment risks** – Undercover operations must avoid coercing criminals into illegal actions.
- **Jurisdictional conflicts** – Laws on Dark Web investigations vary by country.

While the Dark Web remains a hub for anonymity and illicit activities, law enforcement agencies and cybersecurity researchers have developed powerful tools and techniques to monitor, investigate, and disrupt illegal operations.

By using undercover infiltration, blockchain analysis, web crawling, and OSINT methods, investigators can track cybercriminals, identify security threats, and prevent illegal activities before they escalate. However, monitoring the Dark Web also requires strong ethical and legal safeguards to ensure investigations remain within the boundaries of law and privacy rights.

As cybercrime evolves, so must Dark Web intelligence strategies, making continuous research and adaptation critical in the fight against digital threats.

1.6 Case Study: High-Profile Cases Involving the Dark Web

The Dark Web has been at the center of several high-profile cybercrime cases, ranging from massive drug marketplaces and sophisticated hacking groups to ransomware gangs and even high-stakes law enforcement takedowns. These cases highlight both the power and dangers of the Dark Web, as well as the evolving tactics used by criminals—and the agencies working to stop them.

This chapter explores some of the most infamous Dark Web cases, revealing how they operated, how they were dismantled, and what lessons law enforcement, cybersecurity professionals, and OSINT investigators can learn from them.

1. The Silk Road – The Dark Web's Most Infamous Marketplace

Overview

- **Founded**: 2011 by Ross Ulbricht (alias "Dread Pirate Roberts")
- **Operations**: An online black market primarily for drugs but also fake IDs, hacking tools, and illegal services.
- **Technology Used**: Operated on Tor for anonymity and used Bitcoin for payments.

How It Worked

- Silk Road functioned like an illicit eBay, allowing users to buy and sell illegal goods with minimal risk of detection.
- Escrow services ensured sellers got paid only after the buyer confirmed delivery.

- Anonymity tools like PGP encryption and multi-layered security kept users hidden.

How It Was Shut Down

- Law enforcement tracked Bitcoin transactions and used OSINT techniques to connect Ross Ulbricht's online alias to real-world activity.
- A key mistake: Ulbricht once used his real email address in a public forum while discussing Silk Road.
- In October 2013, the FBI arrested Ulbricht in a San Francisco library and seized over 144,000 BTC ($3.6 billion in today's value).

Outcome: Ulbricht was convicted and sentenced to life in prison without parole.

Lesson Learned: Even anonymized Dark Web markets have vulnerabilities, and small operational security (OPSEC) mistakes can lead to exposure.

2. AlphaBay & Hansa – A Double Takedown

Overview

- **AlphaBay**: Launched in 2014, it became the largest Dark Web marketplace, surpassing Silk Road.
- **Hansa**: A smaller but well-established market known for drugs, stolen data, and illicit goods.
- **Technology Used**: Tor network, Bitcoin, Monero (for extra anonymity).

How AlphaBay Operated

- AlphaBay was 10 times larger than Silk Road and hosted transactions worth hundreds of millions of dollars.
- It was popular for selling drugs, hacking tools, stolen credit cards, and personal data.
- It offered Monero transactions, which are harder to trace than Bitcoin.

How It Was Shut Down

- In July 2017, the FBI and Europol identified Alexandre Cazes, AlphaBay's creator, by linking his Hotmail email address to a forum post.
- Thai police arrested Cazes, and he was found dead in his prison cell days later (suspected suicide).

- Meanwhile, law enforcement secretly took over Hansa Market for several weeks.
- **Trap Operation**: They monitored Hansa users, collecting evidence and tracking transactions before taking it down.

Outcome

- Over 10,000 darknet users were identified.
- Thousands of arrests followed across different countries.
- AlphaBay and Hansa were completely shut down.

Lesson Learned: Law enforcement can turn Dark Web markets against criminals by infiltrating them before a takedown, leading to mass arrests and intelligence gathering.

3. Welcome to Video – The Largest Child Exploitation Takedown

Overview

- **What It Was**: A Dark Web site hosting over 250,000 videos of child exploitation.
- **Technology Used**: Tor for anonymity, Bitcoin for payments.

How It Was Shut Down

- Authorities traced Bitcoin payments made by users to fund the platform.
- The site's operator, Jong Woo Son from South Korea, was arrested in 2018.
- Law enforcement agencies from 38 countries worked together to track down users, moderators, and distributors.

Outcome

- Over 300 users arrested worldwide.
- 23 minors rescued from abuse situations.
- Bitcoin transactions played a critical role in exposing the site's operators.

Lesson Learned: Cryptocurrency is not entirely anonymous—tracking transactions can lead to identifying criminals, even in Dark Web networks.

4. The REvil Ransomware Gang – Dark Web Extortion at Scale

Overview

- **What It Was**: A major ransomware gang that extorted corporations, government agencies, and even hospitals.
- **Technology Used**: Dark Web sites for ransom negotiations, Monero for payments.

How They Operated

- REvil offered Ransomware-as-a-Service (RaaS), selling ransomware to affiliates who launched attacks.
- Victims had to pay ransoms through Dark Web portals to receive decryption keys.
- High-profile targets included JBS (a major meat supplier) and Kaseya (IT management firm).

How It Was Shut Down

- In 2021, the FBI and Europol infiltrated REvil's servers, leading to arrests and infrastructure shutdowns.
- Law enforcement seized cryptocurrency wallets linked to ransom payments.
- Some REvil members disappeared, while others were captured and prosecuted.

Outcome

- Major REvil members were arrested in Russia, Ukraine, and the U.S..
- The gang's servers were seized and decryption keys were recovered for victims.

Lesson Learned: International law enforcement cooperation and cryptocurrency tracking are key in fighting Dark Web ransomware operations.

5. DarkSide – The Colonial Pipeline Ransomware Attack

Overview

- In May 2021, DarkSide, a Russian-speaking ransomware group, shut down Colonial Pipeline, causing fuel shortages in the U.S.
- The attack was launched using Dark Web ransomware services.

How They Were Stopped

- The U.S. FBI and cybersecurity teams tracked Bitcoin ransom payments made by Colonial Pipeline.
- They seized $2.3 million worth of Bitcoin linked to the attack.

- DarkSide disbanded shortly after due to law enforcement pressure.

Outcome

- U.S. agencies gained access to ransomware wallets and improved ransomware tracking methods.
- Ransomware attacks became a top national security concern.

Lesson Learned: Even highly sophisticated cybercriminals leave financial trails that can be exploited for investigations.

Conclusion: What We Learn from These Cases

The Dark Web is not as untraceable as criminals believe. Law enforcement and cybersecurity experts have proven that mistakes, financial tracking, and infiltration techniques can expose even the most secretive operations.

Key takeaways from these high-profile cases:

✓ OPSEC mistakes can lead to arrests. Small errors, like using a personal email, can be exploited by law enforcement.

✓ Cryptocurrency tracking is a powerful investigative tool. Even privacy-focused coins like Monero have weaknesses.

✓ Dark Web markets are vulnerable to infiltration. Undercover operations can lead to mass arrests.

✓ International cooperation is essential. Most cases involved multiple countries working together.

The Dark Web is constantly evolving, but so are the techniques used to monitor, track, and dismantle illegal operations. Law enforcement agencies and cybersecurity professionals must continue adapting to new threats while ensuring ethical and legal considerations in their investigations.

2. Tor, I2P & Other Anonymity Networks

This chapter delves into the key anonymity networks that allow users to access the Deep and Dark Web while preserving their privacy. Tor (The Onion Router) is the most widely known, offering encrypted browsing by routing traffic through multiple volunteer-operated relays, masking the user's identity and location. Alongside Tor, I2P (Invisible Internet Project) provides an alternative, focusing on secure, anonymous communication within its own network of routers. We will also touch on other lesser-known anonymity tools and protocols that facilitate access to hidden online spaces. Understanding these networks is crucial for anyone involved in OSINT investigations, as they are the primary gateways to the anonymous activities that often reside in the depths of the internet.

2.1 How Tor Works: The Basics of Onion Routing

The Tor network (short for The Onion Router) is a fundamental technology that enables anonymous communication on the internet. It is widely used by privacy-conscious individuals, journalists, activists, and cybercriminals to conceal their identities and activities. Tor's design ensures that users can browse the web, access hidden services, and communicate securely without revealing their IP addresses.

This chapter explains how Tor works, the concept of onion routing, and how law enforcement and researchers analyze Tor-based activities.

1. What is Tor?

Tor is an open-source, decentralized network designed to provide anonymity and privacy online. It allows users to:

✓ Access websites without revealing their IP addresses.

✓ Communicate anonymously using Tor-based messaging and email services.

✓ Host ".onion" sites, also known as hidden services, which are inaccessible via standard web browsers.

Originally developed by the U.S. Naval Research Laboratory in the 1990s, Tor was later made open-source and is now maintained by the Tor Project, a non-profit organization.

2. The Basics of Onion Routing

Tor's onion routing technology is the key to its anonymity. Instead of sending internet traffic directly from the user to the destination, Tor encrypts the data and routes it through multiple volunteer-operated servers (called nodes or relays).

How Onion Routing Works:

Multi-Layered Encryption:

- When a user sends a request (e.g., opening a website), Tor encrypts the data multiple times, wrapping it in layers—like an onion.
- Each layer corresponds to a different Tor relay (node).

Routing Through Random Nodes:

- The encrypted request is sent through three randomly chosen Tor relays before reaching its destination.

These relays are called:

- **Entry (Guard) Node**: The first relay that receives the request from the user.
- **Middle Node**: The second relay that forwards traffic further into the Tor network.
- **Exit Node**: The final relay that decrypts the last layer and sends the request to the actual destination.

Anonymity Through Layered Decryption:

- Each relay only knows the previous and next node but not the entire route.
- The exit node never knows the original sender, ensuring anonymity.

Example of a Tor Connection

⬣ User → [Entry Node] → [Middle Node] → [Exit Node] → Website

- Each node removes one layer of encryption until the exit node sends the request to the final destination.
- Since each node only sees partial information, no single node can fully identify both the user and the destination.

3. Components of the Tor Network

3.1 Tor Nodes (Relays)

Tor operates through thousands of relays, categorized into:

- **Guard (Entry) Nodes** – First point of contact between a user and the Tor network.
- **Middle Relays** – Forward traffic between nodes to prevent traceability.
- **Exit Nodes** – The final relay that connects to the clearnet (regular internet).

3.2 .onion Domains (Hidden Services)

Tor allows users to host anonymous websites with ".onion" domains that are not indexed by standard search engines.

- **Examples**: Dark Web marketplaces, forums, whistleblower sites (e.g., SecureDrop), and cryptocurrency mixing services.

3.3 Bridges & Obfuscated Nodes

- Tor bridges are special entry nodes that help users bypass censorship in countries where Tor is blocked.
- They prevent governments from detecting and blocking Tor traffic.

4. Who Uses Tor?

Tor serves a wide range of users, including:

4.1 Legal & Ethical Use Cases

✓ **Journalists & Whistleblowers** – Use Tor to protect sources and publish information anonymously (e.g., SecureDrop).
✓ **Activists & Human Rights Defenders** – Communicate securely in censored regions.
✓ **Privacy-Conscious Users** – People who don't want ISPs, corporations, or governments tracking them.

4.2 Criminal Uses

✗ **Dark Web Marketplaces** – Selling drugs, weapons, and stolen data.
✗ **Hacker Forums** – Trading exploits, malware, and ransomware services.

✗ **Illegal Financial Activities** – Laundering money through cryptocurrency mixers.

5. Weaknesses & Risks of Using Tor

Despite its anonymity, Tor is not foolproof, and there are vulnerabilities:

▼ **Exit Node Snooping** – Since exit nodes decrypt the final layer of traffic, malicious exit nodes can intercept unencrypted data.
▼ **Correlation Attacks** – If an attacker controls both entry and exit nodes, they can analyze traffic patterns.
▼ **JavaScript & Browser Exploits** – Attackers can inject malicious scripts to de-anonymize users.
▼ **Compromised Tor Nodes** – Law enforcement and intelligence agencies operate some nodes for surveillance.

Law Enforcement's Strategy Against Tor

- **Seizing Hidden Services** – The FBI has successfully taken down Dark Web marketplaces by infiltrating them.
- **Monitoring Exit Nodes** – Agencies monitor exit nodes for illicit activities.
- **Traffic Analysis Attacks** – Identifying patterns of Tor users' activities to uncover their identities.

Tor is a powerful anonymity tool, but it is not untraceable. While it provides strong privacy protection, it also has vulnerabilities that can be exploited by law enforcement, cybersecurity researchers, and intelligence agencies.

For OSINT analysts, understanding how Tor works is crucial in tracking threat actors, cybercriminals, and Dark Web activities while staying aware of the risks involved.

2.2 I2P vs. Tor: Comparing Anonymity Networks

While Tor (The Onion Router) is the most well-known anonymity network, it is not the only one. The Invisible Internet Project (I2P) is another powerful tool for anonymous communication, offering a different approach to privacy and security. Both networks enable users to hide their identities, but they are designed for different purposes.

This chapter explores how I2P and Tor work, their key differences, and which is better suited for specific use cases—from cybercriminal activities to legitimate privacy-focused communications.

1. What is I2P?

The Invisible Internet Project (I2P) is a decentralized, peer-to-peer anonymity network designed for secure and private communications. Unlike Tor, which focuses on anonymous access to the clearnet (regular internet), I2P is primarily used for internal, anonymous services.

Key Features of I2P:

✅ **End-to-End Encryption** – Unlike Tor, I2P encrypts both inbound and outbound traffic, making tracking even harder.

✅ **Decentralized Network** – I2P does not rely on fixed relay nodes; instead, it dynamically selects paths through a distributed peer network.

✅ **No Exit Nodes** – Unlike Tor, I2P traffic does not exit to the regular internet, reducing risks from compromised nodes.

✅ **Anonymous Services** – Websites on I2P (called "eepsites") are similar to Tor's ".onion" sites, but they operate only within the I2P network.

Who Uses I2P?

- Privacy advocates who want fully anonymous communications.
- Darknet forums and marketplaces that prefer deeper anonymity than Tor.
- Cybercriminals looking for less-policed alternatives to Tor.

2. Tor vs. I2P: Technical Differences

Feature	Tor (The Onion Router)	I2P (Invisible Internet Project)
Primary Use	Anonymous web browsing, access to Dark Web (.onion sites)	Internal anonymous communication (.i2p sites)
Architecture	Uses a network of volunteer-run nodes (relays)	Fully decentralized, peer-to-peer routing
Routing Mechanism	Onion Routing (traffic passes through three fixed relays)	Garlic Routing (traffic is bundled and encrypted across multiple routes)
Exit Nodes	Has exit nodes that connect to clearnet	No exit nodes; only internal network use
Encryption	Partial encryption (exit nodes decrypt traffic)	Full end-to-end encryption
Speed	Slower due to limited relays and high traffic	Faster for internal communications
Susceptibility to Attacks	Exit node monitoring, traffic correlation attacks	More resilient against traffic analysis but still vulnerable

3. How I2P Routing Works (Garlic Routing vs. Onion Routing)

Tor uses onion routing, where traffic passes through a fixed three-node path before reaching its destination. I2P, on the other hand, uses garlic routing, which encrypts and bundles multiple messages together before sending them through the network.

Garlic Routing Process (I2P)

- A user's message is divided into multiple encrypted packets.
- These packets are routed through multiple peer-selected tunnels.
- No single node knows the complete path or original sender.
- Response traffic takes a separate, randomized route, increasing anonymity.

This multi-layered encryption and randomization make I2P more resistant to traffic correlation attacks than Tor.

4. Advantages & Disadvantages of Tor and I2P

4.1 Advantages of Tor

✅ **Best for anonymous web browsing** – Can access both clearnet and Dark Web.

✅ **Large, well-established network** – More relays and greater anonymity support.

✅ **Used by law enforcement & OSINT investigators** – Easier to monitor Dark Web activities.

4.2 Disadvantages of Tor

✖ **Exit node vulnerability** – Traffic is decrypted at the exit node, making it possible to track unencrypted data.

✖ **Frequent law enforcement surveillance** – Many Tor nodes are monitored, increasing risks for illicit users.

✖ **Slower performance** – Due to limited bandwidth and high user volume.

4.3 Advantages of I2P

✅ **No exit node risks** – Everything stays within the encrypted I2P network.

✅ **Better resistance to traffic analysis** – Harder for adversaries to track users.

✅ **Faster for internal services** – Since traffic stays inside I2P, it is generally more efficient.

4.4 Disadvantages of I2P

✖ **Limited external access** – Cannot browse clearnet sites directly.

✖ **Smaller network** – Fewer users mean less anonymity compared to Tor.

✖ **More technical setup required** – I2P requires more configuration than Tor.

5. Use Cases: When to Use Tor vs. I2P

Use Case	Best Choice	Reason
Anonymous web browsing	Tor	Allows access to both clearnet and Dark Web
Accessing Dark Web marketplaces	Tor	Most illegal markets operate on .onion sites
Hosting an anonymous website	I2P	More secure due to garlic routing
Secure messaging and file sharing	I2P	Fully decentralized and encrypted end-to-end
Bypassing censorship	Tor	Bridges help bypass internet restrictions
Criminal activity evasion	I2P	Less monitored than Tor, harder for law enforcement to track

6. How Law Enforcement Monitors Tor & I2P

Law enforcement agencies (FBI, Europol, NSA) use various methods to track Dark Web activities on both Tor and I2P:

▼ **Running exit nodes (Tor only)** – Monitoring unencrypted traffic at exit nodes.
▼ **Traffic correlation attacks** – Analyzing traffic patterns to identify users.
▼ **Undercover operations** – Infiltrating forums and marketplaces.
▼ **Deanonymizing misconfigured servers** – Many hidden services have OPSEC failures.

However, I2P is harder to monitor because it does not have exit nodes, and its dynamic routing makes traffic correlation more difficult.

7. Conclusion: Which Anonymity Network is Better?

The choice between Tor and I2P depends on the use case:

- For accessing the Dark Web, browsing anonymously, and bypassing censorship – use Tor.
- For truly private communications, hosting hidden services, and avoiding surveillance – use I2P.

- For OSINT and law enforcement, monitoring Tor is easier than tracking I2P.

Both networks provide strong anonymity, but neither is completely untraceable. Investigators must stay ahead by understanding how criminals use these networks and adapting OSINT strategies accordingly.

2.3 Accessing the Dark Web Safely & Anonymously

The Dark Web is a hidden part of the internet that is not indexed by traditional search engines and requires special tools, such as Tor or I2P, to access. While it provides anonymity, it is also a hotspot for cybercriminal activity, illicit marketplaces, and hacker forums.

For OSINT analysts, cybersecurity professionals, and law enforcement, accessing the Dark Web safely is essential for conducting investigations without exposing their identity or compromising operational security (OPSEC). This chapter outlines best practices for secure and anonymous access to the Dark Web.

1. Understanding the Risks of Accessing the Dark Web

Before accessing the Dark Web, it is crucial to understand the potential risks:

▼ **Malware & Exploits** – Many Dark Web sites contain malware, trojans, and exploits that can infect your system.

▼ **Tracking & De-anonymization** – Poor OPSEC practices can expose your real IP address or identity.

▼ **Law Enforcement Monitoring** – Some Dark Web forums are monitored or operated by law enforcement agencies.

▼ **Social Engineering & Phishing** – Cybercriminals often deceive users to steal credentials or cryptocurrency.

▼ **Legal Implications** – Accessing or interacting with illegal content can have legal consequences in some jurisdictions.

To mitigate these risks, a layered approach to anonymity and security is essential.

2. Setting Up a Secure Environment for Dark Web Access

Before connecting to the Dark Web, users should establish a hardened, isolated, and anonymous environment.

2.1 Using a Secure Operating System

A secure, privacy-focused operating system is recommended to prevent malware infections and tracking.

✓ **Tails OS (The Amnesic Incognito Live System)** – A Linux-based, portable OS that routes all traffic through Tor and leaves no traces.
✓ **Whonix** – A privacy-focused OS that isolates Tor traffic in a virtual machine (VM) for enhanced security.
✓ **Qubes OS** – A high-security OS that allows for compartmentalized browsing with disposable VMs.

Avoid accessing the Dark Web from your main operating system (Windows/macOS) to prevent malware infections and tracking.

2.2 Using a Virtual Machine (VM) for Isolation

A Virtual Machine (VM) adds an extra layer of protection by isolating the browsing session.

◆ **Step 1**: Install VirtualBox or VMware.
◆ **Step 2:** Set up a Linux-based OS (Tails or Whonix).
◆ **Step 3:** Route all internet traffic through Tor inside the VM.
◆ **Step 4:** Use a fresh instance for each session to avoid tracking.

If malware infects the VM, simply delete and recreate it to remove any threats.

3. Connecting to the Dark Web Securely

Once a secure environment is established, follow these steps to connect to the Dark Web while maintaining anonymity.

3.1 Using the Tor Browser

✓ Download Tor Browser from the official site (https://www.torproject.org).

✓ Avoid modifying default settings, as custom configurations can weaken anonymity.

✓ Disable JavaScript (via NoScript) to prevent browser fingerprinting and exploits.

✓ Do not maximize the browser window, as it can reveal screen resolution details for tracking.

✓ Use bridges or obfuscated nodes if Tor is blocked in your region.

Never access the Dark Web using regular browsers like Chrome or Firefox.

3.2 VPN Over Tor vs. Tor Over VPN

Using a Virtual Private Network (VPN) with Tor adds an extra layer of anonymity.

◆ VPN Over Tor (Less Anonymous, More Secure)

✓ VPN encrypts traffic before it reaches the Tor network.

✓ Prevents ISPs from detecting Tor usage.

✓ May slow down connection speeds.

◆ Tor Over VPN (More Anonymous, But Riskier)

✓ Tor traffic is first encrypted and then passed through a VPN.

✓ The VPN provider cannot see your real IP address.

✓ Some VPNs log activity, potentially exposing users.

For maximum anonymity, use a no-log VPN with anonymous payment options (cryptocurrency).

4. Best Practices for Staying Anonymous on the Dark Web

4.1 Maintaining OPSEC (Operational Security)

To avoid deanonymization, follow these strict OPSEC rules:

⊘ Do NOT use personal email, usernames, or passwords.

⊘ Do NOT enable browser plugins (Flash, JavaScript, WebRTC).
⊘ Do NOT share personal details or real-world information.
⊘ Do NOT download files (PDFs, EXEs) from untrusted sources.
⊘ Do NOT use the same Dark Web identity across different sites.

4.2 Secure Communication & Email on the Dark Web

If communication is necessary, use anonymous and encrypted services:

✓ **ProtonMail / Tutanota** – Secure, encrypted email services.
✓ **PGP Encryption** – Encrypt messages using Pretty Good Privacy (PGP).
✓ **Ricochet / Cwtch** – Anonymous, decentralized messaging apps over Tor.
✓ **Session / Briar** – Secure, peer-to-peer messaging apps with no central servers.

Never use your real-world email, phone number, or personal accounts on the Dark Web.

4.3 Cryptocurrency Anonymity (Avoiding Tracking)

Cryptocurrency transactions on the Dark Web can be traced unless proper privacy measures are taken.

◆ Use privacy coins (Monero, Zcash) instead of Bitcoin.
◆ Mix Bitcoin transactions using coin tumblers/mixers.
◆ Avoid centralized exchanges that require KYC verification.

Law enforcement frequently tracks Bitcoin transactions on the Dark Web, so privacy-focused alternatives are recommended.

5. Identifying and Avoiding Scams on the Dark Web

Because the Dark Web is largely unregulated, scams and phishing schemes are rampant. Common scams include:

✗ **Fake escrow services** – Users send cryptocurrency but never receive goods.
✗ **Phishing pages** – Clone sites designed to steal login credentials.
✗ **Exit scams** – Marketplaces that collect funds and disappear overnight.
✗ **Ransomware extortion** – Threat actors demanding Bitcoin payments for unlocking files.

Always verify PGP-signed messages and never trust new vendors without reviews.

6. Monitoring the Dark Web for OSINT & Cybersecurity

6.1 Passive Dark Web Monitoring

✅ **Threat Intelligence Feeds** – Services like DarkOwl, Intel 471, and Recorded Future track Dark Web activity.
✅ **Onion Search Engines** – Use Ahmia, Haystak, or Dark.fail to find .onion sites.
✅ **Forum & Marketplace Monitoring** – Law enforcement and OSINT analysts monitor criminal chatter, leaked databases, and hacker forums.

6.2 Active OSINT Investigations

✅ **Creating Sock Puppet Accounts** – Fake identities to blend into hacker forums.
✅ **Analyzing Dark Web Leaks** – Investigating data breaches and stolen credentials.
✅ **Tracking Ransomware Groups** – Identifying Bitcoin transactions and communication channels.

7. Conclusion: Accessing the Dark Web Responsibly

The Dark Web offers a mix of privacy, anonymity, and criminal activity. While it is a valuable tool for OSINT investigations and cybersecurity research, it comes with serious risks.

By following strict OPSEC measures, using secure operating environments, and avoiding common pitfalls, investigators and privacy-conscious users can access the Dark Web safely and anonymously—without exposing their identities or compromising their security.

2.4 VPNs, Proxy Chains & OPSEC for Dark Web Investigations

Investigating the Dark Web requires strict operational security (OPSEC) to prevent deanonymization, exposure, or tracking by threat actors and law enforcement. Simply using Tor is not enough—investigators need additional layers of anonymity to avoid leaks that could compromise their identity.

This chapter explores Virtual Private Networks (VPNs), proxy chains, and advanced OPSEC techniques for conducting safe and effective Dark Web investigations.

1. Understanding OPSEC for Dark Web Investigations

OPSEC (Operational Security) refers to the strategic process of protecting identity, location, and investigative activities from adversaries.

◆ Who needs OPSEC on the Dark Web?

✅ OSINT investigators tracking cybercriminals.

✅ Law enforcement & intelligence agencies infiltrating illicit marketplaces.

✅ Journalists & researchers studying censorship-resistant communications.

✅ Cybersecurity analysts monitoring data breaches and malware operations.

Failing to implement proper OPSEC can lead to exposure, hacking, or even legal consequences.

2. VPNs for Dark Web Investigations: Pros & Cons

A Virtual Private Network (VPN) encrypts internet traffic and masks the user's real IP address before it reaches the Tor network.

2.1 Tor Over VPN vs. VPN Over Tor

Configuration	How It Works	Benefits	Risks
Tor Over VPN	Traffic is first routed through a VPN, then into the Tor network	☑ ISP cannot detect Tor usage ☑ Bypasses Tor-blocking firewalls	✖ VPN provider sees real IP ✖ May slow down connection
VPN Over Tor	Traffic goes through Tor first, then into a VPN	☑ Prevents malicious exit nodes from logging data ☑ VPN provider cannot see original IP	✖ Requires special VPN configuration ✖ Tor relays may block VPN traffic

◆ **Recommended Approach**: Tor Over VPN is safer for investigations, as it prevents ISPs from flagging Tor traffic.

◆ **Best VPN Features for Dark Web OPSEC:**

✓ **No-logs policy** – Ensures no user activity is stored.
✓ **Cryptocurrency payments** – Avoids linking payment details to your identity.
✓ **Multihop VPNs** – Routes traffic through multiple servers for extra anonymity.
✓ **Kill switch** – Prevents data leaks if the VPN disconnects unexpectedly.

3. Proxy Chains for Additional Anonymity

3.1 What is a Proxy Chain?

A proxy chain routes traffic through multiple proxy servers before it reaches its final destination. Unlike a single VPN, a proxy chain adds multiple intermediate hops, making tracking more difficult.

3.2 Setting Up a Proxy Chain

To set up a proxy chain:

◆ **Step 1**: Use SOCKS5 proxies (e.g., via Privoxy or ProxyChains).
◆ **Step 2:** Route through at least three different countries for redundancy.
◆ **Step 3**: Combine with Tor for added security (Tor → Proxy → VPN).
◆ **Step 4**: Regularly change proxy servers to prevent tracking.

◆ **Recommended Tools:**

✓ **ProxyChains** – A Linux tool that chains multiple proxies together.
✓ **Privoxy** – A privacy-enhancing proxy that works with SOCKS5.
✓ **SSH Tunneling** – Secure proxying via remote SSH servers.

◆ **Proxy Chain Example (Linux Terminal Command):**

proxychains torbrowser-launcher

◆ **Risks of Proxy Chains:**

✘ Slow speeds due to multiple hops.

✘ Unreliable free proxies (some may log activity).

✘ No encryption unless combined with a VPN or Tor.

4. Advanced OPSEC Techniques for Investigators

To prevent exposure, investigators must use multiple layers of OPSEC beyond VPNs and proxy chains.

4.1 Using Secure Operating Systems

Investigators should never access the Dark Web from a regular Windows/macOS machine. Instead, use:

✓ **Tails OS** – A live, amnesic Linux system that routes all traffic through Tor.
✓ **Whonix** – A VM-based OS that isolates Tor traffic from the main system.
✓ **Qubes OS** – A security-focused OS with sandboxed environments.

Risk: Using an unsecure OS (Windows) increases the chances of malware infection and tracking.

4.2 Preventing Fingerprinting & Tracking

Even with Tor, websites can track users through browser fingerprinting, WebRTC leaks, and metadata collection.

♦ **Disable JavaScript** – Prevents fingerprinting attacks.
♦ **Use Tor's default settings** – Customizing settings makes the user stand out.
♦ **Block WebRTC** – WebRTC leaks can expose the real IP address.

Example: Disabling WebRTC on Tor Browser

- Open about:config in Tor Browser.
- Search for media.peerconnection.enabled.
- Set it to false to disable WebRTC.

4.3 Creating Sock Puppet Accounts for Investigations

When conducting Dark Web investigations, never use personal identities. Instead, create sock puppet accounts:

- Use unique usernames/passwords for each investigation.
- Generate fake identities with tools like FakeNameGenerator.
- Access forums through isolated VMs to avoid linkability.
- Use burner emails (ProtonMail, Tutanota) for registration.

Never reuse usernames across multiple forums—threat actors actively track investigators.

4.4 Isolating Workstations for Dark Web Research

For added security, researchers should use a dedicated, isolated workstation.

✅ **Use a separate laptop** – Never mix investigative and personal activity.
✅ **Air-gap sensitive devices** – Disconnect investigative machines from the internet when not in use.
✅ **Avoid storing notes locally** – Use encrypted USB drives or air-gapped systems.

5. Avoiding Common OPSEC Mistakes

✘ **Accessing the Dark Web from a personal device** – Increases risk of tracking and malware infections.
✘ **Using the same username across multiple sites** – Links investigator activities.
✘ **Forgetting to disable WebRTC, JavaScript, or browser fingerprinting** – Can leak real IP.
✘ **Not using a clean operating system (Windows/macOS)** – Leaves traces that adversaries can analyze.
✘ **Engaging with threat actors using real-world language patterns** – Can be used for linguistic fingerprinting.

6. Conclusion: The Importance of Layered Anonymity

Dark Web investigations require multiple layers of security to prevent exposure. Simply using Tor is not enough—investigators should combine:

✓ VPN + Tor for additional privacy.

✓ Proxy chains for multi-hop anonymity.

✓ Secure OS environments (Tails, Whonix, Qubes).

✓ Strict OPSEC to prevent tracking and deanonymization.

By following these best practices, OSINT professionals, law enforcement, and cybersecurity researchers can safely conduct investigations without compromising their identity or operational integrity.

2.5 How Criminals Use Anonymity Networks to Evade Detection

The rise of anonymity networks like Tor, I2P, and VPNs has allowed cybercriminals to operate undetected, making it increasingly difficult for law enforcement and investigators to track illegal activities. These networks provide encryption, traffic obfuscation, and identity masking, which criminals exploit for various illicit purposes.

This chapter explores the methods cybercriminals use to evade detection, the anonymity tools they rely on, and the challenges investigators face when tracking illegal activities on the Dark Web.

1. Why Cybercriminals Rely on Anonymity Networks

Cybercriminals use anonymity networks for several key reasons:

✓ **IP Address Masking** – Prevents law enforcement from tracing their real-world location.
✓ **Encrypted Communications** – Protects messages from surveillance and interception.
✓ **Decentralized Marketplaces** – Reduces risk of seizure or shutdown by authorities.
✓ **Cryptocurrency Payments** – Enables anonymous financial transactions.
✓ **Multi-layered OPSEC** – Hides identities using VPNs, proxies, and encryption.

Without these anonymity tools, cybercriminals would be far more vulnerable to deanonymization and prosecution.

2. Common Anonymity Tools Used by Criminals

Cybercriminals rely on a combination of darknet services, encrypted communications, and privacy-focused tools to remain undetected.

2.1 Tor (The Onion Router)

Tor is the most widely used anonymity network, allowing users to browse the Dark Web and access hidden services without revealing their real IP address.

◆ **How criminals use Tor:**

✔ Hosting illegal marketplaces (drugs, weapons, stolen data).

✔ Operating ransomware extortion portals.

✔ Coordinating cybercrime operations on hidden forums.

✔ Using dark web email providers (ProtonMail, RiseUp) for secure communication.

◆ **Challenges for investigators:**

✘ Tor encrypts traffic through multiple hops, making IP tracking difficult.

✘ Hidden services (.onion sites) do not rely on centralized hosting, reducing takedown risks.

2.2 I2P (Invisible Internet Project)

I2P is another anonymity network used for peer-to-peer communication and hidden websites (eepsites).

◆ **How criminals use I2P:**

✔ Botnet command & control (C2) servers to manage infected machines.

✔ Hosting scam and phishing sites that avoid detection by law enforcement.

✔ Running decentralized darknet forums for cybercriminals.

◆ **Challenges for investigators:**

✗ Unlike Tor, I2P does not use exit nodes, making traffic harder to intercept.

✗ Stronger resistance to traffic analysis due to end-to-end encryption.

2.3 VPNs & Proxy Chains

VPNs and proxy chains provide an extra layer of anonymity before accessing Tor or I2P.

◆ **How criminals use VPNs & proxies:**

✓ Hiding real IP addresses before connecting to Tor.

✓ Avoiding geolocation tracking by law enforcement.

✓ Evading ISP monitoring and blocking attempts.

◆ **Challenges for investigators:**

✗ VPN providers with a no-logs policy make it impossible to retrieve user data.

✗ Some cybercriminals use multi-hop VPN chains to further obscure their location.

2.4 Cryptocurrencies & Privacy Coins

Cryptocurrencies enable anonymous financial transactions that are difficult to trace.

◆ **Commonly used cryptocurrencies:**

✓ **Bitcoin (BTC)** – Frequently used, but traceable via blockchain forensics.
✓ **Monero (XMR)** – A privacy coin with untraceable transactions.
✓ **Zcash (ZEC)** – Uses zk-SNARK encryption to obscure payment details.

◆ **How criminals use crypto for anonymity:**

✓ **Ransomware payments** – Attackers demand Monero or Bitcoin for decryption keys.
✓ **Dark Web marketplace transactions** – Buying and selling illegal goods.
✓ **Mixers & tumblers** – Laundering Bitcoin to break the transaction trail.

◆ **Challenges for investigators:**

✘ Monero and Zcash transactions cannot be easily traced like Bitcoin.

✘ Cryptocurrency laundering services obfuscate transaction origins.

3. How Criminals Evade Law Enforcement Tracking

3.1 OPSEC Strategies Used by Cybercriminals

Cybercriminals follow strict OPSEC (Operational Security) guidelines to prevent detection.

◆ **Anonymous identities** – Using fake names, disposable emails, and burner phones.
◆ **Air-gapped devices** – Using offline computers to manage cryptocurrency wallets.
◆ **Tails or Whonix OS** – Running secure, amnesic operating systems to avoid tracking.
◆ **No reuse of accounts** – Creating new identities for each cybercrime operation.

These tactics make it extremely difficult for investigators to link criminals to real-world identities.

3.2 Decentralized Marketplaces & Forums

Dark Web marketplaces have evolved to become more resistant to takedowns by law enforcement.

◆ **Decentralized hosting** – Some marketplaces use blockchain-based domain names (e.g., Namecoin) to prevent seizure.
◆ **Mirror sites & backups** – When authorities shut down a marketplace, clones and mirrors quickly appear.
◆ **Private invite-only forums** – Exclusive hacker groups communicate on encrypted chat platforms (e.g., Matrix, Jabber, Tox).

◆ **Examples of marketplaces that evaded detection:**

✓ **Empire Market** – Operated for years by using multiple failover servers.
✓ **Hydra Market** – A Russian-language marketplace that evaded Western law enforcement for years.

✓ **Silk Road 2.0** – Rebuilt after the FBI took down the original Silk Road.

3.3 Secure Communications: End-to-End Encryption

Cybercriminals use encrypted messaging platforms to avoid interception.

◆ **Commonly used encrypted apps:**

✓ **Signal & Telegram** – Popular for secure communication.
✓ **Ricochet & Cwtch** – Decentralized, Tor-based messengers.
✓ **PGP Encryption** – Used for verifying identities and encrypting messages.

◆ **Challenges for investigators:**

✗ Encrypted messages cannot be easily intercepted or decrypted.

✗ Some threat actors use burner accounts that disappear after use.

4. Law Enforcement Challenges & Breakthroughs

Despite advanced anonymity techniques, law enforcement agencies have developed new methods to track criminals on the Dark Web.

4.1 Traffic Analysis & De-anonymization

Investigators use network traffic analysis to identify patterns and correlation attacks.

◆ **Examples of successful deanonymization:**

✓ **FBI's Operation Onymous (2014)** – Took down Silk Road, AlphaBay, and Hansa by infiltrating admin accounts.
✓ **Operation Bayonet (2017)** – Dutch police secretly took over Hansa Market and collected user data for months.
✓ **Europol's takedown of DarkMarket (2021)** – Used blockchain forensics to trace Bitcoin transactions.

These cases prove that even anonymity networks have weaknesses when combined with forensic techniques.

5. Conclusion: The Cat-and-Mouse Game Between Criminals & Investigators

Cybercriminals continue to evolve their OPSEC strategies to evade detection, using Tor, I2P, VPNs, and cryptocurrency to remain anonymous. However, law enforcement agencies are also improving their investigative techniques, utilizing traffic analysis, undercover operations, and blockchain forensics to track illegal activities.

The battle between criminals and investigators in the Dark Web is an ongoing cat-and-mouse game, where both sides constantly adapt to new technologies.

2.6 Case Study: How Tor Hidden Services Were Compromised

While Tor Hidden Services (also known as .onion sites) provide strong anonymity, they are not invulnerable. Over the years, law enforcement agencies and cybersecurity researchers have discovered multiple ways to deanonymize hidden services and track operators of illegal marketplaces, forums, and criminal enterprises.

This case study explores real-world examples of how law enforcement compromised Tor hidden services, the techniques used, and the lessons learned from these investigations.

1. How Tor Hidden Services Work

Tor Hidden Services operate within the Tor network, allowing websites to be hosted anonymously without revealing their IP addresses or server locations.

◆ **How They Stay Anonymous:**

✓ **No direct IP exposure** – The site owner's IP is never directly exposed.
✓ **Rendezvous points** – Users connect through multiple encrypted relays.
✓ **Decentralized hosting** – Often spread across multiple servers to prevent takedowns.

However, despite these safeguards, Tor hidden services have been compromised multiple times.

2. Case Study 1: Silk Road Takedown (2013)

Silk Road was the largest Dark Web marketplace for drugs, fake IDs, and other illicit goods. It operated as a Tor hidden service, using Bitcoin for anonymous payments.

How It Was Compromised

◆ **Operational Security (OPSEC) Failures:**

✓ The Silk Road founder, Ross Ulbricht, reused an old username ("altoid") on both Dark Web and clear web forums.

✓ He accidentally used his real email address in an early post discussing Silk Road.

◆ **Law Enforcement Tactics:**

✓ **Traffic Correlation Attacks** – The FBI monitored Silk Road's server traffic patterns to locate its hosting server.

✓ **Bitcoin Tracing** – Investigators tracked Silk Road's Bitcoin transactions to wallets linked to Ulbricht.

◆ **Outcome:**

✓ Ulbricht was arrested in 2013 and sentenced to life in prison.

✓ Silk Road was seized by the FBI, but Silk Road 2.0 later emerged.

◆ **Lessons Learned:**

✗ Reusing usernames across platforms is dangerous.

✗ Bitcoin is not fully anonymous—blockchain forensics can trace transactions.

✗ Tor does not protect against poor OPSEC.

3. Case Study 2: Playpen Child Exploitation Forum (2015-2017)

Playpen was one of the largest child exploitation forums, hosted as a Tor hidden service. Unlike Silk Road, which was compromised through OPSEC failures, Playpen was directly hacked by the FBI.

How It Was Compromised

◆ FBI's "Operation Pacifier" Hack:

✓ In 2015, the FBI secretly took control of Playpen's servers.

✓ Instead of shutting it down immediately, they left it running for weeks to infect visitors with malware.

✓ The FBI deployed a Network Investigative Technique (NIT) (a form of malware) that unmasked real IP addresses of users.

◆ Outcome:

✓ Over 900 arrests worldwide.

✓ Hundreds of convictions across the U.S. and Europe.

◆ Lessons Learned:

✗ Even Tor hidden services can be hacked with custom exploits.

✗ Law enforcement can use "honey pots" to track criminals.

✗ Exploiting browser vulnerabilities can reveal real identities.

4. Case Study 3: AlphaBay & Hansa Market Takedown (2017)

AlphaBay and Hansa Market were two of the largest Dark Web marketplaces after Silk Road's fall. In 2017, law enforcement successfully shut down both—but in a strategic way that led to mass arrests.

How It Was Compromised

◆ AlphaBay's Administrator Exposed by an Email Address

✓ The creator of AlphaBay, Alexandre Cazes, used his personal email address (pimp_alex_91@hotmail.com) for some site registrations.

✓ Investigators linked this email to AlphaBay's admin accounts.

◆ **Hansa Market Taken Over Secretly**

✓ Dutch police seized Hansa Market before shutting it down.

✓ Instead of closing it immediately, they operated it for a month, secretly collecting user data.

✓ Once AlphaBay was taken down, users flocked to Hansa, unknowingly giving law enforcement more evidence.

◆ **Outcome:**

✓ Cazes was arrested and later found dead in his prison cell.

✓ Thousands of users were tracked and arrested worldwide.

◆ **Lessons Learned:**

✗ Never use personal emails for darknet activity.

✗ Marketplaces are vulnerable to insider takeovers.

✗ Law enforcement often uses deception instead of direct takedowns.

5. How Tor Hidden Services Can Be Compromised

Beyond OPSEC failures, there are technical methods that law enforcement and security researchers use to compromise hidden services.

5.1 Traffic Correlation Attacks

Law enforcement monitors Tor entry and exit nodes to correlate users with Dark Web activity.

◆ **Example**: In 2014, researchers at Carnegie Mellon University allegedly helped the FBI unmask Tor users through traffic analysis.

5.2 JavaScript Exploits & Browser Fingerprinting

Tor Browser has had vulnerabilities in the past, allowing attackers to run JavaScript exploits to leak a user's real IP address.

◆ **Example**: The FBI used a Firefox exploit in 2013 to track users of Freedom Hosting (a hidden service provider).

5.3 Server Misconfigurations & Human Errors

Even if a hidden service is on Tor, if the server is misconfigured, attackers can reveal its real-world IP address.

◆ **Example**: Some darknet sites failed to disable Apache mod_status, which exposed their real IPs.

6. Conclusion: Is Tor Really Anonymous?

Tor provides strong anonymity, but as these cases show, it is not foolproof. The biggest risks come from:

✗ Human errors and OPSEC failures (e.g., reusing usernames, emails).

✗ Traffic correlation attacks by intelligence agencies.

✗ Law enforcement hacking techniques (NIT, malware, JavaScript exploits).

✗ Compromised hosting servers leading to data leaks.

For criminals, assuming Tor is 100% secure is a mistake. For investigators, understanding how hidden services are compromised can improve OSINT, forensic analysis, and cybercrime tracking techniques.

Ultimately, the battle between privacy advocates, cybercriminals, and law enforcement is an ongoing cat-and-mouse game, with each side constantly adapting to new techniques.

3. Accessing Dark Web Marketplaces & Forums

In this chapter, we will explore the process of safely accessing and navigating Dark Web marketplaces and forums, spaces that are often hubs for cybercriminal activity. Using tools like Tor or I2P, investigators can enter these hidden corners of the internet where illicit goods, services, and information are traded anonymously. We will cover how to identify reliable sources, avoid common pitfalls, and understand the complex structures of these platforms, from product listings to user interactions. While these marketplaces and forums often serve as a breeding ground for illegal activities, they also provide valuable intelligence for cybercrime investigations, offering insights into the methods and behaviors of those operating in the shadows of the digital world.

3.1 Overview of Dark Web Marketplaces & How They Operate

Dark Web marketplaces function as hidden online markets where users buy and sell illicit goods and services. These platforms operate anonymously using Tor hidden services and cryptocurrency transactions to protect buyers and sellers from law enforcement.

This chapter provides an in-depth look at how Dark Web marketplaces work, the key features that keep them operational, and the challenges investigators face when trying to take them down.

1. What Are Dark Web Marketplaces?

Dark Web marketplaces are decentralized e-commerce platforms similar to eBay or Amazon but are accessible only via Tor, I2P, or other anonymity networks.

◆ **What's Sold on These Marketplaces?**

✓ **Drugs** – Cocaine, heroin, fentanyl, prescription medications.
✓ **Hacked Data** – Credit card info, passwords, identity documents.
✓ **Weapons & Explosives** – Firearms, ammunition, bomb-making guides.
✓ **Counterfeit Items** – Fake passports, IDs, currency, luxury goods.
✓ **Malware & Cybercrime Services** – Ransomware, botnets, phishing kits.

While some marketplaces allow legal goods, most specialize in illegal trade, making them a target for law enforcement.

2. How Do Dark Web Marketplaces Operate?

Darknet marketplaces use a combination of anonymity, escrow services, and encrypted communication to function securely.

2.1 Anonymity & Access

◆ **Tor Hidden Services** – Most marketplaces are .onion sites, making them difficult to track.

◆ **I2P Sites** – Some platforms prefer I2P for added privacy.

◆ **Invite-Only Markets** – Exclusive markets require vetting before access is granted.

2.2 Cryptocurrency Payments

Most transactions use cryptocurrencies to obscure financial trails.

◆ **Commonly Used Cryptos:**

✔ **Bitcoin (BTC)** – The most widely accepted but traceable.

✔ **Monero (XMR)** – Preferred for private, untraceable transactions.

✔ **Zcash (ZEC)** – Uses encryption to hide transaction details.

Some marketplaces also use mixers or tumblers to launder cryptocurrency, making it harder to track transactions.

2.3 Escrow & Reputation Systems

◆ **Escrow Services** – Funds are held by the marketplace until the buyer confirms delivery.

◆ **Vendor Ratings** – Similar to Amazon, vendors have reputations based on buyer feedback.

◆ **Dead Drops & Fake Addresses** – Buyers use drop locations or false addresses to avoid detection.

This system builds trust while keeping transactions anonymous.

2.4 Encrypted Communications

Darknet marketplaces use PGP encryption to protect messages from being intercepted.

◆ **How Buyers & Sellers Communicate Securely:**

✓ **PGP (Pretty Good Privacy)** – End-to-end encrypted messaging.
✓ **TorChat & Tox** – Anonymous, decentralized messaging platforms.
✓ **Whonix & Tails OS** – Secure operating systems to prevent tracking.

Even if a marketplace is seized, law enforcement cannot easily decrypt messages without access to private keys.

3. Types of Dark Web Marketplaces

Not all darknet markets are the same. They vary in size, focus, and business model.

3.1 Traditional Marketplaces (e.g., Silk Road, AlphaBay, Empire Market)

✓ E-commerce style with vendor listings, reviews, and escrow.

✓ Moderated to prevent scams.

✓ Large user base with multiple product categories.

These were the most common until law enforcement started aggressively shutting them down.

3.2 Decentralized Marketplaces (e.g., OpenBazaar, Agora, Hydra)

✓ No central authority, making takedowns harder.

✓ Uses blockchain-based domains to prevent site seizures.

✓ Often requires private invites for access.

Decentralized marketplaces are more resilient but harder to use.

3.3 Vendor Shops & Private Markets

✓ Some high-profile vendors operate independent stores.

✓ More exclusive and invite-only to avoid law enforcement infiltration.

✓ Transactions often require Monero (XMR) for extra privacy.

These are harder to track but also attract fewer customers.

4. Challenges Law Enforcement Faces in Shutting Them Down

Despite takedowns of major markets like Silk Road, AlphaBay, and Hansa, new ones always emerge.

◆ Challenges Investigators Face:

✕ **Tor Anonymity** – True server locations are hidden.
✕ **Cryptocurrency Laundering** – Tracking payments is difficult.
✕ **Mirror & Backup Sites** – Even if a marketplace is seized, clones quickly appear.
✕ **Decentralized Models** – Some new markets use blockchain-based hosting to resist shutdowns.

However, law enforcement has developed new tactics to infiltrate and dismantle marketplaces.

5. Conclusion: The Future of Dark Web Marketplaces

Dark Web marketplaces continue to evolve, using new encryption, decentralized hosting, and better OPSEC to avoid law enforcement. However, investigators are adapting, using undercover operations, traffic analysis, and blockchain forensics to track and dismantle illegal marketplaces.

The battle between cybercriminals and law enforcement is a continuous cat-and-mouse game, shaping the future of online crime and darknet investigations.

3.2 Investigating Illicit Goods & Services on the Dark Web

The Dark Web serves as a hub for the illegal trade of goods and services, offering everything from drugs and counterfeit money to hacked data and cybercrime tools. Law enforcement agencies, cybersecurity researchers, and OSINT analysts must understand how these marketplaces function, the types of illegal products being sold, and the methods criminals use to evade detection.

This chapter explores how investigators analyze illicit goods and services, the challenges they face, and key OSINT techniques used in Dark Web investigations.

1. Categories of Illicit Goods & Services on the Dark Web

Dark Web marketplaces facilitate a wide range of illegal activities, typically divided into physical and digital goods.

1.1 Physical Goods

- **Drugs & Narcotics** – Cocaine, heroin, fentanyl, LSD, prescription medications.
- **Weapons & Explosives** – Firearms, ammunition, bombs, and chemical weapons.
- **Counterfeit Items** – Fake passports, IDs, driver's licenses, and currency.
- **Human Trafficking & Smuggling** – Illegal migration services, child exploitation materials.

1.2 Digital Goods & Cybercrime Services

- **Hacked Data & Leaked Credentials** – Stolen emails, passwords, banking information.
- **Malware & Ransomware-as-a-Service (RaaS)** – Trojans, botnets, and exploit kits.
- **Credit Card Fraud & Financial Crimes** – Cloned credit cards, PayPal and bank account logins.
- **Hitman & Illegal Services** – Alleged contract killings, extortion, blackmail.

While some of these services are scams designed to steal money from buyers, many operate as sophisticated underground economies that pose serious threats to individuals and organizations.

2. How Investigators Analyze Illicit Goods & Services

Dark Web investigators use various OSINT techniques, data analytics, and forensic methods to track illegal activities.

2.1 Identifying Marketplaces & Vendors

To investigate illicit trade, analysts must first identify the key marketplaces where these transactions occur.

- **Search Engines & Dark Web Directories** – Sites like "Dark.fail" list active darknet markets.
- **Marketplace Forums & Vendor Reviews** – Tracking vendor reputations can reveal major players.
- **Invite-Only Marketplaces** – Some require undercover accounts to access.

Example: Law enforcement monitored AlphaBay and Hansa Market forums to track major vendors before shutting them down.

2.2 Tracking Vendor & Buyer Behavior

- **Transaction Monitoring** – Analyzing vendor sales history and product listings.
- **Cryptocurrency Transactions** – Blockchain forensics can trace payments from buyers to sellers.
- **Undercover Operations** – Law enforcement buys illicit goods to track the supply chain.

Example: In 2020, a Europol operation traced cryptocurrency payments from Dark Web vendors to their real-world bank accounts, leading to multiple arrests.

2.3 Identifying & Analyzing Product Listings

Investigators use automated tools to scrape darknet marketplaces for product data.

- **Text & Image Analysis** – Detecting hidden messages in product descriptions.
- **Metadata Extraction** – Analyzing timestamps, geolocation, or hidden watermarks in product images.
- **Language & Code Patterns** – Identifying seller communication styles to link accounts.

Example: The FBI used image metadata to trace illegal firearms sales on darknet markets.

3. Challenges in Investigating Illicit Goods on the Dark Web

Dark Web investigations are complex due to anonymity technologies and evasive tactics used by cybercriminals.

3.1 Anonymity & Encryption

- ◆ **Tor & I2P Networks** – Hiding marketplace locations.
- ◆ **PGP Encryption** – Protecting buyer-seller communications.
- ◆ **Cryptocurrency Tumbling** – Laundering illegal funds.

3.2 Law Enforcement Risks & Limitations

- ◆ **Jurisdiction Issues** – Servers and users spread across multiple countries.
- ◆ **Undercover Operations Risks** – Potential exposure of law enforcement agents.
- ◆ **False Leads & Scams** – Many illegal service listings are fake or traps.

4. OSINT Techniques for Dark Web Investigations

Despite these challenges, investigators have developed advanced OSINT techniques to track illicit activities.

4.1 Blockchain Analysis for Cryptocurrency Tracking

Law enforcement agencies use blockchain forensics tools like Chainalysis and Elliptic to trace Bitcoin and Monero transactions linked to illicit sales.

Example: In 2021, the DOJ seized $2.3 million in Bitcoin by following blockchain transactions from ransomware payments.

4.2 Market & Vendor Intelligence Gathering

- ◆ **Automated Web Scraping** – Tools like AHOY and Memex help collect Dark Web market data.
- ◆ **Natural Language Processing (NLP)** – AI detects common vendor phrases and slang.
- ◆ **Dark Web Search Engines** – Onion search engines like Ahmia index hidden sites.

Example: Europol used Dark Web monitoring tools to identify and arrest major vendors on Dream Market.

4.3 Undercover Operations & Social Engineering

- ◆ **Creating Fake Buyer Profiles** – Law enforcement builds reliable darknet personas.
- ◆ **Engaging Vendors in Private Chats** – Extracting valuable intelligence.
- ◆ **Tracing Package Shipments** – Monitoring drug shipments for real-world arrests.

Example: FBI undercover agents posed as Bitcoin escrow providers to infiltrate a darknet scam operation.

5. Conclusion: The Future of Dark Web Investigations

Dark Web marketplaces continue to evolve, using better encryption, decentralized hosting, and privacy-focused cryptocurrencies to evade detection. However, law enforcement agencies are adapting, using:

✅ Blockchain forensics to trace illicit payments.

✅ OSINT & AI-powered analytics to monitor vendor activity.

✅ Undercover operations to infiltrate criminal networks.

Despite the cat-and-mouse game between cybercriminals and investigators, OSINT techniques remain a powerful tool in tracking and dismantling illicit Dark Web operations.

3.3 How Marketplaces Maintain Anonymity & Reputation Systems

Dark Web marketplaces thrive on anonymity and trust—two seemingly contradictory concepts. While vendors and buyers operate under layers of encryption and pseudonymity, marketplaces must establish systems that foster reliability and accountability without exposing their users. This chapter explores the anonymity techniques Dark Web marketplaces employ, the reputation systems that govern vendor credibility, and how law enforcement navigates these security measures to track illicit activities.

1. How Dark Web Marketplaces Maintain Anonymity

Darknet marketplaces are designed to conceal user identities, transactions, and server locations from law enforcement and hackers. They achieve this using anonymity networks, encryption, and obfuscation techniques.

1.1 Hosting on Tor & I2P Networks

◆ **Tor Hidden Services (.onion)** – Marketplaces operate as Tor hidden services, making them difficult to locate.

◆ **I2P (Invisible Internet Project)** – Some markets use I2P for an extra layer of anonymity, reducing the risk of tracking.

◆ **Decentralized Hosting** – Some platforms leverage blockchain-based hosting or peer-to-peer networks to prevent takedowns.

Example: After Silk Road was seized, successors like Empire Market switched to more decentralized hosting to avoid a similar fate.

1.2 Bulletproof Hosting & Mirroring

◆ **Bulletproof Hosting** – Some markets use offshore hosting providers with lax regulations to resist legal actions.

◆ **Mirror Sites** – When authorities seize a marketplace, clones and mirror sites appear almost instantly.

◆ **DDoS Protection** – Marketplaces employ anti-DDoS measures to prevent attacks from rival groups or law enforcement.

Example: After AlphaBay was shut down in 2017, multiple mirrors emerged, keeping its user base intact until law enforcement dismantled them.

1.3 Cryptocurrency for Anonymity

◆ **Monero (XMR) for Transactions** – Unlike Bitcoin, Monero transactions are untraceable, making it the preferred cryptocurrency.

◆ **Mixers & Tumblers** – Services that shuffle cryptocurrency transactions to obscure the financial trail.

◆ **Escrow Services** – Marketplaces act as intermediaries, holding funds until both parties confirm the transaction.

Example: Hydra Market required all transactions to be conducted exclusively in Monero, making financial tracking nearly impossible.

1.4 Secure Communication Channels

◆ **PGP Encryption for Messages** – Buyers and sellers use Pretty Good Privacy (PGP) encryption to protect communications.

◆ **Whonix & Tails OS** – Many vendors use anonymized operating systems to avoid leaking metadata.
◆ **Multisig Transactions** – Cryptographic approval from multiple parties ensures secure fund transfers.

Example: Law enforcement compromised Hansa Market by infiltrating its encrypted messaging system, leading to multiple arrests.

2. Reputation Systems: Trust in an Anonymous Economy

To combat scams and fraud, Dark Web marketplaces implement reputation-based ranking systems similar to eBay and Amazon.

2.1 Vendor Ratings & Reviews

◆ **Star Ratings (1-5 Stars)** – Buyers rate vendors based on product quality, delivery time, and communication.
◆ **Detailed** Reviews – Customers leave feedback about their purchases, helping new buyers assess vendors.
◆ **Transaction Volume & Longevity** – Vendors with higher sales and longer histories gain more credibility.

Example: Dream Market allowed users to filter vendors by highest-rated sellers, ensuring customers could buy from trusted sources.

2.2 Escrow & Dispute Resolution

◆ **Escrow Holds Funds** – Buyers deposit money into escrow until they confirm receipt of goods.
◆ **Dispute Mediation** – Market admins step in if there's a dispute between buyer and seller.
◆ **Vendor Bond System** – Some markets require vendors to pay a bond before selling, discouraging scammers.

Example: Empire Market required vendors to pay a $1,000 deposit before selling, preventing short-term scam operations.

2.3 Vendor Verification & Invite-Only Markets

◈ **Verified Vendors Only** – Some markets only allow pre-approved, high-reputation vendors.

◈ **Referral-Based Access** – New members must be invited by existing users.

◈ **Background Checks** – Market admins may vet vendors based on their past transactions.

Example: The White House Market only accepted vendors with an existing track record from other marketplaces, reducing scams.

3. Law Enforcement Challenges in Penetrating Reputation Systems

Despite these security measures, law enforcement has developed tactics to infiltrate marketplaces.

3.1 Undercover Law Enforcement Operations

◈ **Fake Buyer Accounts** – Agencies create trusted profiles by making small purchases before targeting vendors.

◈ **Vendor Honeypots** – Authorities set up fake vendor accounts to collect intelligence on buyers.

◈ **Escrow Manipulation** – By infiltrating marketplace admin roles, law enforcement can seize funds and trace transactions.

Example: The FBI's Operation Bayonet seized Hansa Market in 2017 and ran it covertly for a month, collecting buyer and vendor data before shutting it down.

3.2 Tracking Blockchain Transactions

◈ **Bitcoin Clustering** – Law enforcement uses blockchain analytics tools to link transactions to real-world identities.

◈ **Dusting Attacks** – Sending tiny amounts of cryptocurrency to wallets to track their movements.

◈ **Exchange KYC Compliance** – Many darknet users cash out their funds on regulated exchanges, exposing their identities.

Example: In 2020, the DOJ tracked Bitcoin payments from illicit Dark Web transactions to real-world accounts, leading to multiple arrests.

3.3 Seizing Marketplaces & Arresting Admins

- **Server Takedowns** – Authorities track down and seize darknet servers.
- **Admin Arrests** – Many market administrators get sloppy, revealing their real identities.
- **Vendor & Buyer Arrests** – Buyers who use real-world delivery addresses are often caught.

Example: The AlphaBay admin was arrested in Thailand after using his real email in a marketplace support email.

4. Conclusion: The Future of Dark Web Marketplaces

Despite frequent law enforcement takedowns, Dark Web marketplaces continue to evolve, with new security measures, improved encryption, and decentralized hosting.

However, law enforcement agencies are also improving their tactics, leveraging OSINT techniques, undercover operations, and blockchain forensics to dismantle illegal marketplaces.

The arms race between cybercriminals and investigators is ongoing, shaping the future of anonymity and crime on the Dark Web.

3.4 Dark Web Forums: Cybercrime Intelligence Gathering

Dark Web forums serve as hubs for cybercriminal collaboration, intelligence exchange, and underground commerce. Unlike darknet marketplaces, which focus on transactions, these forums provide a space where hackers, fraudsters, and cybercriminals share tactics, sell stolen data, and coordinate attacks. For law enforcement, cybersecurity researchers, and OSINT analysts, monitoring these forums is critical for gathering threat intelligence, tracking cybercriminals, and preventing cyberattacks.

This chapter explores the structure of Dark Web forums, the types of discussions that occur, and intelligence-gathering techniques used by investigators to monitor cybercriminal activity.

1. Understanding Dark Web Forums & Their Role in Cybercrime

1.1 What Are Dark Web Forums?

Dark Web forums function like underground message boards where cybercriminals:

◆ **Share hacking techniques** – Tutorials on phishing, malware development, and exploit creation.
◆ **Sell and trade stolen data** – Leaked credentials, credit card details, and PII.
◆ **Recruit accomplices** – Ransomware gangs, carding networks, and fraudsters seek new members.
◆ **Discuss law enforcement evasion** – Strategies for OPSEC, secure communications, and avoiding tracking.

These forums are often invite-only or require proof of experience before allowing access.

Example: RaidForums (before its takedown) was a well-known Dark Web forum for trading leaked databases and compromised credentials.

1.2 How Cybercriminals Use Dark Web Forums

◆ **Malware & Exploit Development** – Discussions on vulnerabilities, zero-day exploits, and hacking tools.
◆ **Financial Fraud & Carding** – Selling stolen credit cards, banking logins, and counterfeit documents.
◆ **DDoS & Ransomware Services** – Ransomware-as-a-Service (RaaS) providers offering attack tools.
◆ **Insider Trading & Corporate Espionage** – Employees selling company secrets and access credentials.
◆ **Whistleblowing & Activism** – While most activity is criminal, some forums also host leaks by whistleblowers.

Example: The Russian-speaking forum Exploit.in is known for cybercrime discussions, including selling exploits and malware kits.

2. Intelligence Gathering from Dark Web Forums

Monitoring Dark Web forums provides valuable threat intelligence on emerging cyber threats, vulnerabilities, and criminal networks. OSINT analysts and law enforcement agencies employ various techniques to collect, analyze, and act on intelligence.

2.1 OSINT Techniques for Forum Monitoring

◆ **Automated Web Scraping** – Extracting forum posts, user data, and marketplace listings.

◆ **Natural Language Processing (NLP)** – AI-based keyword analysis to detect trending cyber threats.

◆ **Social Network Analysis (SNA)** – Mapping relationships between forum members and threat actors.

◆ **Behavioral Analysis** – Identifying frequent posters, trusted vendors, and criminal hierarchies.

Example: The FBI used web scraping and undercover accounts to track cybercriminals on the Dark Web forum BlackHatWorld.

2.2 Undercover Operations & Social Engineering

Investigators often infiltrate Dark Web forums using:

◆ **Sock Puppet Accounts** – Fake identities designed to blend into criminal communities.

◆ **Engaging in Forum Discussions** – Gaining trust by posting technical knowledge.

◆ **Buying & Selling Illicit Goods** – Establishing credibility while gathering intelligence.

◆ **Direct Messaging & Social Engineering** – Extracting information from forum members.

Example: Law enforcement agents posed as Bitcoin escrow providers to uncover a Dark Web money laundering scheme.

2.3 Tracking Forum Members & Identifying Threat Actors

◆ **Metadata Analysis** – Examining time zones, writing styles, and language patterns to track users.

◆ **IP Leaks & Mistakes** – Some criminals accidentally expose real IP addresses.

◆ **Cross-Site Profiling** – Matching usernames and PGP keys across different forums.

◆ **Tracking Cryptocurrency Transactions** – Following financial trails from forum transactions.

Example: The FBI identified the admin of Silk Road by cross-referencing his PGP key with an old public forum post.

3. Challenges in Monitoring Dark Web Forums

3.1 Anonymity & OPSEC

◆ **Tor & I2P Networks** – Users hide their identities using encrypted networks.
◆ **Strict Forum Entry Requirements** – Some forums require users to prove criminal activity before granting access.
◆ **Encrypted Messaging Platforms** – Users move private conversations to Jabber, Wickr, or Tox for better security.

3.2 Forum Shutdowns & Migrations

◆ **Law Enforcement Takedowns** – Forums frequently shut down, but members migrate to new platforms.
◆ **Decentralized Forums** – Some platforms now use blockchain-based hosting to resist takedowns.
◆ **Private Telegram & Discord Groups** – Many cybercriminals shift discussions to invite-only chat groups.

Example: After RaidForums was shut down, its users migrated to BreachForums (which was later seized by law enforcement).

4. Case Studies: Law Enforcement Successes

4.1 Operation Bayonet (AlphaBay & Hansa Takedown)

◆ Joint FBI & Europol operation infiltrated and shut down AlphaBay, the largest Dark Web market.
◆ Hansa Market was secretly taken over by law enforcement, leading to mass arrests.

4.2 Joker's Stash Carding Forum Shutdown

◆ One of the largest carding forums, Joker's Stash, was seized in 2021.
◆ Law enforcement tracked cryptocurrency payments and undercover agents gathered intelligence before shutting it down.

5. Conclusion: The Future of Dark Web Intelligence Gathering

Dark Web forums remain valuable sources of cybercrime intelligence, but investigators must adapt to new challenges, including:

✅ Encrypted, decentralized forums that resist takedowns.

✅ Better OPSEC by cybercriminals, making identification harder.

✅ AI-powered OSINT tools that automate forum monitoring.

Despite these challenges, law enforcement agencies continue to evolve, using covert operations, OSINT, and advanced data analytics to infiltrate and dismantle cybercriminal networks.

3.5 OSINT Techniques for Infiltrating Closed Marketplaces

Many of the most notorious Dark Web marketplaces are not openly accessible. Instead, they require invitations, referrals, or proof of criminal activity to gain entry. These closed marketplaces operate in highly secure environments to evade law enforcement and minimize infiltration risks. However, Open-Source Intelligence (OSINT) techniques can be leveraged to infiltrate, monitor, and gather intelligence on these marketplaces.

This chapter explores how cybercrime investigators, law enforcement, and OSINT analysts infiltrate closed marketplaces, uncover illicit networks, and track threat actors.

1. Understanding Closed Dark Web Marketplaces

1.1 What Are Closed Marketplaces?

Unlike public Dark Web markets, closed marketplaces:

◆ Require invitation codes or vouching by existing members.

◆ Vet new members by demanding proof of prior transactions or criminal expertise.

◆ Have strict OPSEC rules (mandatory encryption, limited transactions, verified accounts).

◆ Use encrypted messaging (Jabber, Wickr, Tox) instead of on-site communication.

◆ Are decentralized or mirror-based to prevent law enforcement takedowns.

Example: The Genesis Market required new users to purchase stolen credentials before accessing high-level cybercrime services.

2. OSINT Techniques for Identifying Closed Marketplaces

2.1 Monitoring Open-Source Intelligence Feeds

♦ **Dark Web Monitoring Tools** – Tools like SpiderFoot, DarkOwl, and Intel 471 track market activity.

♦ **Telegram & Discord Channels** – Cybercriminal groups often advertise on encrypted messaging apps.

♦ **Clear Web Mentions** – Some closed marketplaces are referenced on hacking forums, Reddit, or Twitter.

♦ **Vendor Migration Tracking** – When a market shuts down, vendors announce their new locations on forums.

Example: After AlphaBay was shut down, vendors advertised Empire Market as its successor on Dark Web forums.

2.2 Tracking Vendor & Buyer Movements

♦ **Cross-Site Profiling** – Many vendors use the same usernames or PGP keys across different forums and markets.

♦ **Transaction Trail Analysis** – Tracking Monero, Bitcoin, or other crypto payments can lead to marketplace locations.

♦ **Analyzing Breach Dumps** – Marketplace user databases, when leaked, reveal vendor activities.

Example: The takedown of Hansa Market involved law enforcement seizing vendor PGP keys and linking them to transactions on other platforms.

3. OSINT Techniques for Gaining Access to Closed Marketplaces

3.1 Creating a Credible Sock Puppet Identity

♦ **Building a realistic persona** – Crafting a fake cybercriminal identity that fits the marketplace profile.

♦ **Using Dark Web Lingo & Slang** – Proper communication style is crucial to avoid suspicion.

♦ **Establishing Forum Presence** – Posting on hacker forums (e.g., Exploit.in, Dread) to build credibility.

♦ **Purchasing Small Items** – Making low-risk purchases to appear legitimate before escalating.

Example: Law enforcement used sock puppet accounts to purchase malware and stolen data on Joker's Stash before shutting it down.

3.2 Social Engineering & Gaining Trust

◆ **Building relationships with vendors and buyers** – Gaining their trust over time.
◆ **Joining cybercriminal communities** – Becoming active in closed forums to get invitations.
◆ **Impersonating High-Value Targets** – Pretending to be a criminal buyer or hacker-for-hire.
◆ **Leveraging Insider Leaks** – Some marketplaces have disgruntled employees or rival criminals willing to sell access.

Example: FBI agents infiltrated AlphaBay's private vendor channels by posing as high-volume drug buyers.

3.3 OSINT on Marketplace Admins & Weak Points

◆ **Tracking Admin Mistakes** – Many admins reuse usernames, email addresses, or PGP keys.
◆ **Examining Site Metadata** – Some markets reveal server locations or software vulnerabilities.
◆ **Monitoring Cryptographic Signatures** – Marketplaces with weak encryption can be exploited.

Example: The Silk Road takedown was initiated when its admin used his personal email address in an early forum post.

4. Law Enforcement Tactics for Disrupting Closed Marketplaces

4.1 Undercover Law Enforcement Infiltration

◆ **Buying & Selling Illicit Goods** – Establishing credibility before making arrests.
◆ **Operating as Escrow Agents** – Controlling transactions to track payments.
◆ **Becoming Marketplace Moderators** – Seizing control of site infrastructure.

Example: Dutch police secretly ran Hansa Market for a month, gathering data before shutting it down.

4.2 OSINT + Blockchain Forensics

◈ **Tracing Crypto Transactions** – Identifying vendors who cash out on regulated exchanges.

◈ **Analyzing Bitcoin & Monero Tumblers** – Tracking laundering patterns.

◈ **De-anonymizing Wallet Addresses** – Using AI-based OSINT to cluster criminal wallets.

Example: The IRS cracked a major Dark Web fentanyl operation by tracing Bitcoin payments.

5. Conclusion: The Future of OSINT in Closed Marketplace Investigations

As closed marketplaces evolve, OSINT analysts and law enforcement must adapt their techniques by:

✓ Leveraging AI-powered Dark Web monitoring.

✓ Using enhanced blockchain forensics.

✓ Improving cybercriminal infiltration strategies.

While cybercriminals continue to refine their OPSEC, investigators are closing the intelligence gap, making it increasingly difficult for closed marketplaces to remain undetected.

3.6 Case Study: Analyzing a Dark Web Drug Market

The Dark Web has long been a hub for the sale of illicit goods, with drug markets playing a central role. These marketplaces operate under the protection of Tor, I2P, and other anonymity networks, allowing vendors and buyers to conduct transactions away from law enforcement scrutiny. However, despite their attempts at secrecy, OSINT analysts and law enforcement agencies have developed techniques to track, analyze, and disrupt these illegal operations.

This case study explores the rise, operation, and eventual takedown of a major Dark Web drug market, demonstrating OSINT techniques used for intelligence gathering, infiltration, and forensic investigation.

1. The Rise of Dark Web Drug Markets

Dark Web drug markets became prominent with the launch of Silk Road in 2011, which provided:

- A decentralized platform for buying and selling illicit drugs
- Anonymous cryptocurrency transactions using Bitcoin
- End-to-end encrypted communication between vendors and buyers
- A reputation system to ensure trust in transactions

Following the shutdown of Silk Road in 2013, numerous successor markets emerged, including AlphaBay, Dream Market, and Wall Street Market, each improving their security measures and OPSEC practices to evade detection.

2. The Target: Empire Market – A Leading Dark Web Drug Marketplace

2.1 Overview of Empire Market

Empire Market was one of the largest Dark Web markets before it collapsed in 2020. Key features included:

- **Drugs as the primary product** – Listings for cocaine, heroin, LSD, MDMA, and prescription opioids.
- **Strict vendor verification** – Sellers had to pay a bond and pass screening before listing products.
- **Multi-cryptocurrency support** – Accepting Bitcoin (BTC), Monero (XMR), and Litecoin (LTC).
- **DDoS resistance & mirrors** – Market resilience against cyberattacks and takedowns.
- **Escrow & Dispute Resolution** – Funds were held in escrow until buyers confirmed delivery.

At its peak, Empire Market had over 1 million registered users and thousands of vendors worldwide.

3. OSINT Techniques Used to Monitor Empire Market

Despite operating in the Tor network, Empire Market was vulnerable to OSINT-based investigation techniques.

3.1 Dark Web Monitoring & Data Scraping

◆ Automated scraping tools collected marketplace listings, vendor profiles, and customer reviews.

◆ Text analysis & keyword tracking identified drug trends and high-risk vendors.

◆ Historical data analysis revealed changes in market activity over time.

Example: OSINT analysts tracked fentanyl listings on Empire Market and observed price surges following law enforcement crackdowns on real-world suppliers.

3.2 Tracking Vendor Activity & Cross-Site Profiling

Many vendors reused usernames and PGP keys across multiple Dark Web markets and forums.

◆ PGP fingerprinting helped match vendor accounts across different sites.

◆ Username correlation allowed analysts to link vendors to their activities on Reddit, Telegram, and hacking forums.

◆ Analyzing language patterns provided clues about vendors' locations and backgrounds.

Example: A vendor named "DrugKing99" was linked to multiple markets, including Empire Market, Dream Market, and Wall Street Market, using PGP key analysis.

3.3 Blockchain & Cryptocurrency Forensics

Cryptocurrency transactions are pseudonymous, but OSINT analysts use blockchain forensics tools to track illicit financial activity.

◆ **Tracing Bitcoin transactions** – Following the movement of funds from escrow wallets to external exchanges.

◆ **Cluster analysis** – Grouping addresses controlled by the same entity.

◆ **Identifying cash-out points** – Monitoring when funds are converted to fiat currency on regulated exchanges.

Example: Chainalysis and law enforcement identified Empire Market's main Bitcoin wallet by tracking patterns in withdrawal transactions.

4. The Fall of Empire Market

4.1 Law Enforcement Infiltration & Takedown

Despite its sophisticated OPSEC, Empire Market eventually collapsed in August 2020. Key factors included:

◆ **Undercover law enforcement infiltration** – Agents posed as buyers to collect intelligence on vendors.

◆ **Tracking cryptocurrency transactions** – Leading to the identification of administrators and money launderers.

◆ **DDoS attacks & admin exit scam** – The market suffered a massive DDoS attack, and its administrators vanished with millions in escrow funds.

Outcome:

✓ Users lost an estimated $30 million in cryptocurrency due to the exit scam.

✓ Many high-profile vendors were arrested following financial tracing.

✓ The market's fall disrupted global darknet drug distribution networks.

5. Lessons Learned from the Empire Market Case

5.1 How OSINT Can Be Used to Disrupt Dark Web Drug Markets

✓ Monitoring vendor activity across multiple platforms can help identify high-risk sellers.

✓ PGP key tracking and username correlation can expose criminals despite their anonymity efforts.

✓ Cryptocurrency tracing and forensic analysis can link illegal transactions to real-world identities.

✓ Undercover operations and OSINT-based infiltration remain key strategies for law enforcement.

As Dark Web drug markets continue to evolve, OSINT will remain an essential tool in identifying and dismantling illegal online drug networks.

4. Investigating Onion Sites & Hidden Services

This chapter focuses on the unique nature of Onion sites and hidden services that reside within the Tor network, offering both opportunities and challenges for OSINT analysts. Onion sites, identifiable by their ".onion" domain, provide users with enhanced anonymity, making them ideal for cybercriminals seeking to conceal their identity and operations. We will discuss how to access these sites securely, navigate their often complex structures, and identify patterns that could be crucial for investigation. While these sites are frequently associated with illicit activities, they also host valuable intelligence, from encrypted communications to untraceable transactions, which can assist in building profiles, uncovering networks, and solving cybercrime cases. Understanding how to effectively investigate Onion sites is a key skill for any OSINT investigator working in the realm of digital crime.

4.1 The Structure of Onion Sites & How They Work

The Dark Web is primarily accessed through Tor (The Onion Router), which enables users to visit hidden services known as .onion sites. Unlike standard websites, these do not have traditional domain names and rely on a decentralized, anonymity-focused infrastructure. Understanding the architecture, routing process, and security mechanisms of onion sites is critical for OSINT analysts, cybercrime investigators, and security researchers.

This chapter explores how onion sites function, their unique structural components, and how investigators can analyze them effectively.

1. What Are Onion Sites?

1.1 Defining Onion Services

Onion sites are Dark Web domains that use the .onion TLD (top-level domain) and are accessible only through the Tor network. They offer:

⬥ **Anonymity** – Both users and website operators remain hidden.
⬥ **Decentralization** – No central hosting authority, making takedowns difficult.
⬥ **End-to-End Encryption** – Traffic is encrypted multiple times for security.

Unlike surface web domains (e.g., Google.com), onion domains are randomly generated alphanumeric strings, making them harder to remember or search for.

Example:

- A legitimate Dark Web whistleblower site: http://protonirockerxow.onion/
- A well-known former darknet market: http://silkroad7rn2puhj.onion/

1.2 The Difference Between Surface Web & Onion Sites

Feature	Surface Web (Clear Web)	Onion Sites (Dark Web)
Access	Open to all, indexed by search engines	Requires Tor Browser, not indexed by Google
Anonymity	Hosting and users can be tracked	Both users and sites remain anonymous
Domain Names	Human-readable (e.g., example.com)	Randomized (e.g., abcdefghijklmnop.onion)
Hosting	Hosted on public servers (AWS, GoDaddy)	Often decentralized or self-hosted
Security	Uses HTTPS for encryption	Uses multi-layered Tor encryption

2. How Onion Routing Works

2.1 The Onion Routing Process

Onion sites use multi-layered encryption (like an onion) to conceal user identities. The process involves:

1 **Entry Node** – User traffic enters the Tor network via a randomly selected entry node.

2 **Relay Nodes** – Traffic is bounced through multiple middle relay nodes, making it difficult to trace.

3 **Exit Node** – The request reaches the destination (.onion site) via an exit node, which does not reveal the origin IP.

Each layer of encryption peels away at each node, ensuring that no single node knows both the sender and destination.

2.2 Tor Hidden Service Architecture

Onion services use a decentralized directory system to maintain anonymity:

- **Hidden Service Descriptor** – A .onion address is registered on the Tor network.
- **Introduction Points** – These act as proxies that facilitate anonymous connections.
- **Rendezvous Points** – A randomly selected Tor node connects the user to the service, ensuring both parties remain anonymous.

3. How Onion Sites Are Structured

3.1 Onion Site URL Structure

Onion site URLs are randomly generated and consist of 16 or 56 alphanumeric characters. These domains are cryptographic hashes derived from public keys.

Example:

Old 16-character format: http://abcdef1234567890.onion/
New 56-character format: http://3g2upl4pq6kufc4m.onion/

Newer v3 onion addresses provide stronger cryptographic security and resistance against attacks.

3.2 Hosting & Infrastructure of Onion Sites

Onion sites can be hosted in various ways:

- **Self-Hosting** – Run on personal servers with strict OPSEC.
- **Bulletproof Hosting** – Provided by offshore companies that ignore legal requests.
- **P2P Decentralized Hosting** – Using networks like ZeroNet or I2P for resilience.

Example: Many cybercriminal marketplaces use offshore VPS (Virtual Private Servers) in Russia or Eastern Europe to avoid law enforcement takedowns.

4. Challenges in Investigating Onion Sites

4.1 Identifying the Hosting Infrastructure

◆ **Tracking hosting providers** – Some onion sites accidentally reveal server metadata.

◆ **Analyzing uptime patterns** – Monitoring server activity and connection logs can help track movements.

◆ **Investigating Domain Keys** – Some sites reuse PGP keys or SSL certificates, allowing linkage to clear web services.

Example: The Silk Road investigation leveraged server misconfigurations to locate the site's physical host.

4.2 Analyzing Onion Site Metadata

Even though onion sites prioritize anonymity, investigators use OSINT techniques to gather intelligence:

✓ **Tracking mirror sites** – Many onion sites have clear web mirrors or alternative URLs.

✓ **Analyzing source code** – Some sites leave developer comments or reused scripts that reveal clues.

✓ **Cross-referencing forum posts** – Dark Web forum users sometimes mention onion sites or link to them.

Example: The AlphaBay takedown involved cross-referencing usernames across multiple forums to link site admins to real-world identities.

5. Conclusion: The Future of Onion Site Investigations

As onion sites continue to evolve, OSINT techniques must adapt to track and analyze Dark Web activity. Future developments include:

◆ **AI-driven Dark Web monitoring** – Using machine learning to automate pattern detection.

◆ **Blockchain analysis for Dark Web transactions** – Identifying financial trails linked to onion sites.

◆ **Advanced fingerprinting techniques** – Exploiting operational security (OPSEC) mistakes made by site admins.

Despite Tor's anonymity, onion sites are not invulnerable. Investigators can leverage metadata, blockchain forensics, and user behavior analysis to uncover illicit activities while respecting legal and ethical boundaries.

4.2 Tools & Techniques for Mapping Hidden Services

The Dark Web is intentionally designed to be difficult to map and index, making it challenging for researchers, OSINT analysts, and law enforcement agencies to monitor hidden services effectively. However, a combination of specialized tools, investigative techniques, and analytical methodologies can help map and track these elusive sites.

This chapter explores the key tools and techniques used to discover, analyze, and monitor onion services, helping investigators uncover illicit networks and gather intelligence while maintaining operational security (OPSEC).

1. Challenges in Mapping Hidden Services

Onion sites operate differently from traditional surface web domains:

✦ **Not Indexed by Traditional Search Engines** – Google and Bing do not crawl .onion sites.

✦ **Randomized & Changing URLs** – Onion domains are cryptographic hashes, making them difficult to remember or predict.

✦ **Frequent Site Migrations & Shutdowns** – Markets, forums, and criminal networks frequently change addresses to evade detection.

✦ **Use of Captchas & Login Requirements** – Many onion sites restrict automated crawlers.

✦ **Limited Trust & Access Restrictions** – Some hidden services require invites, reputation verification, or cryptocurrency deposits to enter.

Despite these challenges, advanced OSINT techniques and custom Dark Web crawlers can help uncover and analyze these hidden services.

2. Tools for Discovering and Mapping Hidden Services

2.1 Dark Web Search Engines

Although traditional search engines do not index .onion sites, several Dark Web-specific search engines can help locate hidden services.

✦ **Ahmia (https://ahmia.fi/)** – Indexes Tor hidden services and allows users to search for known onion sites.

◈ **OnionLand Search** – A Google-like search engine for onion services, indexing known marketplaces, forums, and wikis.
◈ **Dark.fail** – Maintains an updated list of major onion sites, including darknet markets and whistleblower platforms.

☐ **OSINT Tip**: Many illicit services are not listed on search engines, requiring deeper investigations using forums, leaked databases, and intelligence-sharing communities.

2.2 Dark Web Crawlers & Scrapers

Since onion sites are dynamic and difficult to index, custom crawlers can help map hidden services by scraping URLs, metadata, and content.

◈ **OnionScan** – An open-source tool for analyzing and mapping Dark Web infrastructure, identifying server misconfigurations and vulnerabilities.
◈ **TorBot** – A Python-based web scraper that can crawl and extract links from .onion sites.
◈ **Hunchly** – A tool designed for Dark Web investigations, allowing analysts to archive and analyze onion site data securely.

☐ **OSINT Tip**: Many onion sites use DDoS protection or JavaScript-based defenses, so manual interaction or advanced scraping techniques may be required.

3. Investigative Techniques for Mapping Hidden Services

3.1 Passive Discovery: Collecting Known URLs

Many hidden services are mentioned in forums, paste sites, and leaks, providing valuable intelligence.

◈ **Tracking forum discussions** – Sites like Dread, Raddle, and Telegram groups often share new onion links.
◈ **Monitoring Pastebin & Dark Web leaks** – Criminal groups sometimes publish fresh links in data dumps.
◈ **Analyzing historical onion addresses** – Some site operators reuse URLs or create variations of older domains.

Example: Law enforcement tracked the resurrection of Silk Road 3.0 by analyzing forum discussions and cross-referencing new URLs with previous marketplace addresses.

3.2 Active Discovery: Interacting with Onion Services

Some onion sites require direct interaction to reveal hidden links, services, or invite-only marketplaces.

♦ **Using known directories & link lists** – Services like Hidden Wiki sometimes list underground sites.

♦ **Creating burner accounts on Dark Web forums** – Engaging in low-risk discussions can lead to trusted access to hidden services.

♦ **Social engineering techniques** – Some investigators pose as buyers to infiltrate cybercrime markets.

☐ **OSINT Tip**: Never use personal credentials, emails, or IP addresses when engaging with Dark Web actors—use burner identities and hardened OPSEC measures.

4. Analyzing Hidden Service Metadata

Even if onion sites attempt to remain anonymous, metadata analysis can reveal valuable insights about their infrastructure, operators, and activity patterns.

4.1 Identifying Hosting & Server Misconfigurations

Many onion sites leak metadata due to misconfigured servers or reused infrastructure.

♦ **Checking SSL certificates & PGP keys** – Some sites use the same cryptographic keys across multiple services, linking them together.

♦ **Analyzing uptime patterns** – Some darknet markets go offline at predictable times, revealing server maintenance schedules.

♦ **Reverse image searching logos & banners** – Some onion sites reuse graphics from earlier markets, linking them to past operators.

Example: The AlphaBay takedown involved analyzing PGP keys and reused server configurations, exposing its administrator's real-world identity.

4.2 Tracking Cryptocurrency Transactions

Many Dark Web markets and ransom groups rely on Bitcoin, Monero, and Litecoin for payments. Blockchain forensics can be used to track:

◆ **Escrow wallet movements** – Identifying hot wallets used by major marketplaces.

◆ **Common laundering techniques** – Many criminals use mixers and tumblers, but forensic tools can deanonymize transactions.

◆ **Transaction clustering** – Linking multiple wallets controlled by the same actor.

Example: The FBI used blockchain analysis to track Bitcoin transactions from Silk Road to real-world exchanges, leading to seized funds worth over $1 billion.

5. Future Trends in Mapping Hidden Services

5.1 AI-Powered Dark Web Intelligence

✅ Machine learning models are being trained to detect criminal activity patterns in onion services.

✅ Automated Dark Web monitoring tools are improving, allowing real-time tracking of emerging threats.

✅ AI-based blockchain analysis is enabling faster tracking of illicit transactions.

5.2 Decentralized Dark Web Hosting

⚠️ Newer technologies like I2P, ZeroNet, and blockchain-based hosting are making it harder to map hidden services.

⚠️ Peer-to-peer Dark Web networks reduce the effectiveness of traditional OSINT techniques.

5.3 Ethical Considerations in Dark Web Investigations

◆ **Legal risks** – Engaging with Dark Web actors may violate cybercrime laws.

◆ **Ethical challenges** – Some mapping techniques may infringe on privacy rights.

◆ **Counter-surveillance tactics** – Criminals are increasingly using honeypots, bait URLs, and fake markets to mislead investigators.

6. Conclusion: The Importance of OSINT in Dark Web Mapping

Mapping hidden services requires a combination of OSINT tools, advanced techniques, and secure investigative methods. By leveraging custom crawlers, metadata analysis, and blockchain forensics, analysts can identify, monitor, and disrupt illicit Dark Web networks.

Despite the growing sophistication of anonymity networks, the use of machine learning, AI-driven analytics, and enhanced OPSEC measures will continue to strengthen Dark Web intelligence efforts in the future.

4.3 Tracking Site Operators & Their Digital Footprints

Despite the anonymity offered by the Dark Web, many site operators leave digital footprints that investigators, OSINT analysts, and law enforcement can exploit. Whether through mistakes in OPSEC, reuse of online identities, or blockchain transactions, these breadcrumbs can be used to track, deanonymize, and link individuals to illicit activities.

This chapter explores the methods, tools, and techniques used to track Dark Web site operators, focusing on metadata analysis, behavioral profiling, and cryptocurrency forensics.

1. Understanding Digital Footprints on the Dark Web

Every online action leaves a trace, and even skilled cybercriminals sometimes make mistakes. These mistakes can be leveraged to uncover real-world identities.

1.1 Key Digital Footprints of Dark Web Operators

◆ **Metadata in site configurations** – Leaked information from hosting environments.
◆ **Reused usernames & PGP keys** – Operators often use the same credentials across different platforms.
◆ **Forum & marketplace interactions** – Behavioral patterns can link multiple accounts.
◆ **Cryptocurrency transactions** – Blockchain forensics can track illegal payments.
◆ **Time zone & language markers** – Typing patterns, linguistic clues, and active hours can reveal location data.

Example: Ross Ulbricht, the creator of Silk Road, was arrested after using the same username ("altoid") on Stack Overflow and Bitcoin forums, linking him to the marketplace.

2. OSINT Techniques for Tracking Dark Web Operators

2.1 Identifying Reused Usernames & Aliases

Many cybercriminals reuse usernames, email addresses, or PGP keys across multiple platforms. OSINT analysts use cross-referencing tools to uncover these links.

☐ **Tools for Tracking Usernames:**

◈ **Namechk (https://namechk.com/)** – Checks if a username exists across multiple platforms.

◈ **WhatsMyName (https://whatsmyname.app/)** – OSINT tool for tracking usernames across websites.

◈ **Dehashed (https://www.dehashed.com/)** – Searches leaked databases for email or username associations.

☐ **OSINT Tip**: Try different variations of usernames (e.g., "darkmarket_admin" vs. "darkmarketadmin") to catch subtle reuse patterns.

2.2 Tracking PGP Keys & Digital Signatures

Many Dark Web marketplaces and forums require users to use PGP encryption for secure communication. However, reused PGP keys can be traced back to previous accounts.

☐ **Tools for PGP Key Analysis:**

◈ **MIT PGP Keyserver (https://pgp.mit.edu/)** – Searches for public PGP keys and their associations.

◈ **KeyBase (https://keybase.io/)** – Identifies PGP keys linked to social media accounts.

Example: The administrator of AlphaBay, Alexandre Cazes, was tracked after investigators found his old PGP key matched emails from his personal accounts.

2.3 Analyzing Writing Style & Linguistic Patterns

Even when using anonymous accounts, writing style and linguistic clues can expose a user's identity.

☐ **Techniques for Linguistic Analysis:**

◈ **Stylometry Analysis** – Identifies unique writing patterns (e.g., grammar, punctuation, vocabulary).

◈ **Time Zone & Active Hours** – If a user posts regularly at 3 AM UTC, they may be in North America.

◈ **Language Markers** – Users sometimes forget to translate certain phrases, revealing native language clues.

☐ **Tools for Stylometry:**

◈ **Jstylo-Anonymouth** – Compares writing styles across multiple samples.

◈ **TextRazor (https://www.textrazor.com/)** – AI-powered text analysis tool.

Example: The FBI used stylometry analysis to match Ross Ulbricht's writing style across his Silk Road posts and clear web discussions.

3. Tracking Cryptocurrency Transactions

Since many Dark Web markets rely on Bitcoin, Monero, or other cryptocurrencies, investigators can use blockchain forensics to follow the money.

3.1 Cryptocurrency Analysis Techniques

◈ **Tracking wallet addresses** – Identifying linked transactions and laundering attempts.

◈ **Analyzing mixing & tumbling services** – Criminals use these to obfuscate transaction trails, but forensic tools can sometimes deanonymize them.

◈ **Exchanges & cash-out points** – Many criminals convert crypto to fiat via centralized exchanges, which often require KYC (Know Your Customer) verification.

☐ **Blockchain Forensics Tools:**

◈ **Chainalysis (https://www.chainalysis.com/)** – Tracks cryptocurrency movements for law enforcement.

◈ **CipherTrace (https://ciphertrace.com/)** – Analyzes Bitcoin transactions and mixer patterns.

◈ **Elliptic (https://www.elliptic.co/)** – Identifies suspicious crypto transactions.

Example: Authorities tracked Bitcoin payments made by AlphaBay users, leading to the arrest of multiple vendors.

4. Leveraging Dark Web Forum & Marketplace Interactions

Many site operators engage in public discussions on Dark Web forums, inadvertently revealing information.

4.1 Monitoring Forum Activity

◆ **Tracking IP leaks & OPSEC mistakes** – Some users forget to mask their IPs or use real-world usernames.

◆ **Analyzing interactions with buyers/sellers** – Market admins often use the same alias across multiple sites.

◆ **Cross-referencing clear web & Dark Web posts** – Some users accidentally link their real identity.

☐ **OSINT Tools for Dark Web Monitoring:**

◆ **SpiderFoot (https://www.spiderfoot.net/)** – Automates OSINT analysis, including forum tracking.

◆ **Hunchly (https://www.hunch.ly/)** – Captures Dark Web pages for evidence collection.

◆ **Recon-ng** – Python framework for automated reconnaissance.

☐ **OSINT Tip**: Dark Web forums often use trust and reputation systems—researchers can infiltrate networks by building low-risk credibility over time.

5. Case Studies: Real-World Tracking of Dark Web Operators

Case Study #1: The AlphaBay Takedown

◆ **Mistake**: Alexandre Cazes reused his PGP key and personal email in AlphaBay communications.

◆ **Tracking Method**: Investigators linked his Bitcoin transactions to known exchange accounts.

◆ **Outcome**: Cazes was arrested in Thailand, and AlphaBay was shut down in 2017.

Case Study #2: Welcome to Video (Dark Web Child Exploitation Case)

◆ **Mistake**: The site admin used a traceable Bitcoin wallet for hosting payments.

◆ **Tracking Method**: Blockchain forensics identified cryptocurrency transactions leading to real-world IP addresses.

◆ **Outcome**: Over 300 arrests globally, including in the U.S., South Korea, and the UK.

6. Future Challenges & Trends in Tracking Dark Web Operators

Despite OSINT advancements, Dark Web operators are adapting their tactics to remain anonymous.

Emerging Trends:

☑ **Increased use of Monero (XMR)** – Unlike Bitcoin, Monero is privacy-focused and harder to trace.
☑ **Decentralized Dark Web hosting** – Some criminals are shifting to I2P and ZeroNet for added security.
☑ **AI-powered identity obfuscation** – Deepfake technology may allow criminals to forge fake digital identities.

How Investigators Can Adapt:

◆ Improve blockchain analytics tools to handle privacy coins like Monero.
◆ Enhance stylometry & linguistic profiling to track writing patterns more accurately.
◆ Leverage AI for pattern recognition in Dark Web marketplaces.

7. Conclusion: The Future of Dark Web Intelligence

Tracking Dark Web site operators requires a combination of OSINT, metadata analysis, behavioral profiling, and blockchain forensics. By exploiting small operational mistakes, investigators can unmask hidden identities, ultimately leading to market shutdowns and arrests. However, as anonymity networks evolve, so must the techniques used to track criminals in the ever-changing digital underworld.

4.4 Identifying Mirror Sites & Market Relocations

The Dark Web is a constantly shifting landscape, with marketplaces and illicit services frequently changing domains to evade law enforcement takedowns and DDoS attacks. When a major market shuts down, its administrators often relocate operations to a mirror site or an entirely new domain. Identifying these mirror sites and relocated markets is crucial for OSINT analysts, law enforcement, and cybersecurity researchers tracking criminal activity.

This chapter explores the techniques, tools, and methodologies used to track mirror sites, identify market relocations, and follow the movements of darknet operators.

1. Understanding Mirror Sites & Market Relocations

1.1 What Are Mirror Sites?

A mirror site is a duplicate version of a Dark Web site hosted on a different .onion address. Mirror sites serve several purposes:

⬧ **Backup against takedowns** – If a primary domain is seized, a mirror site allows users to continue accessing the market.

⬧ **Resilience against cyberattacks** – Market admins create mirrors to combat DDoS attacks and server failures.

⬧ **Scams & phishing** – Fake mirror sites often appear after a major shutdown, tricking users into revealing credentials or depositing cryptocurrency.

Example: After the Silk Road takedown in 2013, multiple mirror sites and clones (e.g., Silk Road 2.0, Silk Road Reloaded) emerged, some operated by law enforcement as honeypots.

1.2 How Markets Relocate After Takedowns

When authorities shut down a Dark Web market, operators and vendors often migrate to a new marketplace or create a successor.
Common relocation tactics include:

✓ Announcing new addresses on forums & encrypted chat channels (e.g., Dread, Telegram, and I2P forums).

✓ Using private invite-only markets to vet new users.

✓ Switching to alternative anonymity networks, like I2P or decentralized hosting.

✓ Leveraging blockchain-based websites that cannot be easily seized.

Example: After the AlphaBay seizure in 2017, its users relocated to Dream Market and other emerging alternatives.

2. OSINT Techniques for Identifying Mirror Sites

Tracking mirror sites requires a combination of active and passive reconnaissance techniques, leveraging Dark Web crawling, metadata analysis, and user behavior tracking.

2.1 Monitoring Forum Announcements & Vendor Migration

Dark Web communities often announce new mirror sites or successor markets on forums like:

- **Dread** – A Dark Web forum where market operators post updates.
- **Envoy** – An alternative forum used for discussion on market relocations.
- **Raddle.me (Clear Web)** – A Reddit-like site sometimes used for encrypted announcements.

☐ **OSINT Tools for Forum Monitoring:**

- **Hunchly** – Captures and archives Dark Web posts for evidence collection.
- **OnionScan** – Crawls and analyzes .onion sites to detect mirrors.
- **Recon-ng** – A Python framework for tracking online footprint changes.

✓ **Tip**: Market admins often use the same writing style or branding elements (e.g., similar logos, UI, or PGP keys) across mirrors and successor sites.

2.2 Tracking Onion Site Fingerprints

Many mirror sites share common technical attributes with their original versions, which OSINT analysts can use to correlate them.

- **Server Configuration Similarities** – Using Shodan or OnionScan to analyze backend infrastructure.
- **SSL/TLS Certificates** – Some .onion sites reuse encryption certificates, which can link mirrors to the original site.
- **Metadata Analysis** – Comparing HTML, favicon hashes, and JavaScript libraries across suspected mirror sites.

☐ **Tools for Onion Site Fingerprinting:**

- **OnionScan** – Detects metadata leaks and infrastructure similarities.

- ◆ **ExifTool** – Extracts metadata from images and files used on market pages.
- ◆ **Shodan** – Identifies server configurations used by .onion sites.

2.3 Using Blockchain Analysis to Track Market Payments

Since Dark Web markets rely on cryptocurrency transactions, blockchain forensics can help track vendor migrations and market relocations.

- ◆ **Bitcoin & Monero Transactions** – Identifying reused wallet addresses.
- ◆ **Transaction Clustering** – Grouping related transactions to find new market addresses.
- ◆ **Crypto Exchange Deposits** – Tracking cash-out points linked to market admins.

☐ **Blockchain Forensics Tools:**

- ◆ **Chainalysis** – Tracks illicit Bitcoin transactions.
- ◆ **CipherTrace** – Analyzes Monero and other privacy coins.
- ◆ **Elliptic** – Identifies suspicious crypto wallets tied to Dark Web markets.

Example: After the Empire Market exit scam (2020), researchers tracked Bitcoin payments from Empire vendors to newly emerging markets like White House Market.

3. Case Studies: How Investigators Tracked Dark Web Market Relocations

Case Study #1: AlphaBay's Hidden Rebirth (2021)

- ◆ **Event**: AlphaBay was shut down in 2017, but a former admin attempted to revive it in 2021.
- ◆ **Tracking Method**: OSINT analysts identified reused PGP keys, writing styles, and forum activity.
- ◆ **Outcome**: The relaunch failed after credibility concerns arose within the community.

Case Study #2: Hansa Market Honeypot (2017)

- ◆ **Event**: Dutch law enforcement secretly took control of Hansa Market after AlphaBay's takedown.
- ◆ **Tracking Method**: Investigators monitored vendor migrations and crypto transactions, collecting evidence before shutting it down.

◆ **Outcome**: Over 10,000 users were identified and arrested worldwide.

4. Future Challenges in Tracking Dark Web Market Migrations

Dark Web markets are adapting their tactics to make tracking more difficult.

Emerging Trends:

✓ **Increased use of Monero (XMR)** – Bitcoin tracking has become more effective, so criminals shift to privacy coins.
✓ **Decentralized Marketplaces** – New platforms are being built on blockchain technology, making them harder to seize.
✓ **Tor Alternatives** – Some markets move to I2P, ZeroNet, or Yggdrasil for extra anonymity.
✓ **Invite-Only Markets** – Exclusive, closed-access marketplaces prevent OSINT monitoring.

How Investigators Can Adapt:

◆ Develop AI-driven crawlers for detecting hidden services and market mirrors.
◆ Expand blockchain forensic techniques to handle privacy-focused coins.
◆ Enhance linguistic & stylometric profiling to track market operators across different platforms.

5. Conclusion: The Evolution of Dark Web Market Tracking

Identifying mirror sites and tracking market relocations is an ongoing challenge for OSINT analysts and law enforcement. By leveraging forum monitoring, site fingerprinting, blockchain forensics, and behavioral analysis, investigators can stay ahead of cybercriminals and disrupt illicit operations. However, as anonymity tools and decentralized marketplaces evolve, researchers must continue to adapt their methods to uncover hidden networks and criminal infrastructure.

4.5 OSINT for Verifying the Legitimacy of Hidden Services

The Dark Web is rife with fraud, scams, and law enforcement honeypots, making verification of hidden services a critical step for OSINT analysts, cybersecurity researchers, and investigators. Whether tracking illicit marketplaces, whistleblower platforms, or darknet forums, verifying a site's authenticity, trustworthiness, and operational status is essential.

In this chapter, we explore OSINT methodologies, technical indicators, and social verification techniques to assess whether a hidden service is legitimate or a potential trap.

1. Understanding the Risks of Fake Hidden Services

The anonymity of the Dark Web creates an environment where anyone can set up a .onion site, making it difficult to distinguish between legitimate services, scams, and honeypots.

1.1 Common Types of Fake Hidden Services

◆ **Phishing & Scam Sites** – Fake marketplaces or forums designed to steal credentials and cryptocurrency.

◆ **Law Enforcement Honeypots** – Sites set up by agencies to monitor criminal activity or track users.

◆ **Imposter Markets** – Clones of legitimate markets that trick users into depositing funds without delivering services.

◆ **Defunct or Abandoned Services** – Pages that appear functional but no longer process transactions or user requests.

Example: After the Silk Road shutdown, multiple scam sites appeared claiming to be its successor, defrauding users of their Bitcoin.

2. OSINT Techniques for Verifying Hidden Services

2.1 Technical Analysis of Onion Sites

Investigating a .onion site's metadata, infrastructure, and operational history can reveal key authenticity indicators.

☐ **Tools & Methods:**

✓ **OnionScan** – Identifies security vulnerabilities, duplicate sites, and misconfigurations.

✓ **Shodan & Censys** – Detects linked IPs and hosting infrastructure.

✓ **SSL/TLS Certificate Analysis** – Some Dark Web sites reuse SSL certificates, helping analysts track related services.

Indicators of a Suspicious Hidden Service:

✗ Recently registered or frequently changing domains.

✗ Lack of security features (e.g., no PGP keys, weak SSL configurations).

✗ Hosting similarities with known scam sites.

Example: The Hansa Market honeypot (2017) was exposed due to small inconsistencies in server configurations, which tipped off some users.

2.2 Analyzing Forum Mentions & Reputation Systems

Many darknet users discuss marketplaces and hidden services on forums like Dread, Raddle, and Torum. Monitoring these discussions can help verify a site's legitimacy.

☐ **OSINT Techniques:**

✓ **Keyword Monitoring** – Track market reviews and scam alerts.
✓ **Stylometric Analysis** – Compare administrator writing styles across forums and site announcements.
✓ **PGP Key Verification** – Confirm that site operators sign updates with a known public key.

Example: In 2020, Empire Market's admins failed to sign official updates with their original PGP key, leading to speculation of an impending exit scam—which proved accurate.

2.3 Tracking Cryptocurrency Transactions for Legitimacy

Many Dark Web services rely on Bitcoin and Monero, but fraudulent sites often exhibit suspicious transaction patterns.

☐ **Blockchain OSINT Tools:**

✓ **Chainalysis & CipherTrace** – Track Bitcoin payments linked to known scams.
✓ **Elliptic & Bitquery** – Identify money laundering patterns.

✅ **BTC Explorer** – Check wallet reuse or ties to flagged addresses.

Verification Steps:

◆ Compare payment addresses with those used by legitimate markets.
◆ Check if funds are moving to known exchange cash-out points.
◆ Analyze transaction clusters to detect exit scams or laundering schemes.

Example: The AlphaBay relaunch (2021) failed credibility tests when users discovered wallet addresses tied to scam operations.

3. Case Studies: Real-World Verification of Dark Web Services

Case Study #1: Tracking a Phishing Scam on the Dark Web

◆ **Event**: A fake version of Wasabi Wallet's .onion site appeared, designed to steal Bitcoin.
◆ **OSINT Methodology**: Analysts compared PGP keys, SSL certificates, and transaction history, exposing the scam.
◆ **Outcome**: Warnings were issued on OSINT channels, preventing further theft.

Case Study #2: Law Enforcement Honeypot Discovery

◆ **Event**: Users suspected that DarkMarket was compromised before its shutdown.
◆ **OSINT Methodology**: Behavioral analysis and infrastructure tracking suggested it had been under surveillance.
◆ **Outcome**: The market was seized by Europol, confirming suspicions.

4. Future Challenges & Evolving Verification Methods

With decentralized marketplaces, AI-generated deepfake profiles, and improved anonymity tools, verifying Dark Web services is becoming more complex.

◆ Future OSINT Advancements:

✅ AI-driven linguistic analysis for market admin authentication.

✅ Advanced blockchain forensics for tracking Monero transactions.

✅ Dark Web AI crawlers to detect new scam sites faster.

5. Conclusion: The Importance of OSINT in Dark Web Verification

Infiltrating and verifying hidden services requires a multi-layered OSINT approach, combining technical forensics, user behavior tracking, and cryptocurrency analysis. As the Dark Web evolves, investigators must stay ahead of scammers and threat actors by continuously refining their verification techniques.

4.6 Case Study: Unmasking a Dark Web Administrator

The anonymity of the Dark Web presents a significant challenge for law enforcement, cybersecurity researchers, and OSINT investigators. However, through a combination of operational security (OPSEC) failures, blockchain analysis, linguistic fingerprinting, and infrastructure tracking, several high-profile darknet administrators have been unmasked over the years. This case study explores one such investigation—the takedown of AlphaBay's administrator, Alexandre Cazes, and the techniques used to reveal his identity.

1. Background: The Rise of AlphaBay

In 2014, AlphaBay emerged as the largest Dark Web marketplace, surpassing Silk Road in scale and revenue. The site facilitated the sale of narcotics, weapons, stolen data, malware, and hacking services, making it a prime target for law enforcement.

At its peak, AlphaBay had:

✅ Over 400,000 users

✅ $800 million in total transactions

✅ Acceptance of Bitcoin, Monero, and Ethereum

Despite its advanced anonymity features, the marketplace's founder and administrator, Alexandre Cazes (alias "Alpha02"), made crucial OPSEC mistakes that led to his unmasking.

2. The Investigation: OSINT & Digital Forensics Techniques

2.1 OPSEC Failures: A Slip in the Early Days

One of the earliest mistakes that helped investigators was Cazes' reuse of an old email address.

◆ In 2014, AlphaBay's official welcome emails contained a real-world email address: "pimp.alex_91@hotmail.com".
◆ A simple OSINT query linked this email to social media profiles, tech forums, and an online developer account belonging to Cazes.
◆ The same email was connected to a LinkedIn profile listing him as a web developer, reinforcing his technical background.

✓ **Lesson**: Threat actors often make their biggest mistakes early in their operational timeline, before they fully understand OPSEC.

2.2 Cryptocurrency Forensics: Tracking the AlphaBay Funds

AlphaBay processed millions in Bitcoin, Monero, and Ethereum transactions, but despite the use of mixers and tumblers, investigators were able to follow the money trail.

◆ Blockchain analysis revealed BTC addresses linked to AlphaBay deposits.
◆ Some of these funds were traced to wallets registered under Cazes' real name on crypto exchanges.
◆ His crypto transactions were linked to luxury car purchases and property investments.

✓ **Lesson**: Criminals often struggle to completely launder illicit funds—eventually, they need to cash out, creating opportunities for tracking.

2.3 Server Seizure & Digital Fingerprinting

Law enforcement agencies worked to locate AlphaBay's backend infrastructure, which was hosted across multiple Tor hidden services and encrypted servers.

◆ Through OSINT techniques like passive DNS analysis and metadata fingerprinting, investigators identified servers linked to AlphaBay.
◆ Cazes made a critical error by reusing encryption keys from his personal infrastructure, allowing analysts to connect multiple servers to his identity.

☑ **Lesson**: Even the most careful cybercriminals often reuse digital fingerprints across different networks.

2.4 Behavioral & Linguistic Analysis

Another breakthrough came from analyzing Cazes' writing style across multiple platforms.

◆ Posts made by Alpha02 (Cazes' online alias) on tech forums contained linguistic patterns matching AlphaBay's official communications.
◆ Investigators used stylometric analysis (writing style comparison) to link his forum activity to AlphaBay admin messages.
◆ Similarities in punctuation, phrasing, and emoji usage helped strengthen the connection.

☑ **Lesson**: Even on the Dark Web, writing style is a unique identifier that can be used to unmask administrators.

3. The Takedown: Arrest & Aftermath

In July 2017, an international task force—including FBI, DEA, Europol, and Thai law enforcement—moved to arrest Cazes in Bangkok, Thailand.

◆ During the arrest, Cazes' laptop was found open and logged into the AlphaBay admin panel, providing further irrefutable evidence.
◆ Authorities seized his assets, including luxury cars, Bitcoin holdings, and bank accounts tied to illicit profits.
◆ AlphaBay was taken offline, sending the Dark Web community into chaos.

The Unexpected Outcome

Before he could be extradited to the U.S., Cazes was found dead in his prison cell, with officials ruling it a suicide.

☑ Impact of the Takedown:

◆ AlphaBay's collapse led to the migration of users to competing markets like Dream Market and Hansa Market.

◆ Law enforcement's focus on cryptocurrency forensics became a key strategy for future investigations.

◆ The case highlighted the importance of early OPSEC mistakes and financial tracking in deanonymizing cybercriminals.

4. Key Takeaways for OSINT & Law Enforcement

The unmasking of AlphaBay's administrator provided several lessons for OSINT analysts and law enforcement:

◆ **Early mistakes are the most valuable clues** – Criminals often expose personal details before fully understanding OPSEC.

◆ **Cryptocurrency transactions leave a trail** – Even privacy-focused transactions can be tracked with advanced blockchain forensics.

◆ **Servers and encryption keys can reveal identity** – Reused digital infrastructure can link hidden services to real-world identities.

◆ **Writing style analysis is a powerful OSINT tool** – Stylometric analysis can connect cybercriminals across different platforms.

The AlphaBay takedown proved that no Dark Web marketplace is truly untouchable and highlighted the evolving sophistication of OSINT investigations.

5. Future Challenges in Unmasking Dark Web Operators

While the AlphaBay case was a major success, cybercriminals continue to adapt and improve their OPSEC:

✓ **Shift to Monero (XMR) and privacy coins** – Unlike Bitcoin, Monero transactions are harder to trace.

✓ **Decentralized marketplaces** – New markets are using blockchain-based hosting to prevent takedowns.

✓ **Improved identity masking** – Criminals use AI-generated deepfake profiles and burner devices.

Despite these challenges, OSINT investigators are also evolving, leveraging AI-driven tracking, advanced crypto forensics, and machine learning behavioral analysis to stay ahead.

6. Conclusion: The AlphaBay Case as a Model for Future OSINT Work

The unmasking of Alexandre Cazes and the takedown of AlphaBay demonstrated that no Dark Web criminal is completely anonymous—with the right OSINT techniques, even the most careful operators can be identified.

By combining early OPSEC failure analysis, blockchain tracking, server forensics, and linguistic profiling, law enforcement agencies can continue to unmask Dark Web administrators and dismantle illicit online marketplaces.

5. Cryptocurrency & Blockchain Tracking for OSINT

In this chapter, we will dive into the crucial role of cryptocurrency and blockchain technology in cybercrime investigations. As digital currencies like Bitcoin, Monero, and Ethereum continue to gain popularity, they offer both anonymity and traceability, making them a key focus for OSINT analysts. We will explore how blockchain, the underlying ledger technology, enables the tracking of transactions while also providing opportunities to uncover hidden financial flows and criminal activities. By learning how to utilize blockchain explorers, transaction analysis tools, and cryptocurrency wallet tracing techniques, investigators can trace illicit transactions across the network, identify key players, and uncover the financial aspects of cybercrime operations. This chapter will equip you with the skills to leverage blockchain data for effective intelligence gathering in the fight against digital crime.

5.1 How Cryptocurrency Powers the Dark Web Economy

The rise of cryptocurrencies has fundamentally transformed the Dark Web, providing anonymity, decentralization, and an alternative financial system for cybercriminals, black markets, and privacy-conscious users alike. Unlike traditional banking systems, cryptocurrencies enable pseudonymous transactions, making them the preferred payment method for illicit marketplaces, ransomware groups, money launderers, and fraudsters. However, while cryptocurrencies provide a layer of privacy, blockchain analysis and OSINT techniques have exposed vulnerabilities that law enforcement and security researchers leverage to track criminal activities.

This chapter explores how cryptocurrencies fuel the Dark Web economy, the most commonly used digital assets, and the evolving tactics used to evade detection.

1. Why Cryptocurrencies Are Essential to the Dark Web

Before the advent of Bitcoin in 2009, cash, prepaid cards, and traditional banking were the primary financial tools for illicit transactions. However, these methods were risky, traceable, and inefficient for global cybercriminal networks. Cryptocurrencies changed this landscape by offering:

✓ **Decentralization** – No central authority controls transactions.

☑ **Pseudonymity** – Identities are not directly tied to wallet addresses.

☑ **Fast, Global Transactions** – Funds can be transferred across borders instantly.

☑ **Irreversible Payments** – Unlike credit cards, there are no chargebacks.

◆ **Example**: The Silk Road, the first major Dark Web marketplace (2011-2013), was entirely dependent on Bitcoin for transactions, proving the viability of cryptocurrencies in illicit trade.

2. Most Common Cryptocurrencies on the Dark Web

2.1 Bitcoin (BTC) – The Standard, But Not Fully Private

◆ Bitcoin is still the most widely used cryptocurrency on the Dark Web due to its popularity and liquidity.

◆ However, Bitcoin transactions are recorded on a public ledger (the blockchain), making them traceable with the right forensic tools.

◆ Criminals use mixers, tumblers, and coinjoin services to obscure transaction origins.

☐ **Tracking Bitcoin Transactions:**

☑ Blockchain explorers (e.g., Blockchair, BTCscan) reveal transaction histories.

☑ Chainalysis & CipherTrace can link wallets to known Dark Web entities.

☑ Wallet clustering techniques help identify related addresses.

Example: In the AlphaBay takedown (2017), law enforcement traced Bitcoin transactions to unmask its administrator.

2.2 Monero (XMR) – The Privacy Coin of Choice

◆ Monero has overtaken Bitcoin as the preferred currency for cybercriminals due to its built-in privacy features.

◆ It uses ring signatures, stealth addresses, and confidential transactions to obfuscate sender, receiver, and amount details.

◆ Unlike Bitcoin, Monero transactions cannot be easily traced.

☐ **Challenges in Tracking Monero:**

✗ No public ledger for transaction history.

✗ Law enforcement cannot use standard blockchain analysis techniques.

✗ Exchanges that accept Monero often lack KYC regulations.

Example: The REvil ransomware gang demanded ransom payments exclusively in Monero to evade tracking.

2.3 Other Cryptocurrencies in the Dark Web Economy

◆ **Ethereum (ETH) & Smart Contracts** – Some darknet platforms experiment with smart contracts for escrow services.
◆ **Zcash (ZEC)** – Offers optional privacy features but is less popular than Monero.
◆ **Litecoin (LTC) & Dash (DASH)** – Sometimes used for faster transactions.
◆ **Stablecoins (USDT, DAI, BUSD)** – Increasingly used to counter crypto volatility.

3. How Dark Web Marketplaces Handle Cryptocurrency Payments

3.1 Payment Methods in Illicit Marketplaces

◆ **Escrow Systems** – Funds are held in escrow until buyers confirm the receipt of goods.
◆ **Multisignature Transactions** – Require multiple parties to approve a transaction, increasing security.
◆ **Direct Payments** – Some sellers demand upfront payments, increasing the risk of scams.

3.2 How Criminals Launder Cryptocurrency

To cash out illicit funds, cybercriminals use a mix of techniques:

✓ **Mixers & Tumblers** – Break transaction trails by mixing funds with other users' crypto.
✓ **Privacy Wallets** – Software like Wasabi Wallet and Samourai Wallet use CoinJoin to obfuscate Bitcoin transactions.
✓ **Peer-to-Peer (P2P) Exchanges** – LocalMonero and Bisq allow anonymous fiat-crypto conversions.
✓ **Crypto ATMs & Gift Cards** – Convert crypto to cash without direct banking involvement.

◆ **Example**: The Hydra Market (shut down in 2022) offered integrated money laundering services, including cash-out services through Russian financial institutions.

4. OSINT & Law Enforcement Techniques for Tracking Cryptocurrency Transactions

Despite criminals' efforts to stay anonymous, blockchain forensics tools have made significant progress in tracking illicit funds.

4.1 Blockchain Analysis Tools

☐ **Popular Forensic Tools:**

✅ **Chainalysis** – Used by the FBI to trace Bitcoin payments in ransomware attacks.
✅ **Elliptic** – Identifies connections between wallets and criminal activities.
✅ **CipherTrace** – Analyzes Monero transactions and darknet activity.

Example: In 2021, the Colonial Pipeline ransom payment was tracked through Bitcoin forensics, leading to the recovery of $2.3 million in BTC.

4.2 Tracking Cryptocurrency Through Exchange KYC Regulations

Many cryptocurrency exchanges now enforce Know Your Customer (KYC) and Anti-Money Laundering (AML) regulations, making it harder for criminals to cash out funds.

✅ If a criminal cashes out via a regulated exchange, authorities can subpoena the exchange for identity verification.

✅ Suspicious wallet addresses are blacklisted, preventing easy conversion of illicit funds.

Example: The Bitcoin Fog mixing service was shut down in 2021 after investigators linked transactions to real-world identities via KYC exchanges.

5. The Future of Cryptocurrency in the Dark Web

As law enforcement improves blockchain tracking, cybercriminals are shifting towards more advanced privacy techniques:

✅ Greater reliance on Monero and other privacy coins.

✓ Decentralized finance (DeFi) and privacy-preserving smart contracts for laundering funds.

✓ Atomic swaps to convert Bitcoin to Monero without a traceable exchange.

✓ AI-powered address clustering for more sophisticated laundering techniques.

However, OSINT and blockchain forensics are also evolving, ensuring that even privacy-focused transactions leave digital fingerprints.

6. Conclusion: The Double-Edged Sword of Cryptocurrency in the Dark Web

While cryptocurrencies fuel illicit economies, they also provide investigators with a permanent, immutable record of transactions—a valuable asset in tracing cybercrime. With advances in blockchain forensics, OSINT, and regulatory oversight, the cat-and-mouse game between law enforcement and cybercriminals will continue to evolve.

For OSINT analysts, the key to understanding Dark Web financial activity lies in:

◆ Tracking wallet addresses and clustering transactions
◆ Identifying laundering patterns using blockchain tools
◆ Monitoring exchange compliance with AML/KYC regulations

As the Dark Web adapts, so too must OSINT techniques, ensuring that illicit financial flows remain traceable, disruptable, and ultimately, prosecutable.

5.2 Investigating Bitcoin & Altcoin Transactions

Cryptocurrencies serve as the financial backbone of the Dark Web, facilitating transactions for illicit marketplaces, ransomware payments, and other cybercriminal activities. While Bitcoin (BTC) remains the most commonly used cryptocurrency, criminals increasingly rely on privacy-focused altcoins like Monero (XMR), Zcash (ZEC), and Litecoin (LTC) to evade detection. However, law enforcement agencies, cybersecurity professionals, and OSINT analysts have developed sophisticated techniques for tracing Bitcoin and altcoin transactions, identifying wallets linked to illegal activities, and tracking the flow of funds across the blockchain.

This chapter explores how investigators analyze cryptocurrency transactions, the challenges posed by privacy coins, and real-world techniques used to deanonymize illicit financial flows on the Dark Web.

1. Understanding Cryptocurrency Transactions on the Blockchain

Cryptocurrency transactions operate on decentralized public ledgers, where all transfers between wallets are recorded permanently. Each transaction contains:

✅ **Sender's Address (Public Key)** – The wallet that initiates the transaction.

✅ **Receiver's Address (Public Key)** – The wallet that receives the funds.

✅ **Transaction Hash (TXID)** – A unique identifier for each transaction.

✅ **Timestamp** – When the transaction was processed.

✅ **Transaction Amount** – The number of coins transferred.

♦ **Example**: A Bitcoin transaction from Wallet A to Wallet B will have a traceable TXID on the blockchain, making it possible to follow the movement of funds.

💡 **Key Insight**: While cryptocurrency wallets are pseudonymous, their transactions are fully visible on the blockchain. This allows investigators to track illicit funds by analyzing transaction patterns and connections.

2. Investigative Techniques for Tracking Bitcoin Transactions

2.1 Using Blockchain Explorers for OSINT

Blockchain explorers provide real-time access to cryptocurrency transaction data. Investigators use them to:

✅ Identify wallet addresses linked to known criminal activities.

✅ Follow the movement of stolen or illicit funds.

✅ Map out transaction chains to uncover related wallets.

🔲 **Popular Blockchain Explorers:**

♦ Blockchair (Bitcoin, Ethereum, Litecoin, Monero)
♦ BTCScan (Bitcoin-specific tracking)

◆ Blockchain.com Explorer (Multiple blockchains)

◆ Etherscan (Ethereum transactions & ERC-20 tokens)

◆ **Example**: After the Colonial Pipeline ransomware attack (2021), blockchain analysis helped track the Bitcoin ransom payment, leading to the seizure of $2.3 million by U.S. law enforcement.

2.2 Wallet Clustering & Address Attribution

Bitcoin transactions often involve multiple addresses in a single transaction, making it possible to group related addresses together. This technique, known as wallet clustering, helps analysts:

✅ Identify addresses controlled by the same user.

✅ Distinguish between individual wallets and exchange wallets.

✅ Track criminals attempting to hide funds through multiple addresses.

💡 **Key Insight**: When criminals reuse addresses or fail to properly anonymize transactions, OSINT investigators can link multiple transactions to a single entity.

◆ **Example**: In the Silk Road investigation, law enforcement used wallet clustering to link Bitcoin addresses to real-world individuals, leading to multiple arrests.

2.3 Cryptocurrency Mixing & Tumbling – How Criminals Obscure Transactions

To evade tracking, cybercriminals use mixing services (also known as tumblers) to obfuscate Bitcoin transactions. These services work by:

◆ Pooling transactions from multiple users.

◆ Shuffling the coins to break direct transaction links.

◆ Sending mixed coins back to users, making it harder to trace the original source.

☐ **Popular Mixing Services Used by Criminals:**

✅ **Wasabi Wallet** – Uses CoinJoin to mix transactions.

✅ **Samourai Wallet** – Implements Whirlpool mixing.

✅ **ChipMixer** – Operated on the Dark Web before being shut down.

💡 **Key Insight**: Despite their effectiveness, mixers aren't foolproof—law enforcement agencies like Chainalysis and CipherTrace have developed forensic techniques to deanonymize mixed transactions.

◆ **Example**: In 2021, Bitcoin Fog (a popular mixing service) was taken down after investigators linked transactions to real-world identities.

3. Tracking Altcoin Transactions: Challenges & Solutions

While Bitcoin remains the most frequently investigated cryptocurrency, criminals are shifting to privacy coins and alternative digital assets that offer enhanced anonymity.

3.1 Investigating Monero (XMR) Transactions

Unlike Bitcoin, Monero transactions are private by default, making them far harder to trace. Monero achieves anonymity through:

✅ **Ring Signatures** – Mixing transactions so that multiple senders appear in the record.
✅ **Stealth Addresses** – One-time addresses that prevent recipient identification.
✅ **Confidential Transactions** – Hiding the amount of XMR sent in each transaction.

☐ **Challenges in Tracking Monero:**

✘ No public ledger for viewing transactions.

✘ No direct way to trace sender-receiver relationships.

✘ Privacy features prevent address clustering.

◆ **Example**: Ransomware groups like REvil and DarkSide switched to Monero payments to avoid Bitcoin tracing by law enforcement.

💡 **Key Insight**: While Monero is more resistant to tracking, law enforcement agencies pressure exchanges to flag or ban suspicious Monero transactions to disrupt illicit flows.

3.2 Investigating Ethereum (ETH) & Smart Contract Transactions

Ethereum is increasingly used in the Dark Web for smart contract-based financial schemes, NFT laundering, and DeFi fraud. Investigating Ethereum transactions involves:

✅ Tracking ETH transfers through Etherscan.

✅ Identifying scam smart contracts used in rug pulls.

✅ Analyzing DeFi protocols that criminals use to launder funds.

♦ **Example**: In 2023, the $200M Euler Finance hack involved stolen Ethereum, which investigators tracked through DeFi transaction analysis.

💡 **Key Insight**: Ethereum-based transactions introduce new layers of complexity due to smart contracts and decentralized finance (DeFi) platforms.

4. Case Study: Tracing Bitcoin Ransomware Payments

In 2021, the Colonial Pipeline ransomware attack disrupted fuel supplies across the U.S. The attackers demanded a $4.4 million ransom in Bitcoin. However, blockchain forensics quickly uncovered the money trail:

♦ The FBI tracked the ransom through multiple Bitcoin wallets.
♦ Investigators identified a wallet associated with a centralized exchange.
♦ Authorities issued a subpoena, revealing the attackers' identities.
♦ $2.3 million in Bitcoin was recovered.

💡 **Key Lesson**: Even when criminals attempt to obfuscate their transactions, investigators can leverage blockchain transparency and centralized exchange regulations to track and recover illicit funds.

5. Conclusion: The Future of Crypto Investigations in OSINT

As criminals continue evolving their tactics, OSINT analysts must stay ahead by:

✅ Leveraging blockchain analysis tools like Chainalysis & CipherTrace.

✅ Understanding how altcoins like Monero and Ethereum operate.

✅ Monitoring cryptocurrency exchanges for suspicious activity.

✅ Tracking ransomware payments and illicit financial networks.

Despite the increasing complexity of cryptocurrency laundering techniques, advancements in blockchain forensics and regulatory oversight are making it harder for criminals to operate anonymously. Investigators who master these techniques will play a crucial role in disrupting cybercrime and exposing illicit financial networks in the Dark Web.

5.3 Blockchain Explorers & Transaction Analysis Tools

Blockchain technology provides transparency and immutability, making it possible for investigators, OSINT analysts, and law enforcement to track cryptocurrency transactions in real time. While cybercriminals attempt to launder illicit funds using mixing services, privacy wallets, and alternative cryptocurrencies, advanced blockchain explorers and forensic tools allow analysts to uncover transaction histories, wallet connections, and hidden financial networks.

This chapter explores how blockchain explorers work, the most powerful transaction analysis tools, and the techniques used to trace illicit funds across Bitcoin, Ethereum, and other cryptocurrencies.

1. What Are Blockchain Explorers?

Blockchain explorers are search engines for blockchain transactions. They allow users to:

✅ **View transaction histories** – Find sender and receiver wallet addresses.
✅ **Track wallet balances** – Monitor the holdings of any public wallet.
✅ **Analyze transaction flows** – Identify patterns of illicit activity.
✅ **Locate block confirmations** – Verify whether a transaction is complete.

💡 **Key Insight**: Since Bitcoin and many other cryptocurrencies operate on public ledgers, anyone with access to a blockchain explorer can investigate financial transactions.

1.1 How Blockchain Explorers Work

A blockchain explorer indexes and displays real-time blockchain data. It allows users to enter:

♦ **Transaction Hash (TXID)** – A unique identifier for every transaction.

- **Wallet Address** – To track incoming/outgoing payments.
- **Block Number** – To view transactions within a specific block.

Example: If a hacker's wallet receives Bitcoin from a ransomware victim, investigators can use a blockchain explorer to follow the movement of funds and uncover linked transactions.

2. Popular Blockchain Explorers for OSINT & Investigation

2.1 Bitcoin & Multi-Currency Explorers

- ☐ **Blockchair** – Supports Bitcoin, Ethereum, Litecoin, Monero, and more.
- ☐ **Blockchain.com Explorer** – Tracks Bitcoin, Ethereum, and Bitcoin Cash.
- ☐ **BTCScan** – Focuses on Bitcoin address analytics.
- ☐ **Mempool.space** – Real-time Bitcoin transaction monitoring.

- **Example**: After the Silk Road takedown (2013), law enforcement used blockchain explorers to trace millions in Bitcoin transactions, leading to multiple asset seizures.

2.2 Ethereum & Altcoin Explorers

- ☐ **Etherscan** – The go-to tool for tracking Ethereum and ERC-20 tokens.
- ☐ **Polygonscan** – Analyzes transactions on the Polygon (MATIC) network.
- ☐ **Solscan** – Tracks Solana-based transactions.
- ☐ **BSCScan** – Used for Binance Smart Chain transactions.

- **Example**: In NFT and DeFi fraud investigations, OSINT analysts use Etherscan to track stolen assets moving through Ethereum-based smart contracts.

3. Advanced Blockchain Analysis Tools

While blockchain explorers offer basic transaction tracking, forensic tools provide deeper insights into wallet clustering, laundering techniques, and darknet financial activity.

3.1 Chainalysis – The Gold Standard for Law Enforcement

- Used by the FBI, Europol, and financial regulators to investigate crypto crime.
- Identifies wallet clusters, mixing services, and darknet transactions.

◆ Links crypto addresses to real-world identities when used with subpoenaed exchange data.

◆ **Example**: In 2021, Chainalysis helped track the Colonial Pipeline ransomware payment, leading to the recovery of $2.3 million in Bitcoin.

3.2 Elliptic – AI-Powered Crypto Intelligence

◆ Uses AI-driven analytics to detect fraud and illicit financial flows.
◆ Flags high-risk addresses linked to darknet markets, scams, and hacks.
◆ Helps exchanges comply with AML and KYC regulations.

◆ **Example**: Elliptic assisted in tracing hacked funds from the KuCoin exchange in 2020, preventing criminals from cashing out stolen assets.

3.3 CipherTrace – Tracking Privacy Coins & Monero Analysis

◆ Specializes in tracking Monero (XMR), Zcash (ZEC), and Bitcoin mixing services.
◆ Provides risk scores for wallet addresses.
◆ Used by banks and financial institutions to prevent money laundering.

◆ **Example**: U.S. law enforcement used CipherTrace to track illicit Monero transactions linked to darknet markets.

3.4 TRM Labs – Fraud Detection for Financial Institutions

◆ Monitors crypto transactions in real-time to detect suspicious activity.
◆ Integrates with law enforcement to trace illicit crypto payments.
◆ Used by governments and major banks to fight money laundering.

◆ **Example**: TRM Labs helped track stolen assets from a DeFi rug pull, allowing victims to recover their funds.

4. OSINT Techniques for Crypto Transaction Analysis

4.1 Wallet Address Clustering

◆ Combines multiple related addresses into a single entity.

◆ Helps investigators identify connections between different transactions.

◆ Useful in tracking darknet market administrators and ransomware operators.

💡 Key Insight: If a hacker deposits funds into multiple wallets, clustering can reveal which wallets belong to the same user.

4.2 Tracking Transactions Through Exchanges

◆ Many illicit transactions eventually pass through cryptocurrency exchanges.

◆ Investigators monitor wallets linked to KYC-compliant exchanges.

◆ If a criminal cashes out at an exchange, law enforcement can issue subpoenas to uncover their identity.

◆ **Example**: In 2021, the Bitcoin Fog mixer was dismantled after investigators tracked transactions leading to an exchange account tied to a real identity.

4.3 Following Money Laundering Trails

◆ Criminals use mixers, P2P transactions, and DeFi protocols to hide their tracks.

◆ Blockchain analysis tools can detect laundering patterns and identify high-risk wallets.

◆ Investigators track off-ramping transactions (where illicit funds are converted to fiat).

💡 **Key Insight**: Even when criminals use mixers, advanced AI tools can identify suspicious transaction flows.

5. Case Study: The AlphaBay Takedown & Blockchain Analysis

In 2017, AlphaBay, the largest darknet marketplace, was taken down by law enforcement. Investigators used blockchain forensic techniques to trace payments made on the platform:

◆ They identified wallets used for AlphaBay transactions.

◆ By analyzing withdrawals to fiat exchanges, they linked funds to real-world individuals.

◆ AlphaBay's administrator was arrested, and millions in cryptocurrency were seized.

💡 **Key Lesson**: Even on the Dark Web, cryptocurrency transactions leave a digital trail that investigators can follow.

6. Conclusion: The Future of Blockchain Forensics

As criminals adopt privacy-focused techniques, investigators must stay ahead by:

✅ Leveraging blockchain explorers to track illicit funds.

✅ Using AI-powered forensic tools like Chainalysis and Elliptic.

✅ Monitoring exchange compliance with AML/KYC regulations.

✅ Adapting to new privacy coins and DeFi laundering methods.

Despite criminals' best efforts, blockchain forensics is becoming more advanced, ensuring that illicit financial activity remains detectable, traceable, and ultimately, prosecutable.

5.4 Tracing Cryptocurrency Laundering Techniques

Cryptocurrency laundering has become a key method for cybercriminals to obscure the origins of illicit funds. Criminals use mixing services, privacy wallets, chain-hopping, P2P transfers, and DeFi protocols to cover their tracks. However, OSINT analysts and blockchain forensic investigators employ advanced tracing techniques to identify patterns, follow transaction trails, and ultimately de-anonymize illicit financial flows.

This chapter explores the most common cryptocurrency laundering methods used on the Dark Web and how investigators can trace and disrupt them using blockchain analysis tools and OSINT techniques.

1. How Cryptocurrency Laundering Works

Cryptocurrency laundering is the process of disguising the origin of illicit digital funds to make them appear legitimate. Criminals use multiple techniques to break the link between the source of funds (e.g., darknet markets, ransomware payments, fraud) and their destination (e.g., cash-out exchanges, real-world purchases).

💡 **Key Insight**: Unlike traditional financial systems, blockchain transactions are permanent and publicly recorded, making them traceable if analyzed correctly.

2. Common Cryptocurrency Laundering Techniques

2.1 Mixing (Tumbling) Services

What it is: Mixers, or tumblers, are third-party services that blend multiple users' coins together before redistributing them to new wallets. This process breaks the transaction trail, making it harder to trace the origin of funds.

◆ **Types of Mixers:**

- **Centralized Mixers** – Users send funds to a single service provider, who then redistributes "clean" coins.
- **Decentralized Mixers** – Use protocol-based mixing, such as CoinJoin, to make tracking harder.

◆ **Real-World Example:**

- **Helix (2014-2017)** – A darknet-based Bitcoin mixer processed over $300 million in illicit transactions before being shut down by law enforcement.

OSINT Tracing Method:

✓ Identify large incoming transactions to known mixers.

✓ Monitor wallet addresses associated with mixing services.

✓ Use heuristic analysis and clustering techniques to detect mixing patterns.

2.2 Privacy Coins (Monero, Zcash, Dash)

What it is: Some cryptocurrencies have built-in privacy features that make tracking transactions extremely difficult.

◆ **Most Common Privacy Coins:**

- **Monero (XMR)** – Uses ring signatures, stealth addresses, and confidential transactions to obscure sender/receiver details.
- **Zcash (ZEC)** – Offers shielded transactions that encrypt transaction details.
- **Dash (DASH)** – Uses PrivateSend, a coin-mixing feature for added anonymity.

◆ **Real-World Example:**

Darknet markets like White House Market and Alphabay switched from Bitcoin to Monero to enhance privacy and avoid blockchain tracing.

OSINT Tracing Method:

✓ Monitor entry and exit points where privacy coins are converted to traceable assets (e.g., exchanges, peer-to-peer transactions).

✓ Use blockchain forensic tools like CipherTrace, which has limited Monero tracing capabilities.

✓ Analyze transaction amounts and patterns to identify laundering behavior.

2.3 Chain-Hopping (Cross-Blockchain Swaps)

What it is: Chain-hopping involves rapidly converting funds across different blockchains to obscure their origins. Criminals swap Bitcoin for Ethereum, Monero, or other cryptocurrencies using decentralized exchanges (DEXs) or atomic swaps.

◆ **Key Techniques:**

- **Atomic Swaps** – Direct P2P coin exchanges between different blockchains.
- **DEX Swaps** – Using platforms like Uniswap, PancakeSwap, or THORChain to convert funds.
- **Bridges** – Transferring assets between blockchains via wrapped tokens (e.g., WBTC, renBTC).

◆ **Real-World Example:**

- North Korean hacker groups have used chain-hopping to launder stolen cryptocurrency, making it harder for investigators to track funds.

OSINT Tracing Method:

✓ Monitor transactions moving through cross-chain platforms.

✓ Identify suspicious conversion patterns (e.g., rapid swaps between multiple assets).

✓ Track entry and exit points where funds return to traceable blockchains.

2.4 Peer-to-Peer (P2P) Transactions

What it is: Instead of using exchanges, criminals use direct P2P transactions to sell illicit crypto for cash or goods, avoiding centralized monitoring.

◆ **Common P2P Methods:**

- **OTC (Over-the-Counter) Trades** – Large trades conducted privately.
- **Telegram/WhatsApp Groups** – Used to arrange P2P crypto exchanges.
- **LocalBitcoins & Paxful** – P2P marketplaces that have been exploited for laundering.

◆ **Real-World Example:**

- In 2022, a darknet fentanyl dealer used Telegram and LocalBitcoins to convert Bitcoin into cash without detection.

OSINT Tracing Method:

✓ Monitor known P2P marketplaces and forums for illicit activity.

✓ Analyze trading patterns and connections between multiple wallet addresses.

✓ Use social engineering and sock puppet accounts to infiltrate laundering networks.

2.5 DeFi Laundering (Mixing via Smart Contracts)

What it is: Criminals use decentralized finance (DeFi) platforms to obfuscate fund movements via liquidity pools, lending protocols, and smart contract-based mixers.

◆ **Key Techniques:**

- **Tornado Cash** – A DeFi-based Ethereum mixer that anonymizes transactions.
- **Liquidity Pool Laundering** – Deposit illicit funds into liquidity pools, withdraw them under a different identity.
- **Flash Loans** – Use instant, uncollateralized loans to mix funds and break transaction trails.

◆ **Real-World Example:**

In 2022, the Ronin Bridge hack ($600M) used Tornado Cash to launder stolen funds.

OSINT Tracing Method:

✓ Monitor large inflows/outflows to Tornado Cash and similar services.

✓ Track on-chain smart contract interactions linked to laundering patterns.

✓ Use blockchain forensic tools like Chainalysis Reactor to follow DeFi trails.

3. Case Study: The Colonial Pipeline Ransomware Investigation

In 2021, the Colonial Pipeline ransomware attack resulted in a $4.4 million Bitcoin ransom payment. The U.S. Department of Justice was able to trace the ransom payments through blockchain forensic analysis and recover $2.3 million in stolen Bitcoin.

◆ **How Investigators Traced the Funds:**

- Identified the ransomware wallet that received the payment.
- Used blockchain analysis tools (Chainalysis, Elliptic) to track fund movements.
- Found that the criminals used a mixer, but later moved funds to a regulated exchange.
- Issued a legal request to the exchange, leading to fund seizure.

💡 **Key Lesson**: Even if criminals use mixing services and chain-hopping, they often need to cash out through an exchange, which creates an opportunity for investigators to intervene.

4. Conclusion: Overcoming Cryptocurrency Laundering Challenges

While criminals continue to evolve their laundering tactics, OSINT analysts and investigators can fight back with advanced blockchain forensic tools.

✓ Monitor mixing services and privacy wallets for suspicious transactions.

✓ Track cross-chain movements and smart contract interactions.

✓ Leverage forensic tools like Chainalysis, Elliptic, and CipherTrace.

✓ Identify laundering trails when criminals cash out through exchanges.

Despite increasing privacy mechanisms, cryptocurrency laundering remains traceable—investigators just need the right tools and techniques.

5.5 Identifying Cryptocurrency Exchanges Used by Cybercriminals

Cryptocurrency exchanges play a crucial role in the cybercriminal ecosystem, serving as entry and exit points for illicit funds. While some exchanges enforce strict Know Your Customer (KYC) and Anti-Money Laundering (AML) regulations, others operate in jurisdictions with weak oversight, making them ideal platforms for laundering stolen or illicitly obtained cryptocurrencies.

This chapter explores how cybercriminals exploit cryptocurrency exchanges, the techniques used to identify illicit activities, and OSINT methods for tracking cybercriminal transactions through exchanges.

1. Why Cybercriminals Use Cryptocurrency Exchanges

Cryptocurrency exchanges function as financial hubs, allowing users to buy, sell, and trade digital assets. However, cybercriminals leverage exchanges for the following purposes:

1.1 Cashing Out Illicit Funds

- Cybercriminals convert stolen Bitcoin, Monero, or Ethereum into fiat currency (USD, EUR, etc.).
- Ransomware groups, darknet market vendors, and fraudsters use exchanges to liquidate stolen funds.

1.2 Laundering Stolen Crypto

- Criminals deposit illicit funds, trade them between different cryptocurrencies, and then withdraw to new wallets or offshore accounts.
- They often use low-KYC or no-KYC exchanges to avoid detection.

1.3 Funding Further Criminal Activities

- Threat actors use exchanges to buy tools, malware, stolen credit card data, and hacking services from the dark web.

1.4 Moving Funds to Privacy Coins

- Many criminals exchange Bitcoin for Monero (XMR) or other privacy coins on exchanges that allow anonymous trading.

2. Types of Exchanges Used by Cybercriminals

Not all cryptocurrency exchanges operate under strict regulatory frameworks. Some are more vulnerable to criminal exploitation due to lax security, anonymity features, or regulatory loopholes.

2.1 High-Risk and No-KYC Exchanges

- Some exchanges allow users to trade without ID verification, making them attractive for cybercriminals.
- Example: "Bulletproof" exchanges that openly market themselves as privacy-focused platforms.
- Real-world case: BTC-e, a Russian exchange, facilitated money laundering until it was shut down in 2017.

2.2 Offshore and Unregulated Exchanges

- Some exchanges operate in jurisdictions with minimal financial oversight, making them difficult to regulate.
- **Example**: "Rogue" exchanges in countries with weak AML enforcement.

2.3 Decentralized Exchanges (DEXs)

- DEXs like Uniswap, PancakeSwap, and THORChain allow P2P trades with no intermediaries.
- Criminals swap illicit funds for privacy-focused tokens without going through a central authority.
- **Real-world case**: North Korean hackers have used DEXs to launder stolen funds.

2.4 P2P Exchanges and OTC Desks

- Peer-to-peer (P2P) marketplaces enable direct crypto trades between users, often without KYC.
- Over-the-counter (OTC) desks facilitate large, anonymous trades for high-net-worth individuals, including criminals.
- **Example**: LocalBitcoins was frequently used by darknet market vendors before implementing stricter KYC rules.

3. OSINT Techniques for Identifying Criminal Exchange Use

3.1 Blockchain Analysis & Transaction Tracing

By using blockchain analysis tools, investigators can track suspicious transactions leading to exchanges.

◆ **Key Tools for Blockchain Analysis:**

✅ **Chainalysis Reactor** – Tracks illicit crypto transactions and exchange activity.
✅ **Elliptic Forensics** – Detects money laundering patterns on exchanges.
✅ **CipherTrace** – Identifies risk factors in crypto transactions.
✅ **Crystal Blockchain** – Maps relationships between illicit funds and exchanges.

◆ **How Investigators Use These Tools:**

- Identify wallets associated with darknet markets, ransomware, or fraud.
- Follow transaction trails leading to exchanges.
- Detect suspicious withdrawal patterns and trade behaviors.

Example: After the Colonial Pipeline ransomware attack, the FBI used blockchain analytics to trace ransom payments to a crypto exchange, leading to the recovery of $2.3 million.

3.2 Identifying High-Risk Exchanges Through OSINT

Cybercriminals openly discuss "safe" exchanges on dark web forums, Telegram groups, and hacker marketplaces. OSINT investigators can infiltrate these spaces to collect intelligence.

◆ **OSINT Techniques:**

✅ Monitoring darknet forums for discussions on crypto cashouts.

✅ Tracking mentions of "bulletproof" or "no-KYC" exchanges on social media and dark web sites.

✅ Using sock puppet accounts to interact with cybercriminal communities.

✅ Cross-referencing exchange addresses with known illicit wallets.

Example: In 2021, dark web vendors frequently discussed Paxful and Binance P2P as "low-risk" platforms for laundering stolen funds.

3.3 Exchange Deposit & Withdrawal Analysis

Investigators can monitor suspicious deposit and withdrawal activity on high-risk exchanges.

◆ **Indicators of Illicit Activity:**

▸ Large crypto deposits from darknet markets or mixing services.
▸ Frequent small withdrawals (structuring to avoid detection).
▸ Rapid conversion of Bitcoin to Monero (attempting to hide funds).
▸ Connections to known ransomware or fraud wallets.

Example: The Hydra dark web marketplace used exchanges in Russia to cash out millions in illicit crypto transactions before it was shut down in 2022.

3.4 Identifying Exchange Wallet Addresses

Some exchanges publish their wallet addresses for transparency. Investigators can use these to track illicit transactions.

◆ **How to Find Exchange Wallet Addresses:**

✅ Use blockchain explorers (e.g., BTCscan, Etherscan) to analyze known exchange wallets.

✅ Search crypto forums and GitHub repositories for leaked wallet lists.

✓ Monitor exchange deposit addresses appearing in ransomware notes or darknet vendor profiles.

Example: When investigating the 2020 Twitter Bitcoin scam, analysts identified an exchange wallet used by the scammers to withdraw stolen funds.

4. Case Study: Binance & Cybercrime Investigations

In 2021, Binance, the world's largest crypto exchange, faced scrutiny for allegedly facilitating money laundering. Investigators found that:

- Criminals used Binance P2P trading to convert illicit funds.
- Binance did not enforce strict KYC until 2021, allowing anonymous transactions.
- Some darknet market vendors recommended Binance as a safe cashout option.

As a result, Binance strengthened its KYC requirements and froze accounts linked to illicit activity.

Key Lesson: Even well-known exchanges can be exploited by cybercriminals, and OSINT combined with blockchain analysis can help expose illicit use.

5. Conclusion: Fighting Crypto-Based Money Laundering

Cryptocurrency exchanges remain a critical point in cybercriminal financial networks. OSINT analysts, law enforcement, and financial crime investigators must:

✓ Monitor blockchain transactions leading to exchanges.

✓ Identify high-risk, no-KYC, or offshore exchanges favored by criminals.

✓ Analyze darknet forums and Telegram groups for exchange-related discussions.

✓ Collaborate with blockchain forensic firms to track illicit funds.

Despite criminals' efforts to hide their activities, blockchain transparency and OSINT methods make it possible to uncover and disrupt their financial operations.

5.6 Case Study: Following the Money Trail of a Dark Web Fraudster

Cryptocurrency has become the preferred medium of exchange for cybercriminals operating in the dark web economy. Fraudsters, ransomware groups, and illicit vendors use digital currencies to facilitate transactions while attempting to stay anonymous. However, blockchain transparency and OSINT techniques allow investigators to trace these transactions and uncover hidden networks of criminal activity.

In this case study, we will follow the money trail of a dark web fraudster—a cybercriminal selling stolen credit card data and personal information through an underground marketplace. By using blockchain analysis, OSINT tools, and transaction tracing techniques, investigators were able to identify key wallet addresses, uncover laundering tactics, and ultimately track the fraudster to a cryptocurrency exchange where funds were withdrawn.

1. The Investigation Begins: Identifying the Fraudster

The case started when cybersecurity researchers discovered a dark web marketplace selling stolen credit card details. A particular vendor, operating under the alias "ShadowBrokerX," had been active for over a year and had thousands of transactions linked to his account.

Investigators used OSINT techniques to gather the following intelligence:

◆ **Vendor Profile**: ShadowBrokerX had a well-established reputation on multiple dark web forums and marketplaces.
◆ **Payment Method**: Customers were instructed to send Bitcoin (BTC) payments to a specific wallet address displayed on his vendor page.
◆ **Communication Channels**: The vendor used Telegram and Tox for encrypted messaging with potential buyers.
◆ **Escrow Services**: The marketplace provided an escrow system, but some buyers preferred direct transactions with the fraudster.

With the wallet address in hand, analysts turned to blockchain analysis tools to track the movement of funds.

2. Tracing Transactions on the Blockchain

Using blockchain forensics platforms such as Chainalysis, Elliptic, and CipherTrace, investigators traced the flow of Bitcoin from the vendor's initial wallet address to multiple intermediary wallets.

2.1 Identifying the Initial Wallet

- The fraudster's Bitcoin address received hundreds of small payments from different sources.
- Payments were typically 0.01 to 0.05 BTC, suggesting a steady stream of transactions from buyers.
- Funds were quickly moved to new wallets within 24 hours, a classic tactic to obscure the money trail.

2.2 Spotting a Mixing Service

After receiving payments, ShadowBrokerX used a cryptocurrency mixing (tumbler) service to obfuscate the origin of funds. Tumblers work by:

- Pooling multiple Bitcoin transactions from different users.
- Redistributing the funds to new wallets in randomized amounts.
- Breaking the transaction chain, making it difficult to track.

Despite this, blockchain analysts were able to follow the movement of funds using clustering algorithms, which detected links between the fraudster's addresses and the mixer output.

2.3 Exchange Deposits & Cashing Out

After laundering the funds, ShadowBrokerX sent Bitcoin to a cryptocurrency exchange known for weak KYC regulations.

- The transactions were split into smaller amounts before reaching the exchange to avoid detection.
- Investigators noted that some funds were converted into Monero (XMR), a privacy coin known for its untraceability.
- A portion of the Bitcoin was eventually withdrawn to a PayPal-linked account, providing a key lead in the investigation.

3. OSINT Investigation: Unmasking the Fraudster

Once investigators identified the exchange where the fraudster withdrew funds, they conducted an OSINT investigation to connect the activity to a real identity.

3.1 Scraping Dark Web Forums & Marketplaces

Using specialized web crawlers, investigators gathered information from dark web forums where ShadowBrokerX was active. Key findings:

- The fraudster had multiple profiles across different markets but reused the same PGP key for encrypted communications.
- A leaked database from a hacked forum revealed an email address associated with the fraudster's account.
- The same username was found on a clearnet hacking forum, where the fraudster had accidentally posted using a non-anonymous IP address.

3.2 Tracing Social Media & Exchange Activity

Investigators searched the email address across open-source databases and found a connection to a Twitter account linked to a crypto enthusiast.

- The Twitter user frequently tweeted about Bitcoin trading and darknet markets.
- The profile used a real name and was linked to an Instagram account.
- A LinkedIn profile under the same name suggested the individual worked in IT security.

3.3 Confirming the Fraudster's Identity

By correlating data from:

✅ Dark web transactions

✅ Exchange deposits & withdrawals

✅ Leaked credentials

✅ Social media accounts

Investigators identified a real-world individual—a 27-year-old IT technician in Eastern Europe.

4. Law Enforcement Action & Outcome

With sufficient evidence linking ShadowBrokerX to real-world identities and financial transactions, authorities moved in:

- Law enforcement subpoenaed the crypto exchange, obtaining KYC records of the fraudster.
- The suspect had used a fake ID, but linked his account to a personal phone number.
- Investigators coordinated with Europol and local authorities, leading to the suspect's arrest.

♦ **Seized Assets**: Over $500,000 in Bitcoin, computers, and servers hosting darknet forums.

♦ **Market Shutdown**: Authorities took down the fraudster's marketplace account, warning buyers of ongoing investigations.

♦ **Legal Charges**: The suspect faced charges of fraud, money laundering, and identity theft.

5. Lessons Learned & OSINT Best Practices

Key Takeaways from the Case

✓ Blockchain analysis is critical for tracing illicit transactions, even when mixers are used.

✓ OSINT techniques, such as social media tracking and data correlation, can unmask anonymous criminals.

✓ Dark web investigations require monitoring vendor reputation systems, escrow services, and financial trails.

✓ Exchanges with weak KYC enforcement are frequently exploited—cooperation between investigators and exchanges is essential.

Tools Used in the Investigation

♦ **Blockchain Explorers**: BTCscan, Etherscan, MoneroBlocks
♦ **OSINT Tools**: SpiderFoot, Maltego, Have I Been Pwned
♦ **Dark Web Intelligence**: TOR search engines, forum monitoring, PGP key analysis

Conclusion: Following the Money in the Dark Web Economy

This case study highlights the power of OSINT and blockchain analysis in identifying and dismantling cybercriminal operations. While the dark web provides criminals with anonymity, financial transactions always leave a trace. By combining OSINT techniques, transaction tracking, and real-world investigative methods, law enforcement agencies and cybersecurity professionals can follow the money trail and expose even the most careful fraudsters.

6. Identifying Threat Actors in the Dark Web

In this chapter, we will focus on the critical task of identifying and profiling threat actors operating in the Dark Web. These individuals or groups often engage in cybercrime, such as hacking, fraud, and trafficking, under the veil of anonymity provided by tools like Tor. We will explore methods for uncovering their identities, examining patterns in their online behavior, language, and activities. From analyzing forum posts and marketplace listings to tracing digital footprints and cross-referencing data across multiple platforms, OSINT techniques can reveal connections between threat actors and their broader networks. Understanding how to identify these actors is a vital component of any cybercrime investigation, as it helps build profiles, uncover motives, and ultimately dismantle criminal operations operating in the shadows.

6.1 Profiling Cybercriminals & Their Online Behavior

Understanding cybercriminals and their behavior is a crucial aspect of dark web OSINT investigations. Threat actors operating in illicit marketplaces, forums, and hacker communities often attempt to stay anonymous, but patterns in their digital footprints, linguistic tendencies, transaction behaviors, and operational security (OPSEC) practices can reveal valuable intelligence. By profiling cybercriminals, investigators can uncover hidden identities, track activity across multiple platforms, and attribute specific attacks or illicit operations to known actors.

This chapter explores how cybercriminals operate, common behavioral patterns, and OSINT techniques used to build comprehensive profiles of dark web actors.

1. Understanding the Cybercriminal Mindset

Cybercriminals range from script kiddies testing low-level exploits to sophisticated organized crime groups running global cyber fraud networks. Their motivations typically include:

1.1 Financial Gain

- **Fraudsters & Carders** – Sell stolen credit card details and banking credentials.
- **Ransomware Operators** – Conduct extortion schemes demanding cryptocurrency payments.

- **Dark Web Market Vendors** – Sell illegal drugs, hacking tools, counterfeit documents, and weapons.

1.2 Ideological or Political Goals (Hacktivism & Cyberterrorism)

- Groups like Anonymous or nation-state hackers conduct cyber attacks to promote political agendas.
- Cyberterrorists engage in attacks against governments and infrastructure.

1.3 Ego & Notoriety (Script Kiddies & Black Hat Hackers)

- Some cybercriminals are motivated by status within hacker communities.
- Forum reputation systems encourage competition for higher ranks.
- Each cybercriminal type exhibits unique digital behaviors, risk tolerance, and operational techniques that can be analyzed for intelligence gathering.

2. Digital Footprints & Behavioral Patterns

Even though cybercriminals attempt to remain anonymous, they leave behind digital footprints that investigators can analyze. These include:

2.1 Reused Aliases & Handles Across Platforms

- Many cybercriminals use the same or similar usernames (handles) across multiple forums, social media, and marketplaces.
- OSINT investigators can cross-reference handles to track their activities.
- **Example**: The infamous "Dread Pirate Roberts" (Silk Road administrator) reused a handle linked to a real identity.

2.2 Linguistic Analysis & Writing Style (Stylometry)

- Cybercriminals have distinct writing styles, grammar, slang, and word choices.
- Stylometric analysis can compare forum posts, ransom notes, and emails to identify potential matches.
- **Example**: The FBI used stylometry to link Ross Ulbricht to Silk Road communications.

2.3 Time Zone & Posting Activity Patterns

- Analysis of posting times on forums and dark web markets can reveal time zones.

- Cybercriminals unknowingly reveal geographical hints based on when they are most active.
- **Example**: A Russian-speaking hacking group might post during Moscow business hours.

2.4 Cryptocurrency Transaction Behavior

- Bitcoin wallets, Monero transactions, and cash-out methods provide insight into cybercriminal funding.
- Repeated use of specific exchanges can help track their activity.
- **Example**: The Colonial Pipeline hackers laundered ransom payments through Russian crypto exchanges.

3. OSINT Techniques for Cybercriminal Profiling

Investigators use various OSINT tools and methodologies to profile cybercriminals:

3.1 Tracking Dark Web Aliases

◆ **Tools: Dark Web Crawler, DeHashed, Have I Been Pwned**

✓ Search for reused usernames and email addresses across darknet forums and data leaks.

✓ Look for mentions in hacking communities, vendor feedback, and escrow transactions.

✓ **Example**: A vendor on Empire Market was linked to a real-world identity due to an email reuse mistake.

3.2 Social Media & Clearnet Correlation

◆ **Tools: Maltego, SpiderFoot, Google Dorking**

✓ Search for dark web handles on Twitter, LinkedIn, and Facebook.

✓ Check for hacking conference talks, GitHub activity, or leaked credential databases.

✓ **Example**: A hacker on RaidForums was linked to a real identity via a matching GitHub account.

3.3 Cryptocurrency Transaction Analysis

◆ **Tools: Chainalysis, Elliptic, CipherTrace**

✅ Investigate Bitcoin wallets used in ransomware payments or darknet purchases.

✅ Track funds flowing from illegal activities to known crypto exchanges.

✅ **Example**: Lazarus Group (North Korean hackers) laundered stolen funds via DeFi exchanges.

3.4 Dark Web Forum Infiltration

◆ **Tools: Sock Puppet Accounts, TOR Browsers, Cyber Threat Intelligence Feeds**

✅ Join dark web forums under a fake identity to monitor discussions.

✅ Analyze vendor reputation systems and dispute resolutions for clues.

✅ **Example**: Law enforcement infiltrated AlphaBay forums before shutting down the marketplace.

4. Case Study: Profiling a Dark Web Ransomware Operator

Background

A ransomware gang known as "BlackVenomLocker" had been conducting high-profile attacks against companies worldwide.

Step 1: Identifying Their Digital Footprint

- The ransom notes contained similar phrasing and grammatical patterns as past ransomware groups.
- The ransomware demanded payments to a known Bitcoin wallet already flagged for suspicious activity.

Step 2: Tracking Cryptocurrency Movements

- Investigators used blockchain analysis to follow ransom payments.
- The payments were laundered through multiple wallets, but a portion ended up on Binance.
- Binance's compliance team identified an account that had KYC verification.

Step 3: OSINT & Social Media Cross-Referencing

- The Binance account was linked to an email address used on a dark web hacking forum.
- The email was tied to a real-world social media profile, revealing a Russian cybersecurity student.

Outcome

- Authorities linked BlackVenomLocker's ransomware operation to a real-world suspect.
- International law enforcement issued an arrest warrant and seized crypto assets.

5. Conclusion: The Importance of Cybercriminal Profiling

Cybercriminals operate under the illusion of anonymity, but OSINT, blockchain forensics, and behavioral analysis make it possible to track and unmask them. By understanding:

✅ How cybercriminals interact on dark web forums

✅ Their linguistic patterns and time zone activities

✅ Their cryptocurrency laundering methods

✅ Their social media and clearnet activity

Investigators can develop detailed profiles that aid in attribution, tracking, and takedowns. Profiling cybercriminals is a key intelligence technique that enables law enforcement agencies, security researchers, and financial crime units to stay ahead of evolving threats in the dark web ecosystem.

6.2 Dark Web Personas: Sock Puppets & Alias Management

Operating on the dark web—whether as an investigator, journalist, or cybersecurity researcher—requires maintaining strict anonymity. Cybercriminals are highly skilled at detecting outsiders, and failure to properly manage online identities can lead to exposure, targeting, or operational failure. This is where sock puppets and alias management become crucial.

A sock puppet is a fake online identity used to gather intelligence, infiltrate closed communities, or communicate anonymously. However, creating and maintaining a convincing persona requires careful planning and strict operational security (OPSEC). This chapter explores how to build, maintain, and protect sock puppets for dark web investigations while avoiding common mistakes that could compromise anonymity.

1. Understanding Sock Puppets & Their Role in OSINT

A sock puppet is more than just a random username—it's a carefully crafted digital identity designed for a specific purpose. These personas are used in:

✅ **Dark web investigations** – Monitoring cybercriminal forums, marketplaces, and hacker communities.
✅ **Threat intelligence gathering** – Engaging with fraudsters, ransomware operators, and illicit vendors.
✅ **Law enforcement sting operations** – Undercover work to expose criminal activities.
✅ **Corporate security & brand protection** – Tracking phishing campaigns and counterfeit goods sales.

To be effective, a sock puppet must appear legitimate, consistent, and active while avoiding detection.

2. Building a Realistic Dark Web Persona

A poorly constructed sock puppet will raise suspicion and get banned from forums before valuable intelligence can be gathered. A well-crafted one blends in and can operate for months or years undetected.

2.1 Choosing a Believable Alias (Username & Handle)

Your alias must match the language, style, and community you are infiltrating. Consider:

◆ **Dark Web Forum Conventions**: Handles like "ShadowCipher" or "CryptoDrainer" are common in cybercrime forums.
◆ **Consistency**: Do not re-use a username that is linked to your real-world identity.
◆ **Cultural Relevance**: A Russian hacking forum may be suspicious of an English-speaking alias.

Pro Tip: Use random username generators and modify results for uniqueness.

2.2 Creating a Fake Digital History

Cybercriminals verify each other's reputations, so a brand-new account with no history is suspicious. Build credibility by:

✅ **Posting non-sensitive content first** – Ask basic questions about software, security, or cryptocurrency.

✅ **Creating multiple accounts over time** – Interact with your main sock puppet from secondary personas.

✅ **Referencing old but harmless cyber events** – "I remember when Empire Market was at its peak…"

2.3 Establishing a Consistent Persona

Think of your sock puppet as a character with:

◆ **A Background Story** – Are they a hacker? A carder? A drug vendor?

◆ **A Writing Style** – Do they use slang? Proper grammar? A specific dialect?

◆ **Interests & Opinions** – What forums or topics do they engage with?

A lack of consistency raises red flags in tight-knit dark web communities.

3. Maintaining Anonymity & OPSEC

Even the best-crafted sock puppet can be deanonymized if OPSEC is weak. Here's how to avoid common mistakes:

3.1 Isolating Sock Puppets from Your Real Identity

🚫 Never log in to dark web accounts from your real IP or device.

🚫 Do not mix real-world email addresses or social media accounts with your sock puppet.

🚫 Avoid using phrases, slang, or writing styles that match your real identity.

✅ **Use a Dedicated Virtual Machine (VM)** – Running Tails or Whonix isolates dark web activities.

✅ **Create Separate Email & PGP Keys** – Use ProtonMail, Tutanota, or dark web email services.

⊘ **Mask Your Time Zone & Location** – Interact at random times and avoid patterns that match your real-life routine.

3.2 Using Proper Anonymity Tools

A real hacker or dark web user would never browse without protection. To stay credible:

- Use Tor or I2P for all interactions
- Use a VPN before connecting to Tor (VPN > Tor for extra anonymity)
- Disable JavaScript & WebRTC leaks in your browser
- Use an isolated machine for all sock puppet activity

4. Engaging with Dark Web Communities Without Raising Suspicion

Once your sock puppet is established, you must gain trust before obtaining valuable intelligence.

4.1 Understanding Forum Reputation Systems

Most dark web forums have ranking systems based on post history and interactions. To avoid suspicion:

⊘ Start by commenting on general topics (security, cryptocurrency, software).

⊘ Engage in low-risk trades or discussions before requesting access to VIP sections.

⊘ Avoid asking too many questions upfront, as this is a common trait of law enforcement infiltrators.

4.2 Avoiding OPSEC Mistakes That Can Get You Banned

⊘ **Asking for personal details too soon** – Cybercriminals are extremely paranoid.
⊘ **Using inconsistent writing styles** – Switching between formal and slang can seem unnatural.
⊘ **Logging in from different locations too frequently** – Some forums track login IP geolocation.

4.3 Joining Private Marketplaces & Gaining Trust

Many dark web markets require vouching from existing members. To gain access:

✅ Build a reputation by contributing useful knowledge.

✅ Participate in low-value transactions to establish credibility.

✅ Use dummy sock puppets to interact with your primary identity.

5. Case Study: How an OSINT Researcher Infiltrated a Dark Web Ransomware Forum

Step 1: Creating a Sock Puppet

- An investigator built a persona of a cybersecurity professional interested in cryptography.
- They crafted a backstory of being frustrated with corporate security jobs and wanting to "explore the underground."
- The username "CryptoPhantom" was chosen, reflecting an interest in privacy and anonymity.

Step 2: Engaging in Low-Risk Discussions

- The sock puppet posted about cryptocurrency mixing services to appear knowledgeable.
- They avoided law enforcement-style questioning and instead offered insights on cybersecurity topics.

Step 3: Gaining Access to Ransomware Negotiation Logs

- After three months, "CryptoPhantom" was invited into a VIP forum where ransomware groups discussed their operations.
- By analyzing ransom negotiation tactics, the investigator gathered valuable intelligence on target selection and payment demands.

Outcome:

The research contributed to law enforcement action against ransomware affiliates by identifying cryptocurrency wallets and ransom demand templates.

6. Conclusion: Mastering the Art of Sock Puppetry

Sock puppets are essential tools for dark web OSINT investigations, but maintaining anonymity requires careful planning, consistency, and strict OPSEC. By:

✅ Creating believable personas with established digital histories

✅ Avoiding real-world identity leaks through strict device & network isolation

✅ Building trust within dark web communities before attempting infiltration

Investigators, journalists, and security professionals can gather intelligence safely while minimizing risks.

In the world of dark web OSINT, the best sock puppets are the ones that never get exposed.

6.3 Language & Communication Patterns in Criminal Networks

The dark web operates as a global underground economy, with cybercriminals, fraudsters, and illicit vendors communicating through specialized language, slang, and coded terminology. Understanding how criminals communicate is crucial for OSINT investigators, cybersecurity professionals, and law enforcement working to infiltrate and analyze these networks.

Cybercriminals use a mix of linguistic strategies to obscure their intentions, evade law enforcement, and establish trust within their communities. From coded phrases in ransomware negotiations to trust signals in fraud marketplaces, this chapter explores the key communication patterns used in criminal networks.

1. The Role of Language in Cybercriminal Networks

Cybercriminals use language strategically for several reasons:

✅ **Anonymity & Evasion** – To avoid detection by automated monitoring tools and law enforcement.
✅ **Trust & Reputation** – To establish credibility within closed communities.
✅ **Operational Security (OPSEC)** – To prevent undercover infiltration.

✓ **Efficiency in Transactions** – To quickly communicate pricing, services, and trade terms.

Different criminal groups—hackers, fraudsters, drug traffickers, ransomware gangs, and human traffickers—each have their own unique communication styles.

2. Common Cybercriminal Communication Patterns

Dark web criminals communicate primarily via forums, encrypted messaging apps (like Telegram, Tox, and Jabber), and PGP-encrypted emails. Their language varies based on their expertise, region, and purpose.

2.1 Coded Language & Euphemisms

Cybercriminals avoid direct references to illegal activities. Instead, they use euphemisms to describe illicit goods and services.

Illicit Activity	Coded Terms Used	Example Phrase
Stolen Credit Cards	"CCs" / "Dumps"	"Selling fresh CC dumps, high balance only."
Bank Fraud	"Cashout Services"	"I can help cashout PayPal accounts, DM for details."
Ransomware	"Pentesting" / "Locker"	"We provide pentesting services for targeted clients."
Stolen Databases	"Logs" / "Leads"	"HQ email logs available for bulk purchase."
Drug Sales	"Party favors" / "Research chemicals"	"Selling party favors, EU shipping only."
Hiring a Hitman	"Problem Solving"	"Need professional problem solvers? Serious inquiries only."

◆ **Why It Works**: These terms help criminals avoid detection from automated monitoring systems, while experienced buyers understand the hidden meaning.

2.2 Regional Variations & Multilingual Criminal Networks

Cybercriminals operate globally, but regional variations in language exist:

◈ **Russian Cybercriminals** – Often discuss malware and banking fraud in Russian-only forums to deter Western investigators.

◈ **Chinese Fraud Networks** – Use platforms like WeChat and obscure slang for illicit trade.

◈ **Spanish & Portuguese Markets** – Focus on drug trafficking and human smuggling.

◈ **English-Speaking Criminals** – Use Telegram and Discord for fraud schemes like carding and phishing.

🔍 **Example**: Russian forums often use transliterated English terms (e.g., "skimmer" becomes "скиммер") to prevent keyword detection by Western law enforcement.

2.3 Trust Signals & Reputation Systems in Criminal Forums

Trust is critical in dark web transactions. Many forums and marketplaces have built-in reputation systems, where vouches, escrow services, and "reps" (reputation points) signal credibility.

💬 **Example Conversation in a Fraud Forum:**

- **User 1**: "Selling fresh CVVs, non-VBV, high success rate. DM me!"
- **User 2**: "Any vouches? Escrow accepted?"
- **User 1**: "Plenty of vouches, check my thread. I take escrow for first-timers."

📷 **Key Trust Signals:**

✓ "**Vouches**" – Positive reviews from previous buyers.

✓ "**Escrow**" – Holding funds with a trusted third party until a transaction is complete.

✓ "**HQ**" (**High Quality**) – Used to describe good data, software, or logs.

3. Encryption & Secure Communication Methods

Cybercriminals never use regular email or messaging apps. Instead, they rely on encrypted and decentralized platforms to protect their anonymity.

3.1 Preferred Communication Platforms

Platform	Usage
PGP-Encrypted Email	Used for ransomware negotiations & high-value transactions.
Telegram & Jabber (XMPP)	Common in fraud, drug markets, and cybercrime coordination.
Tox Messenger	A decentralized, peer-to-peer messaging system used for malware discussions.
Wickr & Signal	Used for high-anonymity communications.

⬧ **Example**: Ransomware gangs use PGP encryption for communication with victims. A typical ransom note might include:
"Contact us via our secure email and encrypt all messages using our provided PGP key."

4. Case Study: Ransomware Negotiations & Dark Web Communication

🔍 **Background**: In 2021, a ransomware gang compromised a major corporation and demanded payment in Bitcoin. The company engaged in negotiations through an encrypted Tor-based chat portal provided by the attackers.

⬧ **Step 1: Initial Contact** – The company was instructed to visit an onion site and enter a chat room.

⬧ **Step 2: Ransom Demand** – The criminals used coded language:

- "Your network is now in our hands."
- "We offer a professional recovery service for a donation." (Ransom request)

◆ **Step 3: Payment Discussion** –

- "We only accept BTC. No funny business, or files will be leaked."
- "Use a clean wallet, no exchange transactions."

📌 **Key Takeaway**: Ransomware gangs use formalized, structured language in negotiations, avoiding emotional responses while maintaining control over the victim.

5. Implications for OSINT & Dark Web Investigations

Understanding cybercriminal communication patterns helps OSINT analysts, law enforcement, and cybersecurity teams:

- Identify criminal networks by analyzing common phrases & slang.
- Track cybercriminal transactions through marketplace reviews and trust signals.
- Monitor dark web threats by infiltrating forums & encrypted messaging groups.
- Enhance threat intelligence by decoding ransomware negotiation strategies.

🔍 **Example OSINT Method:**

1️⃣ Scraping dark web forums for coded terms related to stolen data sales.

2️⃣ Analyzing message structures in Telegram fraud groups.

3️⃣ Linking usernames & aliases across different forums using linguistic fingerprinting.

6. Conclusion: Decoding the Dark Web's Hidden Language

Cybercriminal networks have complex communication methods, using coded slang, reputation-based trust systems, and encrypted messaging to conduct their operations.

For OSINT analysts, understanding and infiltrating these networks requires:

✓ Familiarity with cybercriminal slang and coded language.

✓ Awareness of regional differences in cybercrime operations.

✓ Use of OSINT tools to monitor forum discussions & marketplace listings.

✓ Strong OPSEC when engaging with cybercriminal communities.

As cybercrime continues to evolve, language and communication analysis will remain a key investigative tool for law enforcement, researchers, and security professionals.

6.4 Connecting Dark Web Activity to Real-World Identities

The anonymity provided by the dark web is not absolute. While cybercriminals take extensive measures to hide their identities, mistakes and investigative techniques allow law enforcement, OSINT researchers, and cybersecurity professionals to link online personas to real-world individuals. This process—often referred to as deanonymization—relies on tracking digital footprints, OPSEC failures, blockchain analysis, and social engineering.

In this chapter, we will explore the key methods used to connect dark web activity to real-world identities, including OSINT techniques, metadata analysis, linguistic fingerprinting, and past law enforcement successes.

1. Common Mistakes Cybercriminals Make

Despite their use of Tor, VPNs, burner accounts, and encryption, many cybercriminals slip up, making them vulnerable to tracking. Some of the most common mistakes include:

✅ **Reusing usernames & email addresses** – Criminals often use the same alias across multiple platforms, making it easier to link their activities.

✅ **Poor OPSEC on social media** – They sometimes reveal personal information in unguarded moments, such as posting about wealth or bragging in hacker forums.

✅ **Leaking metadata in images or documents** – Files uploaded to the dark web can contain EXIF metadata, revealing IP addresses, device details, or GPS locations.

✅ **Using personal Bitcoin wallets** – Cryptocurrency transactions can be traced, especially when cybercriminals use exchanges that require Know Your Customer (KYC) verification.

✅ **Connecting to the dark web without proper anonymity** – Accessing hidden services without using VPNs or clean devices can expose real IP addresses.

📌 **Case Example**: In 2013, Ross Ulbricht (Dread Pirate Roberts), the creator of Silk Road, was caught partly because he used the same alias on Stack Overflow and dark web forums.

2. OSINT Techniques for De-Anonymization

OSINT (Open-Source Intelligence) plays a crucial role in unmasking cybercriminals. Investigators use a variety of data correlation techniques to connect dark web identities to real-world individuals.

2.1 Username & Alias Tracking

Many dark web users reuse usernames across different forums, making it possible to link them back to clear-net profiles.

🔍 Example:

- A hacker selling stolen credentials on a dark web marketplace uses the alias "ShadowX99."
- The same alias appears on a gaming forum with an email attached.
- A LinkedIn profile uses that email.

📌 OSINT Tool: Check username availability across platforms using sites like Namechk or WhatsMyName.

2.2 Metadata Analysis from Leaked Files

Criminals sometimes upload files containing hidden metadata that can reveal their real identity.

🔍 Example:

- A ransomware operator shares a sample decryption key in a Microsoft Word document.
- The document's EXIF metadata reveals the author's username and time zone.
- This information is cross-checked with other known cybercriminal aliases.

📌 OSINT Tool: Use ExifTool to extract metadata from documents, images, and PDFs.

2.3 Linguistic Fingerprinting & Writing Style Analysis

Each person has a unique way of writing, even when using different aliases. Linguistic analysis can help investigators identify authors across different platforms.

🔍 Example:

- A dark web vendor posts advertisements in a marketplace.
- Their writing style, grammar, and word choice is compared to known social media posts.
- A match is found, revealing their identity.

📌 OSINT Tool: JStylo & Writeprint analyze writing patterns for authorship attribution.

2.4 Cryptocurrency & Blockchain Analysis

Although Bitcoin transactions are pseudonymous, they are publicly recorded on the blockchain. Law enforcement and researchers use blockchain forensics to track payments linked to dark web activities.

🔍 **Example:**

- A cybercriminal receives Bitcoin ransom payments.
- They send Bitcoin to an exchange that requires KYC verification.
- Investigators subpoena the exchange for customer data, revealing the real-world identity.

📌 **OSINT Tool**: Use Blockchain Explorers (like Blockchain.info, Blockchair) and Chainalysis for transaction tracking.

3. Law Enforcement Techniques & Case Studies

Many cybercriminals have been arrested due to OPSEC failures and investigative techniques. Here are a few notable cases:

3.1 Ross Ulbricht (Silk Road) – Username & OPSEC Mistake

Ross Ulbricht, creator of Silk Road, was caught when:

- He used the same alias (Dread Pirate Roberts) across multiple sites.
- His LinkedIn profile mentioned creating an "economic simulation" similar to Silk Road.
- Law enforcement linked his Bitcoin transactions to real-world exchanges.

3.2 AlphaBay Admin (De-Anonymization via Email & Metadata)

Alexandre Cazes, the administrator of AlphaBay, was caught because:

- His email address ("pimp_alex_91@...") was embedded in AlphaBay's welcome emails.
- He used the same alias in clearnet tech forums.
- His Bitcoin wallet transactions were traced to luxury purchases.

3.3 Welcome To Video (Child Exploitation Site) – Bitcoin Tracking

A global pedophile ring was dismantled when:

◆ Law enforcement analyzed Bitcoin transactions linked to payments for illegal content.

◆ The funds led to real-world crypto exchanges where suspects had verified accounts.

◆ Over 337 arrests were made worldwide.

4. Tools & Techniques for OSINT Investigators

Investigators use a variety of OSINT tools to track cybercriminals. Here are some key resources:

Tool Name	Purpose
Namechk / WhatsMyName	Check username reuse across platforms.
ExifTool	Extract metadata from files & images.
Maltego	Visualize connections between aliases, emails, and IPs.
Blockchain Explorers	Track cryptocurrency transactions.
Hunchly	Capture and organize OSINT investigations.

📌 **Pro Tip**: Always use secure environments (such as air-gapped machines or VMs) when conducting dark web investigations.

5. Best Practices for Dark Web Investigations

◆ Never engage directly with cybercriminals unless authorized.

◆ Use VPNs, Tor, and burner accounts to protect anonymity.

◆ Correlate multiple data points (usernames, writing styles, crypto transactions).

◆ Check OPSEC mistakes made by suspects on clearnet platforms.

◆ Leverage blockchain forensics to trace illicit funds.

6. Conclusion: The Challenge of Anonymity

While the dark web provides a high level of anonymity, it is not foolproof. Cybercriminals often make critical mistakes, which OSINT analysts and law enforcement can exploit.

By using username correlation, metadata analysis, linguistic fingerprinting, and blockchain forensics, investigators can successfully de-anonymize criminals and link their dark web activities to real-world identities.

The fight against cybercrime is an ongoing battle, but as techniques evolve, so do the capabilities of OSINT professionals in uncovering hidden threats.

6.5 OSINT Tools for Tracking Threat Actor Movements

Tracking cybercriminals across the dark web requires a combination of OSINT techniques, specialized tools, and strategic intelligence gathering. Threat actors frequently migrate between forums, marketplaces, and encrypted communication platforms, making it essential for investigators to use automated tools, data correlation methods, and digital forensics to follow their movements.

This chapter explores the best OSINT tools and methodologies used by cybersecurity professionals, law enforcement, and threat intelligence analysts to monitor and track cybercriminals operating within the dark web.

1. Why Tracking Threat Actor Movements is Crucial

Understanding how and where cybercriminals operate enables investigators to:

✓ Identify emerging threats before they gain traction.

✓ Track cybercriminal groups across multiple platforms.

✓ Monitor affiliations and partnerships within underground networks.

✓ Attribute cyberattacks to specific individuals or groups.

✓ Gather intelligence for proactive mitigation of future threats.

Many criminals mistakenly believe that anonymity networks like Tor and I2P make them untraceable. However, OSINT investigators can track them by correlating usernames, monitoring cryptocurrency transactions, analyzing language patterns, and following forum migrations.

2. Essential OSINT Tools for Tracking Threat Actors

Investigators use a range of tools to follow threat actors across the dark web. Below are some of the most effective OSINT tools:

2.1 Dark Web Crawlers & Search Engines

Unlike the surface web, dark web sites are not indexed by Google. However, specialized dark web crawlers and search engines help locate hidden services, forums, and marketplaces.

📌 **Key Tools:**

- ◆ **Ahmia** – A Tor search engine indexing onion sites.
- ◆ **OnionLand Search** – Searches dark web marketplaces and forums.
- ◆ **Recon** – A dark web intelligence tool for searching vendor profiles and marketplace listings.
- ◆ **DarkEye** – Collects intelligence from multiple hidden services.

🔍 **Use Case**: When a marketplace is shut down, OSINT analysts can monitor forum discussions using search tools to find where vendors and customers are relocating.

2.2 Monitoring Username & Alias Reuse

Cybercriminals often reuse usernames, email addresses, and aliases across different platforms. By tracking these identities, investigators can link threat actors to multiple sites.

📌 **Key Tools:**

- ◆ **WhatsMyName** – Checks username availability across platforms.
- ◆ **Namechk** – Identifies where a username is used on different sites.
- ◆ **Sherlock** – Searches for aliases on social media and forums.

🔍 **Use Case**: If a hacker uses the same alias on both a dark web forum and a clearnet hacking site, OSINT analysts can connect their activities and extract more intelligence.

2.3 Cryptocurrency & Blockchain Tracking

Dark web transactions are often conducted using Bitcoin, Monero, or other cryptocurrencies. By tracing blockchain transactions, OSINT investigators can link wallet addresses to illicit activities.

📌 **Key Tools:**

◈ **Blockchain.com Explorer** – Analyzes Bitcoin transactions.
◈ **Blockchair** – Tracks multiple cryptocurrencies.
◈ **Chainalysis Reactor** – A law enforcement-grade tool for investigating crypto laundering.
◈ **CipherTrace** – Identifies high-risk transactions linked to criminal activities.

🔍 **Use Case**: If a darknet vendor receives Bitcoin payments, investigators can trace the wallet and look for transactions involving crypto exchanges that require KYC verification.

2.4 Monitoring Dark Web Marketplaces & Forums

Cybercriminals frequently shift between marketplaces, vendor shops, and encrypted chat groups. OSINT analysts use intelligence tools to monitor discussions, track vendor movements, and identify emerging threats.

📌 **Key Tools:**

◈ **DarkOwl Vision** – Provides real-time monitoring of dark web marketplaces.
◈ **Intel 471** – Tracks cybercriminal activities and data leaks.
◈ **Hunchly** – A browser extension that helps OSINT analysts capture and catalog dark web research.
◈ **SpiderFoot** – An OSINT automation tool that gathers intelligence on domain names, emails, and IP addresses.

🔍 **Use Case**: When a dark web marketplace is taken down, OSINT tools help identify where vendors and buyers are migrating to resume their activities.

2.5 Language & Communication Analysis

Many cybercriminals belong to specific geographical and linguistic groups, making language and writing style analysis a powerful OSINT technique.

📌 **Key Tools:**

◈ **JStylo & Writeprint** – Analyzes writing styles to match cybercriminal aliases.

◆ **Tineye & Google Reverse Image Search** – Identifies re-used images across different sites.

◆ **Maltego** – Visualizes connections between dark web profiles, email addresses, and domains.

🔍 **Use Case**: If a cybercriminal frequently posts in Russian and uses a specific slang or phrasing, investigators can match their language patterns to other forums and potentially identify their nationality or location.

3. Tracking Threat Actor Movements Across Platforms

3.1 Marketplaces & Vendor Migrations

When a dark web marketplace shuts down, vendors often relocate to new platforms or start their own independent shops. OSINT analysts use monitoring tools to:

◆ Identify alternative markets where vendors reappear.
◆ Cross-check vendor PGP keys and Bitcoin addresses.
◆ Monitor forum discussions to track where users migrate.

🔍 **Example**: After the AlphaBay takedown, many vendors moved to Dream Market, and OSINT tools were used to track their movements.

3.2 Encrypted Messaging & OPSEC Mistakes

Many cybercriminals use Telegram, Wickr, Tox, and Jabber for secure communication. However, investigators can still extract intelligence by:

✓ Monitoring invite links shared on dark web forums.

✓ Identifying reused usernames across messaging platforms.

✓ Tracking leaks and internal disputes within hacker groups.

📌 **Case Example**: The REvil ransomware gang had an internal dispute that led to leaked chat logs, allowing OSINT analysts to uncover their internal operations.

3.3 Social Media & Clearnet Footprints

Many cybercriminals inadvertently expose themselves on clearnet platforms.

- They brag about exploits on Twitter or Reddit.
- They accidentally reuse email addresses linked to personal accounts.
- They post hints about their location or lifestyle.

🔍 **Example**: A hacker selling stolen credit card data on a dark web forum used the same Telegram handle on a public hacking subreddit, allowing investigators to track their real-world activity.

4. Best Practices for OSINT Investigations

- Use burner devices & VPNs to avoid exposure.
- Automate data collection using OSINT scrapers.
- Monitor cryptocurrency movements for laundering patterns.
- Cross-check aliases across multiple platforms.
- Never interact directly with cybercriminals unless authorized.

5. Conclusion: The Power of OSINT in Dark Web Investigations

While cybercriminals rely on anonymity networks, encryption, and OPSEC, OSINT tools and techniques make it possible to track their movements, uncover real-world identities, and prevent cybercrime.

By leveraging username tracking, blockchain forensics, forum monitoring, and language analysis, OSINT investigators can stay one step ahead in the fight against dark web threats.

6.6 Case Study: Unmasking a Dark Web Fraud Ring

Dark web fraud rings operate under the assumption that anonymity networks like Tor and I2P, combined with cryptocurrency laundering and OPSEC best practices, make them untraceable. However, through OSINT (Open-Source Intelligence), blockchain analysis, and digital forensics, investigators have successfully identified and dismantled multiple organized fraud operations.

This case study examines a real-world investigation into a dark web fraud ring, detailing the tools, techniques, and intelligence-gathering strategies that led to the unmasking and prosecution of its key members.

1. The Fraud Ring: Operation Phantom Market

In 2021, cybersecurity analysts identified an emerging fraud marketplace on the dark web, operating under the name Phantom Market. The platform specialized in selling:

- Stolen credit card data (CC dumps & CVVs)
- Compromised PayPal and bank accounts
- Forged IDs, passports, and driver's licenses
- Money laundering and cash-out services

Unlike larger, well-known dark web markets, Phantom Market restricted access to only trusted members and operated with an invitation-only model. It also implemented enhanced OPSEC measures, including:

✅ Mandatory PGP encryption for communications

✅ Monero (XMR) transactions only to evade blockchain tracking

✅ Frequent mirror site updates to avoid takedowns

✅ Strict vetting of new buyers and sellers

Despite these precautions, OSINT analysts and law enforcement agencies began monitoring Phantom Market's activities, looking for potential weaknesses in its security.

2. Identifying the Key Actors

2.1 Tracking Usernames & Aliases

OSINT specialists used username correlation techniques to track Phantom Market vendors across multiple dark web forums.

- Using tools like WhatsMyName and Sherlock, analysts discovered that some sellers used similar usernames on clearnet hacking forums.
- A fraud vendor with the alias "PhantomX" was found discussing hacking techniques on a clearnet forum, where he had linked his Telegram account.

✅ **Breakthrough**: This Telegram handle led investigators to additional social media accounts, revealing PhantomX's real-world identity.

2.2 Tracing Cryptocurrency Transactions

Although Phantom Market used Monero (XMR) for most transactions, some vendors accepted Bitcoin (BTC).

◆ Investigators used Blockchain Explorers and Chainalysis to trace Bitcoin payments from Phantom Market to known crypto exchanges.

◆ A vendor selling stolen credit card data withdrew BTC from a dark web wallet to a Binance account, which required KYC verification.

◆ This provided law enforcement with a real-world identity linked to the transaction.

✅ **Breakthrough**: One of the market's key financial operators was identified through his crypto transactions.

2.3 Monitoring Vendor & Buyer Migrations

After Phantom Market suddenly went offline, OSINT analysts monitored dark web forums and Telegram groups to track where users were relocating.

◆ Using tools like Recon and DarkOwl Vision, analysts searched for vendors mentioning "Phantom Market" closures.

◆ Several vendors reappeared on a new dark web site, using similar product listings and usernames.

◆ PGP keys associated with Phantom Market vendors were reused on new sites, confirming their identities and connections.

✅ **Breakthrough**: The new marketplace was linked to the same operators, allowing investigators to track their next moves.

2.4 Language & Metadata Analysis

OSINT specialists performed linguistic analysis on forum posts, identifying:

◆ Repeated phrases and slang indicating a Russian-speaking cybercrime group.

◆ Metadata analysis on leaked documents and seller-provided PDFs, revealing time zones and software versions.

◆ Forum activity logs showing that most posts were made between 10 AM and 6 PM Moscow time.

✔ **Breakthrough**: Analysts narrowed down the fraud ring's location to Eastern Europe.

3. The Takedown: Law Enforcement Intervention

With intelligence gathered from OSINT techniques, cryptocurrency tracing, and alias tracking, law enforcement executed a coordinated operation to dismantle the fraud ring.

◆ Arrests were made in Russia, Ukraine, and the UK, targeting the ring's operators and key vendors.

◆ Server infrastructure hosting Phantom Market was seized, providing access to buyer and seller transaction logs.

◆ Cryptocurrency wallets linked to the fraud ring were frozen, preventing further financial transactions.

✔ **Final Outcome**: Phantom Market was permanently shut down, and its operators were charged with financial crimes, identity theft, and cyber fraud.

4. Key Takeaways from This Investigation

◆ **No cybercriminal is truly anonymous** – Even with strong OPSEC, mistakes like username reuse and metadata exposure can unmask identities.

◆ **Cryptocurrency tracking is a powerful OSINT tool** – Even privacy coins like Monero can be traced indirectly by following exchange deposits and withdrawals.

◆ **Marketplace shutdowns don't stop crime** – they just relocate it – Tracking vendor movements across dark web platforms is essential.

◆ Language and time zone analysis can reveal geographical locations of criminal groups.

This case study highlights how OSINT-driven investigations can successfully identify and dismantle organized cybercrime operations on the dark web. By using a combination of blockchain forensics, alias tracking, and intelligence gathering, investigators can unmask even the most well-hidden fraud rings.

7. Monitoring Dark Web Breaches & Leaks

In this chapter, we will examine the process of monitoring and investigating data breaches and leaks that surface on the Dark Web. These breaches, often involving stolen personal, financial, or corporate data, are a significant source of intelligence for OSINT analysts tracking cybercrime activity. We will explore methods to identify leaked data across Dark Web forums, marketplaces, and underground communities, and discuss how to monitor specific targets or sectors for potential compromises. By understanding how to detect and track the spread of these leaks, investigators can assess the scope of damage, identify compromised entities, and gather key evidence that can aid in mitigating risks and preventing future attacks. This chapter will provide you with the tools and strategies to effectively monitor and respond to Dark Web data leaks.

7.1 The Role of Data Breaches in Cybercrime

Data breaches have become one of the most significant drivers of cybercrime, fueling identity theft, fraud, and underground market economies on the dark web. Every year, millions of personal records, login credentials, financial information, and corporate data are stolen and sold to cybercriminals. These breaches not only compromise individual privacy but also enable phishing attacks, account takeovers, financial fraud, and even corporate espionage.

This chapter explores how stolen data fuels cybercrime, the lifecycle of breached data on the dark web, and how OSINT analysts and law enforcement track and mitigate threats stemming from data leaks.

1. How Data Breaches Fuel Cybercrime

Once data is breached, it follows a well-established underground economy, passing through multiple layers of cybercriminals. The typical flow includes:

1️ **Initial Breach** – Hackers exploit vulnerabilities (e.g., weak passwords, phishing attacks, unpatched software) to steal sensitive data.
2️ **Data Dump or Private Sale** – Stolen data is either dumped for free (to gain reputation in hacker communities) or sold on dark web forums and marketplaces.

3⃞ **Criminal Exploitation** – Buyers use the stolen credentials for account takeovers, credit card fraud, SIM swapping, and blackmail.

4⃞ **Resale & Reuse** – As more criminals obtain the data, it spreads across multiple platforms, prolonging the lifespan of the stolen information.

🔍 **Example**: The 2021 Facebook breach exposed 533 million user records, including phone numbers and emails, which were later used in phishing campaigns and SIM swap frauds.

2. The Lifecycle of Stolen Data on the Dark Web

2.1 Initial Leak: Private Forums & Telegram Channels

When a breach first occurs, the stolen data is often privately sold on invite-only dark web forums, Telegram groups, and Jabber chats. These groups act as exclusive marketplaces where only verified buyers can access fresh breaches before they become public.

📌 **Key Criminal Platforms:**

✅ **Exploit.in** – A hacking forum for selling databases.
✅ **RaidForums (defunct, replaced by BreachForums)** – Hosted leaked databases.
✅ **Telegram & Discord Groups** – Used for private transactions.

🔍 **Example**: The 2023 T-Mobile breach was first spotted in private Telegram groups, where hackers auctioned off customer data, including SSNs and addresses.

2.2 Public Dumping on Dark Web Marketplaces

After the initial sales phase, stolen data often gets resold or publicly dumped on dark web marketplaces. Criminals use these databases for:

◆ **Credential stuffing** – Trying leaked usernames/passwords on other sites.
◆ **Phishing attacks** – Targeting exposed email addresses.
◆ **Financial fraud** – Selling stolen credit card data (CC dumps).

📌 **Common Dark Web Marketplaces for Data Leaks:**

🕯 **Genesis Market (Seized)** – Specialized in stolen browser fingerprints.

◈ **BreachForums (Successor to RaidForums)** – Hosted leaked credentials.
◈ **Russian Market** – A dark web hub for stolen bank accounts and SSNs.

🔍 **Example**: The Marriott Hotels breach (500M records) led to a surge in phishing scams targeting hotel customers.

2.3 Weaponization: Account Takeovers, Blackmail & Fraud

Once data is widely available, it is weaponized for various criminal activities:

✓ **Identity Theft** – Stolen personal info is used to open bank accounts, credit lines, and fake passports.
✓ **SIM Swapping** – Attackers hijack phone numbers to bypass 2FA and steal cryptocurrency.
✓ **Corporate Espionage** – Leaked employee credentials allow hackers to infiltrate corporate networks.
✓ **Doxxing & Blackmail** – Exposed personal data is used to threaten individuals.

🔍 **Example**: The Ashley Madison hack leaked personal details of users on an affair website, leading to blackmail schemes and even suicides.

3. OSINT Techniques for Tracking Data Breaches

3.1 Monitoring Dark Web Leaks & Forums

OSINT analysts actively monitor dark web forums and Telegram groups to track new breaches before they spread.

📌 **Key OSINT Tools for Dark Web Monitoring:**

◆ **IntelX** – Searches leaked databases and forums.
◆ **DarkOwl Vision** – Provides real-time alerts on dark web leaks.
◆ **DeHashed** – Checks if credentials have been exposed.

🔍 **Use Case**: Law enforcement used DarkOwl Vision to track discussions around the LinkedIn breach, which exposed 700 million user profiles.

3.2 Identifying Credential Reuse & Password Spraying

Since many users reuse passwords, breached credentials are tested on other platforms to gain unauthorized access (credential stuffing).

📌 **Key Tools for Checking Compromised Credentials:**

✅ **Have I Been Pwned** – Checks if an email/password has been leaked.
✅ **H8mail** – Searches multiple breach databases for compromised accounts.
✅ **Snusbase** – Provides access to leaked credential databases.

🔍 **Use Case**: OSINT analysts discovered that leaked passwords from the 2012 Dropbox breach were reused in a 2022 attack on GitHub accounts.

3.3 Blockchain Analysis for Stolen Cryptocurrency

When financial data is breached, criminals often convert stolen money into cryptocurrency to evade detection. OSINT tools help track these transactions on the blockchain.

📌 **Key Cryptocurrency OSINT Tools:**

♦ **Chainalysis** – Tracks illicit crypto transactions.
♦ **CipherTrace** – Monitors crypto wallets linked to fraud.
♦ **Elliptic** – Detects stolen funds in crypto exchanges.

🔍 **Example**: After the Mt. Gox hack, authorities used blockchain analysis to track stolen Bitcoin movements, leading to the arrest of a crypto launderer.

4. How Companies & Law Enforcement Respond to Data Breaches

✔ **Dark Web Takedowns** – Law enforcement targets major dark web marketplaces (e.g., AlphaBay, BreachForums).
✔ **Corporate Security Measures** – Companies enforce multi-factor authentication (MFA) and encryption to reduce breach risks.
✔ **OSINT Threat Intelligence** – Cybersecurity teams proactively monitor leaked credentials to prevent unauthorized access.

🔍 **Example**: The FBI's Operation DisrupTor led to 179 arrests and the seizure of $6.5M in cryptocurrency from dark web vendors selling stolen data.

5. Conclusion: Data Breaches as a Continuous Threat

✦ Data breaches are fueling the cybercrime ecosystem, from identity theft to corporate espionage.
✦ Dark web forums and marketplaces play a crucial role in the dissemination of stolen data.
✦ OSINT techniques allow investigators, cybersecurity experts, and companies to monitor and mitigate the risks associated with data leaks.

As breach incidents continue to rise, OSINT will remain a critical tool in tracking, preventing, and responding to cybercriminal activities fueled by stolen data.

7.2 Investigating Leaked Databases & Stolen Credentials

Leaked databases and stolen credentials are among the most valuable commodities on the dark web. Cybercriminals buy, sell, and trade stolen login credentials, credit card details, personally identifiable information (PII), and corporate records, fueling cyber fraud, identity theft, and hacking campaigns. Investigating these leaks is crucial for law enforcement, cybersecurity analysts, and OSINT professionals to mitigate risks and track cybercriminal activities.

This chapter explores how to investigate leaked databases, the tools used for tracking stolen credentials, and OSINT techniques for identifying victims and threat actors.

1. How Leaked Databases Appear on the Dark Web

1.1 Initial Leak & Distribution

When a data breach occurs, attackers either hoard the stolen data for private use, sell it in dark web markets, or leak it publicly. The distribution usually follows these stages:

1️⃣ **Private Sale** – Hackers sell fresh databases to select buyers via dark web forums and Telegram groups.

2️⃣ **Broader Distribution** – After high-value buyers purchase the data, it may resurface on dark web marketplaces for resale.

3️⃣ **Public Dump** – Eventually, the data is either leaked for free to gain reputation in hacker circles or indexed on breach databases.

📌 **Example**: The Yahoo breach (2013-2014) exposed 3 billion accounts but was only made public years later when the data appeared for sale on dark web forums.

1.2 Common Types of Stolen Data

Leaked databases often contain various types of sensitive information, including:

♦ **Username & Password Dumps** – Used for credential stuffing and hacking accounts.

♦ **Credit Card Data (CC Dumps)** – Sold for fraudulent transactions and carding schemes.

♦ **Personal Identifiable Information (PII)** – Includes names, addresses, SSNs, and phone numbers for identity theft.

♦ **Corporate & Government Records** – Used in espionage, ransomware attacks, and blackmail.

📌 **Example**: The LinkedIn breach (2021) exposed 700 million user profiles, later used in phishing and impersonation scams.

2. OSINT Techniques for Investigating Leaked Databases

2.1 Searching for Leaked Credentials

OSINT analysts can track stolen credentials using breach databases and dark web monitoring tools.

📌 **Key OSINT Tools for Investigating Stolen Credentials:**

✅ **Have I Been Pwned (HIBP)** – Checks if an email/password has been exposed in past breaches.

✅ **DeHashed** – Searches leaked data for emails, usernames, IPs, and passwords.

✅ **Snusbase** – Provides access to breached databases for investigation.

✅ **IntelX** – Searches the dark web for compromised credentials.

🔍 **Use Case**: A cybersecurity firm used HIBP and DeHashed to warn employees about exposed credentials in the Dropbox and LinkedIn breaches, preventing account takeovers.

2.2 Monitoring Dark Web Forums & Telegram Channels

Cybercriminals frequently trade stolen data in underground forums and encrypted messaging apps like Telegram and Jabber. OSINT investigators monitor these channels for leaked data.

📌 **Common Dark Web Forums for Leaked Databases:**

❖ **BreachForums (Successor to RaidForums)** – Hosts stolen credentials and databases.
❖ **Exploit.in** – A Russian-language forum for hacking discussions and data sales.
❖ **Genesis Market (Seized)** – Sold stolen browser fingerprints and login credentials.

🔍 **Use Case**: Law enforcement monitored BreachForums to track the sale of stolen banking credentials from a major financial institution breach.

2.3 Identifying Cybercriminals Behind Leaked Databases

Many cybercriminals believe they are anonymous, but OSINT techniques can uncover their real identities through alias tracking, metadata analysis, and username correlation.

📌 **OSINT Methods for Tracking Threat Actors:**

✓ **Username Correlation** – Using tools like WhatsMyName to check if cybercriminals reuse usernames across different platforms.
✓ **PGP Key Matching** – Many dark web users sign messages with PGP keys, which can be linked to previous accounts or emails.
✓ **Metadata Analysis** – Extracting data from leaked documents or images to find IP addresses, timestamps, or software versions.
✓ **Dark Web to Clearnet Tracking** – Some cybercriminals accidentally link their dark web aliases to real-world social media.

🔍 **Example**: OSINT analysts tracked a hacker's alias from BreachForums to his GitHub and Twitter accounts, revealing his real-world identity.

3. Case Study: Investigating a Dark Web Credential Dump

Background:

In 2022, a dark web vendor named "CyberX" leaked a 1.2 million record database from a compromised e-commerce platform. The dump contained:

* Emails & hashed passwords
* Credit card transaction logs
* Customer addresses & phone numbers

Investigation Steps:

1️ **Searching OSINT Databases** – Analysts used HIBP and DeHashed to confirm the breach's authenticity.

2️ **Monitoring Dark Web Forums** – BreachForums discussions revealed that CyberX was also selling bank credentials from past breaches.

3️ **Alias Tracking** – Investigators found that "CyberX" had a Telegram channel where he discussed new leaks.

4️ **Metadata & IP Analysis** – A leaked JSON file in the database contained a timestamp and server location, indicating a possible hosting provider in Eastern Europe.

Outcome:

* Law enforcement identified "CyberX" as a 21-year-old Ukrainian hacker, leading to his arrest.
* The stolen database was taken down, preventing further fraud.
* Victims were notified to reset passwords and enable multi-factor authentication (MFA).

4. Preventative Measures & Mitigation Strategies

* **Use Unique Passwords & MFA** – Prevent credential stuffing attacks.
* **Regularly Monitor Breach Databases** – Detect if your data is leaked.
* **Encrypt Sensitive Data** – Protect personal and financial information.
* **Monitor Dark Web Activity** – Identify emerging threats from leaked credentials.
* **Train Employees on Cyber Hygiene** – Reduce phishing risks from exposed emails.

5. Conclusion: The Growing Threat of Stolen Credentials

With billions of credentials leaked online, stolen databases remain a critical cybercrime threat. OSINT techniques provide investigators, cybersecurity teams, and law enforcement with the tools to track leaks, identify criminals, and mitigate risks. By combining dark web monitoring, breach database searches, and threat actor tracking, investigators can stay ahead of cybercriminals and reduce the impact of stolen credentials on individuals and businesses.

7.3 OSINT Tools for Tracking Data Leaks on the Dark Web

Data leaks are a growing concern, with cybercriminals constantly sharing and selling stolen information on the dark web. Whether it's personal credentials, corporate databases, or sensitive government records, tracking these leaks is crucial for cybersecurity professionals, law enforcement, and OSINT analysts.

This chapter explores OSINT tools and techniques used to monitor, investigate, and mitigate the impact of data leaks on the dark web.

1. Why Tracking Data Leaks Matters

Cybercriminals exploit stolen data for fraud, identity theft, ransomware attacks, and corporate espionage. Proactively monitoring leaks can help organizations:

✅ Detect breaches early before criminals exploit them.

✅ Identify compromised accounts and force password resets.

✅ Monitor threat actors discussing or selling stolen data.

✅ Gather evidence for law enforcement investigations.

🔍 **Example**: In 2023, cybersecurity researchers used OSINT tools to track a leaked database of 200 million Twitter accounts, allowing affected users to secure their credentials before attackers misused them.

2. OSINT Tools for Tracking Data Leaks

2.1 Dark Web Search Engines & Crawlers

Since traditional search engines don't index dark web content, specialized OSINT tools are needed to crawl and index onion sites.

📌 **Top OSINT Tools for Searching Leaked Data:**

🔎 **OnionSearch** – Indexes hidden services and lets users search for breached data.

🔎 **Ahmia** – A Tor-based search engine that helps find leaked credentials.

🔎 **Dark.fail** – A directory tracking dark web marketplaces and forums.

🔎 **Hunchly** – Captures and archives web evidence for OSINT investigations.

🔍 **Example**: Investigators used Ahmia and OnionSearch to find a data dump containing stolen medical records, leading to its removal.

2.2 Breach & Credential Monitoring Databases

OSINT analysts rely on breach databases to check if sensitive information has been exposed in past leaks.

📌 **Best Breach Monitoring Tools:**

✅ **Have I Been Pwned (HIBP)** – Checks if an email/password was exposed in past breaches.

✅ **DeHashed** – Lets users search for leaked emails, usernames, IPs, and passwords.

✅ **IntelX** – A powerful search engine for dark web leaks, documents, and credentials.

✅ **Snusbase** – Provides access to hacked databases and PII dumps.

🔍 **Example**: A financial firm used HIBP and DeHashed to detect employee credentials leaked in a phishing campaign, forcing immediate password resets.

2.3 Dark Web Market & Forum Monitoring Tools

Cybercriminals often sell or distribute stolen data on dark web marketplaces, hacker forums, and Telegram channels.

📌 **OSINT Tools for Monitoring Dark Web Markets:**

◆ **DarkOwl Vision** – Continuously scans the dark web for leaks.

◈ **Cybercrime Tracker** – Monitors malware campaigns and stolen credentials.

◈ **SOCMINT Telegram Scrapers** – Extracts data from Telegram groups selling leaked credentials.

◈ **Threat Intelligence Platforms (Recorded Future, Cybersixgill)** – Offer real-time monitoring of leaked data.

🔍 **Example**: Law enforcement used DarkOwl Vision to identify a forum selling government employee credentials, leading to an undercover investigation.

2.4 Blockchain & Cryptocurrency Tracking

Many dark web transactions for stolen data involve cryptocurrency payments. OSINT analysts track crypto transactions to follow the money trail behind leaks.

📌 **Top Crypto Tracking Tools for OSINT:**

💰 **Blockchain Explorers** – Monitor Bitcoin and altcoin transactions.

💰 **Chainalysis & Elliptic** – Analyze illicit crypto transactions.

💰 **Crystal Blockchain** – Helps link wallets to known cybercriminal activity.

🔍 **Example**: After a ransomware group leaked stolen hospital data, analysts traced Bitcoin payments to an exchange where attackers attempted to launder funds.

3. Techniques for OSINT Leak Investigations

3.1 Monitoring Leaked Credentials in Real-Time

◈ Set up alerts on IntelX, DeHashed, and Have I Been Pwned to track new breaches.

◈ Use DarkOwl Vision or SOCMINT tools to monitor Telegram channels.

◈ Deploy automated scripts to scrape leaked data for investigation.

3.2 Connecting Leaks to Threat Actors

◈ Use username correlation with WhatsMyName to find reused aliases.

◈ Extract metadata from leaked files (e.g., timestamps, server logs).

◈ Investigate forum accounts and PGP keys to link hackers to real-world identities.

3.3 Mapping Leak Sources

- Identify if leaks originate from phishing, malware, or insider threats.
- Compare stolen data formats to previous breaches to find patterns.
- Analyze crypto payments and dark web transactions for connections.

4. Case Study: Tracking a Corporate Data Leak

Background:

In 2022, an unknown hacker leaked a database containing 500,000 corporate emails and passwords on a dark web forum.

Investigation Steps:

1. **Searching Breach Databases** – Analysts used HIBP and IntelX to verify that these credentials hadn't been leaked before.
2. **Dark Web Forum Monitoring** – Using DarkOwl Vision, investigators found the hacker advertising more stolen corporate data.
3. **Tracking Cryptocurrency Transactions** – Blockchain analysis revealed the hacker received payments in Monero (XMR) from a dark web escrow service.
4. **Threat Actor Profiling** – The hacker's PGP key and alias were linked to previous forum posts from 2020, revealing connections to past breaches.

Outcome:

- The organization reset compromised accounts and enhanced security protocols.
- Law enforcement traced the hacker's crypto transactions, leading to their arrest.
- Cybersecurity teams monitored dark web forums for further leaks.

5. How to Protect Yourself & Your Organization from Leaks

✓ Regularly check breach monitoring services (HIBP, IntelX).

✓ Enable MFA on all accounts to prevent unauthorized access.

✓ Encrypt sensitive data to reduce exposure in case of leaks.

✓ Use dark web monitoring tools to detect stolen credentials.

✓ Educate employees on phishing risks and data security.

6. Conclusion: OSINT as a Key Tool for Leak Investigations

The dark web remains a hotbed for data leaks, but OSINT tools provide powerful ways to detect, track, and mitigate threats. By combining dark web crawlers, breach databases, forum monitoring, and blockchain analysis, investigators can proactively fight cybercrime and protect sensitive data.

7.4 How Cybercriminals Monetize Stolen Data

The dark web is a thriving underground economy where stolen data is transformed into profit. Cybercriminals leverage various methods to monetize breached databases, stolen credentials, financial information, and personal identities. From selling data in bulk to using it for fraud and extortion, the dark web offers multiple avenues for criminals to turn illicit information into money. Understanding these techniques is crucial for OSINT analysts, cybersecurity professionals, and law enforcement agencies aiming to track and disrupt cybercrime.

1. The Value of Stolen Data

Not all stolen data holds the same value. The price of leaked information depends on factors such as rarity, recency, sensitivity, and demand. The following are some of the most commonly monetized data types:

◆ **Personal Identifiable Information (PII):** Names, addresses, phone numbers, Social Security Numbers (SSNs), and dates of birth. Used for identity theft and fraud.

◆ **Financial Data**: Credit card numbers, bank account details, PayPal logins. Directly exploited for unauthorized transactions.

◆ **Login Credentials**: Emails and passwords for various accounts. Often sold in bulk for credential stuffing attacks.

◆ **Corporate Data**: Employee information, internal documents, customer records, and trade secrets. Used for corporate espionage or extortion.

◆ **Medical Records**: Stolen health records are valuable due to their detailed personal information, often used for fraudulent insurance claims.

🔍 **Example**: In 2023, a hacker sold millions of LinkedIn credentials on a dark web marketplace, allowing cybercriminals to launch phishing campaigns and business email compromise (BEC) scams.

2. Methods Cybercriminals Use to Monetize Stolen Data

2.1 Selling Stolen Data on Dark Web Marketplaces

One of the most direct ways criminals make money is by selling stolen data on dark web forums and marketplaces. These platforms function similarly to legitimate e-commerce sites, with escrow services, reputation systems, and customer reviews to build trust among buyers and sellers.

📌 **Where Stolen Data Is Sold:**

💰 **Dark Web Marketplaces**: Sites like Genesis Market, Russian Market, and BreachForums specialize in selling credentials and stolen data.
💰 **Hacker Forums**: Cybercriminal communities where users trade, sell, and share breach data.
💰 **Telegram & Discord Channels**: Many cybercriminals now use private Telegram groups to sell stolen credentials and bypass law enforcement monitoring.

🔍 **Example**: A hacker sold stolen Uber employee credentials on BreachForums, which were later used to infiltrate internal systems and gain access to sensitive company data.

2.2 Using Stolen Data for Identity Theft & Fraud

Cybercriminals often exploit PII to commit identity fraud, taking out loans, opening credit cards, or applying for government benefits under false identities.

📌 **Common Identity Fraud Techniques:**

◆ **Synthetic Identity Fraud**: Combining real and fake personal information to create a new identity.
◆ **Tax Fraud**: Filing fraudulent tax returns to steal refunds.
◆ **Loan & Credit Fraud**: Opening lines of credit using stolen Social Security numbers (SSNs).

🔍 **Example**: A fraud ring used stolen Social Security numbers from a hospital breach to create fake identities and secure fraudulent car loans worth millions.

2.3 Credit Card Fraud & Carding

Credit card data, also known as "CVVs", is one of the most frequently sold commodities on the dark web. Criminals use carding techniques to exploit stolen credit card numbers.

📌 **How Carding Works:**

💳 **Purchase Card Details**: Stolen card data is sold in dark web marketplaces.
💳 **Test Small Transactions**: Criminals test the card with a small online purchase to see if it's still active.
💳 **Buy & Resell Goods**: If the card is valid, they purchase expensive electronics, gift cards, or luxury goods to resell for cash.
💳 **Use Drop Services**: Criminals use "drop addresses" to receive fraudulently purchased goods before reselling them.

🔍 **Example**: In 2022, a hacker group sold 1 million stolen credit card numbers on a dark web forum, leading to millions in fraudulent transactions before banks detected the breach.

2.4 Ransomware & Extortion Schemes

Some criminals don't sell stolen data outright but instead use it for extortion and ransom attacks. Ransomware gangs steal and encrypt data, demanding a ransom in cryptocurrency in exchange for returning access.

📌 **How Extortion Schemes Work:**

💀 **Ransomware Attacks**: Criminals infect a company's system with ransomware, encrypting critical files and demanding payment.
💀 **Data Leak Extortion**: Hackers threaten to publicly release sensitive data unless a ransom is paid.
💀 **Sextortion Scams**: Cybercriminals blackmail individuals by claiming to have compromising personal information.

🔍 **Example**: The ALPHV/BlackCat ransomware gang hacked a major healthcare provider, encrypting patient records and demanding millions in Bitcoin to prevent data leaks.

2.5 Exploiting Stolen Credentials for Account Takeovers (ATO)

Many people reuse passwords across multiple sites, making stolen credentials highly valuable for account takeovers (ATO).

📌 **How ATO Attacks Work:**

🔑 **Credential Stuffing**: Cybercriminals use automated bots to test stolen usernames and passwords across multiple sites.
🔑 **Brute Force Attacks**: Using software to guess weak or reused passwords.
🔑 **SIM Swapping**: Hijacking a victim's phone number to bypass two-factor authentication (2FA).

🔍 **Example**: A hacker used credentials from a massive Facebook breach to take over thousands of Instagram accounts, demanding ransom payments from victims.

2.6 Selling Access to Compromised Systems (RDP & VPN Credentials)

Instead of using stolen credentials themselves, cybercriminals often sell access to compromised systems, including Remote Desktop Protocol (RDP) logins, VPN credentials, and corporate networks.

📌 **How System Access Is Sold:**

◆ **Initial Access Brokers (IABs):** Criminal groups that sell access to hacked corporate systems.
◆ **RDP Shops**: Marketplaces where attackers buy and sell remote desktop access to infected machines.
◆ **Ransomware-as-a-Service (RaaS):** Some ransomware groups purchase access from IABs to deploy malware.

🔍 **Example**: The REvil ransomware gang bought corporate VPN credentials from an Initial Access Broker to launch ransomware attacks on Fortune 500 companies.

3. How OSINT Analysts Can Track & Prevent Monetization

🔎 **Monitor Dark Web Marketplaces** – Track the sale of stolen credentials on hacker forums and Telegram groups.

🔎 **Search Breach Databases** – Use Have I Been Pwned, DeHashed, and IntelX to check for leaked credentials.

🔎 **Investigate Cryptocurrency Payments** – Analyze ransomware payments and stolen funds using blockchain explorers.

🔎 **Track Threat Actor Behavior** – Use OSINT tools to monitor cybercriminal discussions and detect upcoming attacks.

4. Conclusion: Disrupting the Cybercriminal Economy

The dark web operates as a multi-billion-dollar underground economy, but cybersecurity professionals and OSINT analysts can intervene, track, and disrupt these illicit activities. By understanding how criminals monetize stolen data—whether through sales, fraud, extortion, or ransomware—investigators can develop strategies to mitigate cyber risks, track financial transactions, and prevent future breaches.

7.5 Preventive Measures & Monitoring Services for Data Breaches

As cybercriminals continuously exploit stolen data on the dark web, organizations and individuals must implement preventive measures and leverage monitoring services to detect and mitigate the risks associated with data breaches. Proactive security strategies, OSINT-based monitoring, and collaboration with cybersecurity firms can significantly reduce the impact of leaked credentials, financial data, and personally identifiable information (PII). This section explores key measures for preventing breaches, detecting data leaks, and responding effectively to protect digital assets.

1. Preventive Measures: Strengthening Security to Reduce Data Breach Risks

Preventing data breaches requires a multi-layered security approach that includes robust cybersecurity policies, user awareness, and proactive monitoring. Below are essential preventive measures:

1.1 Implement Strong Authentication & Access Controls

🔐 **Enforce Multi-Factor Authentication (MFA):** Requires a second form of verification (e.g., SMS codes, authenticator apps) to prevent unauthorized logins.

🔐 **Use Strong, Unique Passwords**: Encourage employees and users to create long, complex passwords and avoid password reuse.

🔐 **Apply Zero-Trust Security Models**: Limit access based on user roles, device trust levels, and behavioral analytics.

🔍 **Example**: Google reported a 50% drop in phishing-related account takeovers after enforcing MFA across all employee accounts.

1.2 Secure Sensitive Data with Encryption & Tokenization

🔒 **Encrypt Data at Rest & In Transit**: Protects data stored in databases and transmitted over networks.

🔒 **Use End-to-End Encryption (E2EE):** Ensures only authorized recipients can decrypt sensitive communications.

🔒 **Tokenization**: Replaces sensitive data (e.g., credit card numbers) with non-sensitive placeholders to limit exposure.

🔍 **Example**: After adopting end-to-end encryption, major financial institutions reduced fraudulent transactions by 30%.

1.3 Regular Security Audits & Patch Management

🔲 **Conduct Regular Vulnerability Scans & Penetration Testing**: Identifies weak points before cybercriminals can exploit them.

🔲 **Apply Security Patches & Software Updates**: Prevents attacks exploiting outdated systems.

🔲 **Monitor Third-Party Vendors**: Ensure suppliers and partners follow strict cybersecurity protocols.

🔍 **Example**: The Equifax data breach (2017) was caused by an unpatched Apache Struts vulnerability, leading to the leak of 147 million records.

1.4 Educate Employees & Users on Cyber Threats

👥 **Security Awareness Training:** Educate employees on phishing attacks, social engineering, and credential security.

✉@ **Phishing Simulations**: Conduct internal tests to assess employee responses to phishing attempts.

🔍 **Monitor Insider Threats**: Use behavioral analytics to detect suspicious activity within an organization.

🔍 **Example**: A major bank reduced phishing attack success rates by 75% after implementing a company-wide security awareness program.

2. Monitoring Services: Detecting & Responding to Data Breaches

While preventive measures reduce breach risks, continuous monitoring is critical to detect leaked credentials and stolen data before they can be exploited.

2.1 Dark Web Monitoring Services

Specialized dark web monitoring tools track hacker forums, marketplaces, and breach dumps for stolen data. These tools help detect leaks early and mitigate potential threats.

⬜⬜ **Popular Dark Web Monitoring Services:**

✅ **SpyCloud** – Tracks compromised credentials and provides automated alerts.

✅ **Have I Been Pwned (HIBP)** – Checks if emails and passwords have been exposed in known breaches.

✅ **DeHashed** – Allows OSINT investigators to search leaked data by email, IP, or username.

✅ **IntelX** – Scans breach databases, dark web forums, and paste sites for leaked information.

🔍 **Example**: After discovering leaked credentials on a dark web forum, a company used SpyCloud to reset affected employee passwords, preventing account takeovers.

2.2 Breach Detection in Real Time

📡 Intrusion Detection Systems (IDS) & Security Information and Event Management (SIEM) tools can detect unusual activity and unauthorized data access.

⚠⬜ Automated Alert Systems: AI-driven threat intelligence platforms can flag suspicious login attempts and credential stuffing attacks in real time.

🔍 **Example**: A global retailer detected unauthorized API access through real-time SIEM monitoring, stopping an attack before customer data was stolen.

2.3 Blockchain & Cryptocurrency Transaction Monitoring

Since many cybercriminals use cryptocurrencies for ransom payments and money laundering, blockchain analysis tools can help track illicit funds.

☐ **Best Tools for Cryptocurrency Monitoring:**

✅ **Chainalysis** – Tracks cryptocurrency transactions to detect suspicious wallet activity.
✅ **Elliptic** – Provides real-time blockchain monitoring for fraud and money laundering prevention.
✅ **CipherTrace** – Identifies cryptocurrency addresses linked to criminal activities.

🔍 **Example**: Law enforcement agencies used Chainalysis to trace ransomware payments made in Bitcoin, leading to the seizure of millions in illicit funds.

3. Incident Response: What to Do If Your Data Is Found on the Dark Web

Despite preventive efforts, breaches can still occur. A rapid incident response can mitigate damage and prevent further exploitation.

3.1 Immediate Steps After a Breach

☐ **Reset Affected Passwords & Enable MFA**: Prevents attackers from using stolen credentials.
🔎 **Investigate Breach Scope:** Determine what data was exposed and potential risks.
🔊 **Notify Affected Users & Authorities**: Inform users and regulators (e.g., GDPR, CCPA compliance).

🔍 **Example**: After discovering leaked customer passwords, a tech company forced password resets and implemented MFA to block future unauthorized access.

3.2 Long-Term Recovery & Prevention

☐ **Monitor for Fraudulent Transactions**: Keep track of suspicious financial activity post-breach.

□□ **Enhance Security Policies**: Learn from past incidents and improve password policies, employee training, and data encryption.

⚏ **Conduct Post-Breach Security Audits**: Identify vulnerabilities and patch them before further exploitation.

🔍 **Example**: Following a massive customer data breach, a major airline strengthened encryption, enforced stricter authentication measures, and hired a dedicated threat intelligence team to monitor for future threats.

4. Conclusion: A Proactive Approach to Dark Web Data Protection

Cybercriminals will continue to exploit stolen data, but organizations and individuals can take proactive measures to prevent breaches, detect leaks, and respond swiftly when data is compromised. Implementing robust security measures, leveraging dark web monitoring services, and maintaining a strong incident response plan can help minimize risks and disrupt cybercriminal operations. In an era where data breaches are inevitable, real-time monitoring and swift action are the keys to staying ahead of cyber threats.

7.6 Case Study: Investigating a Massive Data Dump on the Dark Web

In early 2021, cybersecurity researchers and law enforcement agencies uncovered one of the largest data dumps ever discovered on the dark web—a staggering 3.2 billion email-password pairs leaked from multiple breaches. This case study examines how OSINT investigators and cybersecurity professionals analyzed the data dump, identified affected individuals and organizations, and traced the origins of the leak.

1. Discovery of the Data Dump: COMB (Compilation of Many Breaches)

In February 2021, cybersecurity analysts monitoring dark web forums and underground marketplaces found references to a newly released database titled "COMB" (Compilation of Many Breaches). Unlike previous breaches, COMB was not the result of a single hack but an aggregation of data stolen from multiple companies over several years.

🔍 **Key Findings:**

3.2 billion unique email-password pairs

- Data collected from past breaches, including LinkedIn, Netflix, Gmail, Yahoo, and others
- Credentials indexed and searchable through a user-friendly interface
- Shared for free or at a minimal price on hacker forums

👤💻 OSINT Techniques Used to Identify the Leak:

✅ Dark web monitoring tools (SpyCloud, IntelX, DeHashed) detected hacker forum posts discussing the database.

✅ Search engines for breached data allowed investigators to analyze sample leaks.

✅ Pastebin and Telegram channels were monitored for further distribution.

2. Analyzing the Data: Tracking the Origin and Impact

To assess the risks posed by COMB, analysts needed to determine:

- Which organizations were affected?
- How recent was the stolen data?
- Whether passwords were encrypted or stored in plaintext?

2.1 Clues from the Metadata

🗂️ The leak contained metadata suggesting aggregation from multiple sources, including timestamps that revealed when each dataset was stolen.

🔍 Example:

- Some credentials were linked to the 2012 LinkedIn breach (167M records).
- Others were traced to the Yahoo breach (2013-2014), which exposed 3 billion accounts.
- Newer breaches suggested that cybercriminals had updated stolen credentials with more recent hacks.

2.2 Investigating the Criminal Actors Behind the Leak

Researchers analyzed dark web marketplaces, Telegram groups, and underground forums to find out who was distributing the COMB dataset and their motives.

💰 Findings:

- The dataset was initially leaked for free, likely to gain credibility and reputation in the hacker community.
- Other actors repackaged and sold access to premium versions with additional filtering and indexing features.
- The hacker group responsible had ties to previous breaches and password leaks.

☐ Law Enforcement Action:

- Agencies flagged the IP addresses and servers hosting the COMB database.
- Hosting providers were notified, leading to the removal of some download links.
- Ongoing investigations sought to trace cryptocurrency transactions from forum purchases.

3. Impact on Individuals & Organizations

Unlike smaller, single-company breaches, COMB was particularly dangerous because it aggregated credentials from multiple breaches.

⚠☐ Risks to Users:

- **Credential Stuffing Attacks**: Hackers used the leaked data to automate login attempts on banking, email, and e-commerce sites.
- **Phishing & Identity Theft**: Personal details from emails allowed for targeted scams.
- **Account Takeovers**: Reused passwords gave attackers access to social media, financial, and business accounts.

🏢 Risks to Organizations:

- Companies with employee emails in the leak faced corporate account hijacking.
- Reputation damage and regulatory fines for failing to secure user data.
- Dark web monitoring became essential to track credential exposure.

4. Response & Mitigation: How Victims Reacted

Once news of the COMB breach spread, organizations and cybersecurity firms took immediate action to mitigate damage.

4.1 Incident Response by Major Companies

✅ Google & Microsoft forced password resets for affected users.

✅ Banks & financial institutions enhanced fraud detection for compromised accounts.

✅ Security firms released breach detection tools for users to check if their credentials were leaked.

4.2 OSINT-Based User Protection

🔍 Dark web monitoring platforms sent automated alerts when corporate or personal emails appeared in the dataset.

🔍 Government agencies advised the public to change passwords and enable multi-factor authentication (MFA).

5. Lessons Learned: The Future of Dark Web Data Monitoring

The COMB data leak reinforced the importance of proactive security measures and OSINT-based monitoring to track breached credentials.

🔲 Key Takeaways:

- Massive data dumps will continue as cybercriminals aggregate stolen information from multiple breaches.
- Monitoring the dark web is crucial to detect leaks before they are exploited.
- Organizations must enforce MFA to prevent credential stuffing attacks.
- Users should use password managers to generate unique passwords for each site.

👤💻 Future Strategies:

- AI-driven threat intelligence platforms will automate dark web monitoring.
- Blockchain technology could prevent unauthorized access by providing decentralized identity verification.
- More aggressive takedowns of hacker forums and data marketplaces will disrupt cybercriminal activity.

6. Conclusion: The Ongoing Battle Against Data Breaches

The COMB data leak was a wake-up call for both cybersecurity experts and the general public. While stolen credentials remain a lucrative resource for cybercriminals, OSINT investigations, dark web monitoring, and proactive cybersecurity measures can limit their impact. As long as massive breaches continue, continuous vigilance and advanced security strategies will be essential to protect digital identities in an increasingly vulnerable cyber landscape.

8. Cybercriminal Communication Channels & OPSEC

In this chapter, we will delve into the secretive communication channels used by cybercriminals operating in the Dark Web and their emphasis on operational security (OPSEC). Threat actors often rely on encrypted messaging platforms, private forums, and even custom-built communication tools to coordinate illegal activities while protecting their identities. We will explore the various methods cybercriminals use to maintain secrecy, from PGP encryption to secure, anonymous chat services, and how OSINT investigators can monitor these channels without compromising their own security. Understanding the significance of OPSEC in cybercrime is essential for analysts to gather intelligence effectively and safely, ensuring that investigations do not inadvertently expose the identity of those involved. This chapter will provide insight into how these communication channels operate and the techniques for safely infiltrating or monitoring them.

8.1 Encrypted Messaging Apps & Dark Web Forums

Cybercriminals rely on encrypted messaging apps and dark web forums to communicate, share intelligence, and conduct illicit transactions while maintaining anonymity. These platforms provide secure channels for organizing cybercrime operations, selling stolen data, and discussing exploits without law enforcement detection. This section explores the most commonly used encrypted communication tools, how dark web forums function, and how OSINT investigators monitor these platforms for intelligence gathering.

1. The Role of Encrypted Messaging in Cybercrime

Encrypted messaging apps are vital for cybercriminals, offering end-to-end encryption (E2EE), self-destructing messages, anonymity features, and hidden group chats. These platforms allow users to:

✅ Coordinate cyberattacks, ransomware negotiations, and fraud operations

✅ Sell or trade stolen data, malware, and hacking tools

✅ Recruit new members into cybercrime syndicates

✅ Evade law enforcement by masking digital footprints

1.1 Most Popular Encrypted Messaging Apps Used by Cybercriminals

◆ **Telegram** – Encrypted channels and private groups make it a hub for stolen data sales, fraud tutorials, and ransomware negotiations.

◆ **Signal** – Offers strong encryption and disappearing messages; used by high-level cybercriminals.

◆ **Wickr** – Anonymous registration and auto-deleting messages make it popular for darknet drug markets.

◆ **Threema** – No phone number required, providing extra anonymity.

◆ **Session** – A decentralized, blockchain-based app used to prevent tracking.

🔍 **Example**: In 2023, a Telegram channel named "@darkleaks" was found selling millions of breached credentials from corporate hacks.

2. Dark Web Forums: The Underground Cybercrime Ecosystem

Unlike traditional social media, dark web forums operate on Tor, I2P, and ZeroNet, allowing cybercriminals to exchange knowledge, sell illicit goods, and discuss hacking techniques without being easily traced.

2.1 How Dark Web Forums Operate

🖥 **Access via Onion Services**: Requires Tor or I2P to access hidden sites.

☐ **Strict Membership Requirements**: Many forums require vouching, paid memberships, or proof of criminal activity to join.

🔐 **Private Messaging & Encrypted Chat Rooms**: Enable secure communications between members.

☐☐ **Law Enforcement Infiltration**: Some forums are monitored or even secretly operated by authorities.

3. OSINT Techniques for Monitoring Encrypted Apps & Forums

3.1 Tracking Cybercrime Activities on Messaging Apps

🔍 **Keyword & Hashtag Monitoring**: Researchers track common dark web terms like "fullz," "dump," and "CVV" on Telegram and other platforms.

☐☐ **Bot Analysis**: Many fraud groups use automated bots to distribute stolen credentials—OSINT analysts track bot activity.

Undercover Operations: Law enforcement creates fake accounts to infiltrate groups and collect intelligence.

3.2 Investigating Dark Web Forums

Forum Crawlers: Automated tools scrape forum discussions for relevant cybercrime topics.

Analyzing Language & Behavior: Patterns in language, timestamps, and user behavior help identify threat actors.

Linking Forum Identities to Real-World Accounts: Investigators use OSINT techniques to track usernames, PGP keys, and cryptocurrency wallets.

Example: In 2021, the FBI infiltrated RaidForums, a notorious hacking forum, leading to multiple arrests and the forum's shutdown.

4. Conclusion: Balancing Privacy & Cybersecurity

Encrypted messaging apps and dark web forums provide both legitimate privacy and opportunities for cybercriminals to operate anonymously. OSINT analysts and law enforcement must continuously develop advanced monitoring techniques to track illegal activities while respecting legal and ethical boundaries. By leveraging automated tracking tools, infiltration tactics, and cryptocurrency tracing, investigators can effectively counter cyber threats emerging from these hidden communication networks.

8.2 Investigating PGP Encryption in Cybercrime Networks

Pretty Good Privacy (PGP) encryption is a cornerstone of cybercriminal operational security (OPSEC) on the dark web. It enables secure messaging, digital signatures, and identity verification, making it a crucial tool for threat actors, dark web vendors, and hacking groups. Understanding how cybercriminals use PGP—and how investigators can analyze it—is essential for OSINT (Open Source Intelligence) investigations.

1. What is PGP & Why Do Cybercriminals Use It?

PGP is a public-key cryptography system that allows users to encrypt and sign messages to ensure confidentiality, authenticity, and integrity. It uses:

📍 **Public & Private Keys** – A user shares their public key for others to encrypt messages, while only they can decrypt them with their private key.

✍️ **Digital Signatures** – Used to verify identity and prevent message tampering.

💼 **File & Email Encryption** – Ensures secure transactions between cybercriminals.

1.1 Why PGP is Popular in Cybercrime Networks

✅ **Trusted Identity Verification** – Dark web vendors use PGP keys to prove their legitimacy.

✅ **Secure Communications** – Encrypted messages prevent law enforcement from intercepting private chats.

✅ **Protection Against Impersonation** – Fraudsters can't easily fake another vendor's PGP-signed messages.

✅ **Used in Ransomware Operations** – Attackers include PGP keys in ransom notes to receive decryption key requests securely.

2. Where PGP Appears in Cybercrime Networks

◆ **Dark Web Marketplaces** – Vendors share PGP keys for encrypted communication with buyers.

◆ **Hacking Forums** – Cybercriminals use PGP signatures to verify malware, exploit kits, and stolen data sales.

◆ **Ransomware Negotiations** – Attackers sign ransom demands with PGP to confirm authenticity.

◆ **Leaked Databases** – Hackers encrypt sensitive data dumps with PGP before selling them.

🔍 **Example**: In 2021, the REvil ransomware group used PGP encryption to verify decryption keys for victims who paid ransom.

3. OSINT Techniques for Investigating PGP Encryption

3.1 Identifying & Extracting PGP Keys

Investigators analyze PGP keys in dark web vendor profiles, forum posts, and leaked communications. OSINT tools can:

✅ Extract public PGP keys from dark web sites

✓ Cross-reference keys with known cybercriminal identities

✓ Identify reused PGP fingerprints across different forums

🔍 OSINT Tools for PGP Analysis:

- **MIT PGP Keyserver** – Searches for public PGP keys.
- **Keybase.io** – Links PGP keys to social media profiles.
- **Hagrid (GnuPG keyserver)** – Helps track PGP key usage.
- **pgpdump** – Analyzes PGP key details.

3.2 Linking PGP Keys to Real Identities

🔲 **Investigative Steps:**

1️⃣ Check if a cybercriminal's PGP key appears on multiple sites under different usernames.

2️⃣ Analyze email addresses associated with public keys to find real-world connections.

3️⃣ Search old data breaches to see if a PGP-verified user previously used a non-anonymous email.

4️⃣ Look for reused PGP key fingerprints—many threat actors recycle encryption keys.

🔍 **Example**: Law enforcement tracked a dark web weapons vendor after discovering his PGP key was linked to a personal email from an old forum post.

4. How Law Enforcement De-anonymizes PGP-Protected Communications

While PGP encryption is strong, investigators use several methods to uncover hidden links between criminals:

◆ **Metadata Analysis** – Even if a message is encrypted, PGP leaves metadata (timestamps, key fingerprints) that can be analyzed.

◆ **Operational Security (OPSEC) Mistakes** – Criminals sometimes reuse PGP keys across personal and dark web accounts.

◆ **Forum Infiltration** – Undercover agents pose as buyers, request PGP-encrypted messages, then analyze the sender's patterns.

◆ **Compromising Private Keys** – Law enforcement agencies seize servers and devices to extract stored PGP keys.

🔍 **Example**: In 2017, Dutch police seized Hansa Market's servers, gaining access to PGP-encrypted vendor messages, which helped track drug traffickers.

5. Case Study: The Fall of AlphaBay & PGP Mistakes

AlphaBay, one of the largest dark web markets, used PGP encryption extensively. However, its administrator, Alexandre Cazes, made critical mistakes:

✗ Reused his PGP key across multiple forums.

✗ Linked his real email to his PGP key.

✗ Stored his private PGP key on his personal laptop—which was seized.

✹ **Outcome**: Law enforcement unraveled his identity, leading to the takedown of AlphaBay.

6. Conclusion: The Double-Edged Sword of PGP in Cybercrime

PGP encryption remains a powerful tool for dark web criminals, but OSINT investigators can exploit key weaknesses to track them down. By monitoring PGP usage, analyzing metadata, cross-referencing keys, and leveraging OPSEC mistakes, law enforcement and researchers can de-anonymize cybercriminals and disrupt illegal activities on the dark web.

8.3 Understanding OPSEC Practices of Threat Actors

Operational Security (OPSEC) is the foundation of cybercriminal activity on the dark web. Threat actors meticulously follow OPSEC protocols to evade law enforcement, maintain anonymity, and protect their illicit operations. Understanding these tactics, techniques, and procedures (TTPs) is crucial for OSINT investigators, cybersecurity professionals, and law enforcement agencies attempting to track and unmask cybercriminals.

This section explores the core OPSEC principles used by dark web actors, common mistakes they make, and how investigators can exploit these weaknesses.

1. What is OPSEC & Why Do Cybercriminals Use It?

OPSEC is a risk management strategy designed to minimize exposure, prevent identification, and maintain anonymity. Cybercriminals use OPSEC to:

✅ **Avoid digital fingerprints** – Preventing law enforcement from linking online activity to real-world identities.

✅ **Evade tracking & surveillance** – Using encryption, VPNs, and anonymity networks (Tor, I2P, ZeroNet).

✅ **Ensure compartmentalization** – Separating criminal activities across different aliases, devices, and networks.

✅ **Secure communications & transactions** – Using PGP encryption, cryptocurrency tumblers, and secure drop sites.

2. Core OPSEC Practices of Dark Web Threat Actors

2.1 Identity & Alias Management

◆ **Multiple Aliases**: Cybercriminals operate under different pseudonyms across various platforms to avoid pattern detection.

◆ **Compartmentalization**: They separate identities for different activities—e.g., one alias for ransomware, another for fraud.

◆ **Use of Disposable Accounts**: Temporary email providers, burner phones, and one-time-use usernames are common.

🔍 **OSINT Exploitation**: Investigators track username reuse, avatar patterns, and writing styles to link multiple accounts.

2.2 Secure Network & Device Usage

◆ **Tor, I2P & VPNs**: Used to mask IP addresses and location.

◆ **Air-Gapped Systems**: Some actors operate on offline devices to prevent malware tracking.

◆ **Tails OS & Whonix**: Privacy-focused operating systems prevent forensic tracking.

◆ **MAC Address Spoofing**: Prevents hardware tracking.

🔍 **OSINT Exploitation**: Misconfigured VPNs, time zone leaks, and repeated login locations can reveal identities.

2.3 Encrypted Communication & Data Handling

◆ **PGP Encryption**: Used for secure messaging and identity verification.
◆ **Self-Destructing Messages**: Wickr, Signal, and Telegram's "secret chats" help erase traces.
◆ **Steganography**: Hiding messages in images or files to evade detection.
◆ **Dark Web Dead Drops**: Cybercriminals sometimes use dark web sites to exchange information anonymously.

🔍 **OSINT Exploitation**: Investigators analyze PGP key reuse, metadata, and timestamps to track identities.

2.4 Cryptocurrency Anonymization

◆ **Bitcoin Mixers & Tumblers**: Used to obfuscate transaction trails.
◆ **Privacy Coins**: Monero, Zcash, and Dash are preferred for untraceable transactions.
◆ **OTC Trading & Peer-to-Peer Sales**: Avoids exchanges that require KYC (Know Your Customer) verification.

🔍 **OSINT Exploitation**: Tracking money flows via blockchain analysis tools like Chainalysis, CipherTrace, and Elliptic.

3. Common OPSEC Mistakes That Expose Cybercriminals

Despite their expertise, threat actors frequently make OPSEC mistakes, leading to their identification and arrests. Some key errors include:

▼ **Reusing Usernames & Email Addresses**: Investigators track aliases across forums, leaks, and social media.
▼ **Logging into Anonymous Accounts Without VPN/Tor**: Accidental real IP exposure is a common mistake.
▼ **Forgetting to Scrub Metadata from Files & Images**: Photos, documents, and videos often contain geolocation data.
▼ **Leaving Digital Fingerprints on Marketplaces & Forums**: Time zone leaks, writing styles, and browsing habits can reveal identities.
▼ **Using Weak or Leaked Passwords**: Law enforcement checks for reused passwords in breached data dumps.

🔍 **Case Study**: Ross Ulbricht, the creator of Silk Road, was caught because he used his real email in early forum posts before switching to a pseudonym.

4. How Investigators Exploit OPSEC Failures

Cybercrime investigators and OSINT analysts use advanced techniques to identify OPSEC mistakes and track cybercriminals:

◆ **OSINT Tools for Username Tracking**: Have I Been Pwned, Namechk, and Sherlock help match usernames across platforms.

◆ **Metadata Analysis**: Extracts hidden data from images and files using tools like ExifTool.

◆ **Forum & Marketplace Infiltration**: Law enforcement poses as buyers or vendors to gather intelligence.

◆ **Language Pattern Analysis**: Examines writing styles and vocabulary to match multiple aliases.

◆ **Time Zone & Activity Pattern Tracking**: Helps correlate dark web activity with real-world behaviors.

5. Case Study: OPSEC Mistakes That Led to Arrests

5.1 The Fall of AlphaBay & Its Founder

🔍 **OPSEC Mistakes by Alexandre Cazes (AlphaBay Admin):**

✗ Used a personal email in early forum registrations.

✗ Reused passwords from old hacked databases.

✗ Stored personal documents on his server, which was seized by law enforcement.

✅ **Outcome**: Law enforcement tracked his OPSEC failures and seized AlphaBay, one of the largest dark web markets.

5.2 Tracking the FBI's Honeypot: Anom Encrypted Phones

🔍 **How Cybercriminals Were Caught:**

- The FBI secretly ran "Anom," a fake encrypted phone network.

- Criminals used it for illegal transactions, thinking it was secure.
- Law enforcement had backdoor access, monitoring every message.

✅ **Outcome**: Over 800 arrests worldwide in a massive cybercrime bust.

6. Conclusion: OPSEC is Not Perfect

While cybercriminals invest heavily in OPSEC strategies, mistakes and human error expose them over time. By understanding these tactics, vulnerabilities, and tracking techniques, OSINT investigators and law enforcement agencies can effectively de-anonymize cybercriminals and dismantle illicit operations on the dark web.

Key Takeaway: No OPSEC is perfect—every cybercriminal eventually makes a mistake.

8.4 How Law Enforcement Monitors Criminal Communication Channels

Cybercriminals rely on encrypted communication channels, dark web forums, and private messaging apps to conduct illicit activities while avoiding detection. Law enforcement agencies, however, have developed sophisticated OSINT (Open Source Intelligence), SIGINT (Signals Intelligence), and HUMINT (Human Intelligence) techniques to infiltrate, monitor, and disrupt these criminal networks.

This section explores the methods law enforcement uses to track cybercriminal communication channels, common challenges, and real-world case studies where these techniques have led to major arrests.

1. Where Do Cybercriminals Communicate?

Criminals leverage multiple platforms to sell stolen data, coordinate attacks, and exchange intelligence. Law enforcement monitors:

⬧ **Dark Web Marketplaces & Forums** – Places where criminals buy/sell drugs, weapons, malware, and stolen data.
⬧ **Encrypted Messaging Apps** – Telegram, Wickr, Signal, and Jabber are used for private, self-destructing messages.
⬧ **Decentralized Networks (I2P, Matrix, ZeroNet)** – Privacy-focused networks resistant to takedowns.

◆ **Social Media & Encrypted Email** – Threat actors use Twitter, Discord, and ProtonMail to share updates.

◆ **Gaming Platforms & VoIP Services** – Some criminals communicate via PlayStation, Xbox Live, or TeamSpeak to evade monitoring.

2. Law Enforcement Monitoring Techniques

2.1 OSINT: Gathering Intelligence from Public & Private Sources

OSINT analysts scrape, analyze, and track digital footprints across forums, marketplaces, and social media.

✅ Automated Scraping Tools:

- **SpiderFoot & Maltego** – Map connections between criminal profiles.
- **Hunchly & Hyphe** – Capture forensic evidence from dark web sites.
- **Have I Been Pwned & Dehashed** – Search leaked credentials linked to cybercriminals.

✅ Forum & Marketplace Monitoring:

- Law enforcement monitors vendor feedback, transaction history, and aliases to track criminal activity.
- Infiltration & Undercover Operations: Officers pose as buyers to gather intelligence.

2.2 SIGINT: Intercepting & Analyzing Communications

Signals intelligence (SIGINT) focuses on tracking and intercepting digital communications.

◆ **Dark Web Honeypots** – Law enforcement sets up fake darknet markets or forums to lure criminals.

◆ **Metadata Analysis** – Even if a message is encrypted, metadata (timestamps, IP logs, and device fingerprints) can expose users.

◆ **Botnet & Malware Tracking** – Monitoring Command & Control (C2) servers used by ransomware gangs.

⧫ **Monitoring Encrypted Messaging Apps** – Telegram and Discord channels are often infiltrated by intelligence agencies.

✓ **Case Study: The FBI's TrojanShield Operation (2021)**

- The FBI ran a fake encrypted phone service (ANOM), allowing them to monitor 12,000 devices used by criminals worldwide.
- Over 800 arrests were made as criminals unknowingly shared plans with law enforcement.

2.3 HUMINT: Infiltrating Cybercriminal Networks

Human intelligence (HUMINT) plays a key role in gathering intelligence from within cybercriminal groups.

✓ **Undercover Law Enforcement Agents:**

- Pose as buyers or hackers to build trust and extract information.
- Gain access to invite-only forums and private Telegram groups.
- Buy stolen data or illicit goods to track sellers' locations and identities.

✓ **Flipping Criminal Informants:**

- Arrested cybercriminals cooperate with law enforcement in exchange for reduced sentences.
- Informants leak chat logs, PGP keys, and crypto wallets of active cybercrime groups.

🔍 **Example**: The takedown of the Silk Road market was aided by an informant who provided access to vendor transactions and messages.

3. Challenges Law Enforcement Faces

Despite advanced techniques, several factors make monitoring cybercriminal communications difficult:

✗ **End-to-End Encryption (E2EE):** Platforms like Signal and ProtonMail prevent law enforcement from reading messages.

✘ **Decentralized Networks**: Some services (Matrix, I2P) operate without central servers, making takedowns nearly impossible.

✘ **Anonymity Tools**: Criminals use Tor, VPNs, and encrypted devices to hide their identities.

✘ **AI-Powered Anonymity**: Some actors now use deepfake voices and AI-generated text to evade forensic analysis.

✅ **Law Enforcement Countermeasures:**

- **Metadata Analysis** – Even encrypted messages leave timestamps, IP logs, and behavior patterns that can be analyzed.
- **Device Seizures** – Arrested criminals often store unencrypted messages and PGP keys on their devices.
- **Legal Backdoors & Subpoenas** – Authorities demand chat records from messaging services (when applicable).

4. Case Study: The Fall of Dark Web Markets & Cybercrime Networks

4.1 AlphaBay & Hansa Market Takedown (2017)

✅ **How Law Enforcement Monitored Communications:**

- Undercover agents posed as buyers & vendors, gaining access to encrypted messages.
- FBI & Dutch police hacked the Hansa Market servers and monitored vendor transactions.
- AlphaBay's admin, Alexandre Cazes, made an OPSEC mistake by linking his real email to vendor accounts.

✹ **Outcome**: Both markets were shut down, and hundreds of arrests were made.

4.2 EncroChat & Sky ECC: The End of "Untraceable" Phones

✅ **Law Enforcement's Tactic:**

- European police hacked the servers of EncroChat & Sky ECC, two encrypted phone providers used by criminals.

- Millions of messages were intercepted, revealing drug trafficking and money laundering operations.
- Thousands of criminals were arrested worldwide based on intercepted messages.

✹ **Outcome**: Criminal networks collapsed, and authorities seized billions in assets.

5. Conclusion: The Future of Law Enforcement Monitoring

While criminals continuously adapt and evolve their communication tactics, law enforcement agencies leverage OSINT, SIGINT, and HUMINT to track, infiltrate, and dismantle dark web cybercrime networks.

Key Takeaway: No communication channel is 100% secure. Mistakes, metadata, and infiltrations always leave traces.

8.5 Challenges in Decrypting Dark Web Communications

Dark web communications are heavily protected by encryption, anonymity networks, and advanced operational security (OPSEC) techniques, making them difficult to monitor and decrypt. Law enforcement agencies, cybersecurity researchers, and OSINT investigators face significant technical, legal, and ethical hurdles when attempting to intercept and analyze these communications.

This section explores the key challenges in decrypting dark web messages, the methods used to overcome these obstacles, and real-world cases where encrypted cybercriminal communications were successfully compromised.

1. Why Is Decrypting Dark Web Communications So Difficult?

Dark web users take extreme precautions to conceal their messages and protect their identities from law enforcement and intelligence agencies. Here are the main reasons why decrypting these communications is so challenging:

1.1 End-to-End Encryption (E2EE)

⬥ Dark web criminals use encrypted messaging apps (Signal, Wickr, Telegram, Threema, Tox, Ricochet) that prevent third parties from intercepting messages.

◆ Messages are only decrypted on the sender's and receiver's devices, making it nearly impossible to access without device seizure.

◆ Some platforms use forward secrecy, meaning even if a key is compromised, past messages remain encrypted.

✅ **Example**: Law enforcement struggled to monitor EncroChat and Sky ECC, encrypted phone networks used by drug cartels, until they hacked the devices.

1.2 Onion Routing & Anonymity Networks

◆ Tor, I2P, and ZeroNet protect communication by routing traffic through multiple encrypted nodes.

◆ Law enforcement cannot easily track IP addresses or identify the message's origin.

◆ Even if an investigator accesses an onion service, messages remain encrypted.

✅ **Example**: Silk Road's admin, Ross Ulbricht, was caught only after his device was physically seized, as law enforcement couldn't decrypt Tor-based messages remotely.

1.3 PGP Encryption & Secure Email Services

◆ Many cybercriminals use Pretty Good Privacy (PGP) encryption for email and document exchange.

◆ Even if emails are intercepted, without the private key, decryption is computationally infeasible.

◆ Secure email providers like ProtonMail, Tutanota, and CTemplar do not store user decryption keys, limiting law enforcement access.

✅ **Example**: Investigators seized PGP-encrypted emails during the AlphaBay takedown but couldn't decrypt them without the admin's private key.

1.4 Cryptocurrency Transactions & Blockchain Privacy

◆ Privacy coins (Monero, Zcash, Dash) use ring signatures, stealth addresses, and zero-knowledge proofs to hide transaction details.

◆ Even Bitcoin transactions can be obfuscated using mixers, tumblers, and CoinJoin.

◆ Dark web markets use multi-signature wallets and escrow systems to further conceal financial trails.

✅ **Example**: FBI tracked Bitcoin transactions from Silk Road, but Monero-based transactions in later dark web markets remain largely untraceable.

2. Methods Used to Decrypt Dark Web Communications

Despite these challenges, investigators have developed several methods to intercept and analyze dark web messages:

2.1 Metadata & Traffic Analysis

◆ Even when messages are encrypted, metadata (timestamps, IP logs, device fingerprints) can provide clues.
◆ Analyzing Tor entry/exit nodes helps correlate online activity.
◆ Investigators use network traffic monitoring tools like Wireshark & Zeek to detect suspicious patterns.

✅ **Example**: FBI tracked Silk Road's admin by monitoring Tor login timestamps matching Ross Ulbricht's activity.

2.2 Device Seizures & Exploiting OPSEC Mistakes

◆ Law enforcement targets endpoints (laptops, phones) instead of breaking encryption directly.
◆ Seizing an active device can bypass encryption if messages are already decrypted.
◆ Investigators exploit poor OPSEC (username reuse, leaked credentials, metadata in uploaded files).

✅ **Example**: Alexandre Cazes, AlphaBay's founder, was caught when law enforcement found his laptop open and logged in, bypassing encryption.

2.3 Undercover Operations & Honeypots

◆ Law enforcement infiltrates dark web forums, Telegram groups, and marketplaces to gather intelligence.
◆ Agencies sometimes set up honeypots—fake encrypted services to lure criminals.

✅ **Example**: The FBI's Operation TrojanShield created the ANOM encrypted phone network, which criminals used, unaware that law enforcement was monitoring every message.

2.4 Hacking & Backdoor Exploits

◆ In some cases, law enforcement hacks servers, implants spyware, or exploits software vulnerabilities.
◆ Malware & keyloggers can be deployed to capture passwords and decryption keys.

✅ **Example**: Dutch police hacked the Hansa dark web marketplace and logged vendor communications before shutting it down.

3. Legal & Ethical Challenges

Even when decryption is possible, law enforcement faces legal and ethical limitations:

✖ **End-to-End Encryption Protections**: Many countries have laws preventing companies from providing backdoor access.
✖ **Jurisdiction Issues**: Dark web servers may be hosted in countries with no extradition or legal cooperation.
✖ **Privacy Rights & Abuse Risks**: Bulk surveillance and decryption programs raise human rights concerns.

✅ **Example**: The Apple-FBI encryption dispute (2016) highlighted the tension between security and privacy, as Apple refused to unlock an iPhone for the FBI.

4. Case Study: The FBI vs. Silk Road 2.0

Silk Road 2.0, a successor to the original Silk Road, was an anonymous dark web drug marketplace. Law enforcement struggled to decrypt communications but ultimately succeeded.

🔍 Challenges Faced:

- Tor & PGP encryption protected vendor-buyer interactions.
- Bitcoin transactions were obfuscated using tumblers.
- Admins used strict OPSEC, rotating aliases and credentials.

📷 How Law Enforcement Bypassed Encryption:

✅ Undercover agents infiltrated Silk Road 2.0, posing as buyers.

✓ The FBI exploited a server misconfiguration, accessing unencrypted transaction logs.

✓ The site's admin, Blake Benthall (Defcon), was careless, using a personal email linked to his dark web identity.

✹ **Outcome**: Silk Road 2.0 was shut down in 2014, and its administrator was arrested.

5. The Future of Dark Web Decryption

As encryption and anonymity technologies become more advanced, law enforcement agencies are developing AI-driven analytics, quantum computing decryption methods, and enhanced infiltration techniques.

◆ **Artificial Intelligence (AI) in Dark Web Monitoring** – AI is improving law enforcement's ability to track encrypted discussions, detect behavioral patterns, and analyze metadata.

◆ **Quantum Computing & Post-Quantum Cryptography** – Future quantum computers could potentially break encryption algorithms, making today's protected communications vulnerable.

◆ **Legislation & Policy Debates** – Governments continue to push for "lawful access" backdoors, though privacy advocates strongly oppose these measures.

6. Conclusion: No Encryption is Perfect Forever

While dark web criminals continue to evolve their encryption methods, law enforcement finds new ways to exploit OPSEC mistakes, infiltrate networks, and track digital footprints. However, encryption remains a significant barrier, and new privacy technologies will continue to challenge traditional decryption methods.

Key Takeaway: The cat-and-mouse game between cybercriminals and law enforcement will continue, but no encryption system is foolproof forever.

8.6 Case Study: How OPSEC Mistakes Led to an Arrest

Despite using advanced encryption, anonymity networks, and strict operational security (OPSEC), many cybercriminals have been arrested due to small yet critical mistakes. One of the most famous examples is the case of Ross Ulbricht, the founder of Silk Road, the first major dark web drug marketplace. His downfall was not due to a breakthrough in decryption technology, but rather a series of OPSEC failures that allowed law enforcement to connect his real-world identity to his dark web persona, "Dread Pirate Roberts" (DPR).

1. Background: The Rise of Silk Road

Silk Road, launched in 2011, was a Tor-based hidden marketplace where users could buy and sell illicit goods, primarily drugs, using Bitcoin for payments. The platform operated on strict anonymity principles, using PGP encryption, escrow services, and pseudonyms to protect vendors and buyers.

Ulbricht took extreme measures to conceal his identity, using:

- ◆ Tor & VPNs to mask his real IP address.
- ◆ Multiple aliases to interact with users.
- ◆ Encrypted communication for internal team discussions.
- ◆ A separate laptop and dedicated Wi-Fi networks to access Silk Road.

Yet, despite these precautions, he made crucial mistakes that led to his capture.

2. OPSEC Mistakes That Led to Ross Ulbricht's Arrest

Even the most careful cybercriminals can slip up. Ulbricht's downfall resulted from small OPSEC errors that investigators pieced together to reveal his identity.

2.1 Reusing a Real-World Email in Early Forum Posts

One of Ulbricht's first mistakes was using his personal Gmail address in an early post about Silk Road on a public forum.

✅ What Happened?

- In January 2011, before Silk Road gained traction, Ulbricht posted on the Bitcointalk forum asking about running a Tor-based marketplace.
- He used the handle "altoid" and included his personal email, rossulbricht@gmail.com, in a follow-up post.
- The email was later linked to his LinkedIn profile, which described him as a "freedom advocate" with an interest in economic theory.

☐ **OPSEC Lesson**: Using a real-world email address on forums related to illicit activities created a digital breadcrumb that linked Ulbricht to Silk Road.

2.2 Logging into Silk Road Admin Accounts Without a VPN

In another key mistake, Ulbricht once logged into a Silk Road admin account without masking his real IP address.

✅ What Happened?

- The FBI was monitoring Silk Road's backend infrastructure.
- One login attempt from an IP address traced to a San Francisco coffee shop was flagged.
- This coffee shop was located near Ulbricht's residence.

☐ **OPSEC Lesson**: Always use a VPN or Tor when managing dark web operations. A single unprotected login can expose a hidden identity.

2.3 Leaving a Digital Footprint on Reddit & Coding Forums

Ulbricht discussed topics related to Silk Road's encryption, anonymity, and Bitcoin transactions on various forums.

✅ What Happened?

- Investigators searched for mentions of Silk Road across Reddit, Stack Overflow, and coding websites.
- Ulbricht had posted technical questions about running a Tor hidden service and using PGP encryption.
- Some of these posts were linked back to accounts that had previously interacted with his known email addresses.

☐ **OPSEC Lesson**: Cybercriminals should avoid discussing technical aspects of their operations on public forums, as even generic inquiries can provide investigative leads.

2.4 Keeping an Unencrypted Laptop Open During Arrest

The FBI finally arrested Ulbricht in October 2013 at a public library in San Francisco. They needed to seize his laptop while it was still unlocked to access Silk Road's encrypted records.

✅ What Happened?

- FBI agents staged a fake argument behind him to distract him.
- When Ulbricht turned to look, an agent snatched his laptop before he could close or encrypt it.
- The laptop was logged into Silk Road's admin panel, providing immediate access to transaction logs, messages, and other critical data.

☐ **OPSEC Lesson**: Always have a kill switch or automatic encryption setup to lock devices immediately when left unattended.

3. How Investigators Connected the Dots

By piecing together various OPSEC mistakes, law enforcement linked Ulbricht to Silk Road:

🔍 **Bitcointalk & Reddit Posts** – His early forum posts discussing Silk Road and Tor-related topics provided the first leads.

🔍 **Gmail Address Link** – His personal email was tied to early Silk Road promotions, connecting him to the platform.

🔍 **IP Tracking & Location Data** – His IP address was flagged when he accessed Silk Road admin tools without Tor.

🔍 **Laptop Seizure** – The final, crucial mistake—keeping his laptop unencrypted while logged into Silk Road.

4. The Arrest & Legal Outcome

Following his arrest, Ulbricht was charged with:

✅ Conspiracy to commit money laundering

✅ Conspiracy to commit computer hacking

✅ Conspiracy to traffic narcotics

◆ In 2015, he was sentenced to life in prison without parole.

◆ Authorities seized $3.6 billion worth of Bitcoin from Silk Road-related wallets.

Despite his extreme caution, minor OPSEC mistakes allowed investigators to unmask him.

5. Key Takeaways for Cybercrime Investigations

The Silk Road case highlights crucial lessons for OSINT investigators and law enforcement:

🔎 **Even small OPSEC mistakes can lead to arrests** – Cybercriminals can protect their identity for years, but one lapse can expose them.

🔎 **Forum activity & old digital traces matter** – Early posts, usernames, and leaked credentials provide valuable leads.

🔎 **VPNs, Tor, & encryption must be used consistently** – A single unprotected login can compromise an entire operation.

🔎 **Metadata & traffic analysis are powerful tools** – Even encrypted communications leave traces investigators can exploit.

🔎 **Physical device security is crucial** – If law enforcement gains access to an unlocked device, encryption becomes irrelevant.

6. Conclusion: OPSEC Failures Are Inevitable

No matter how skilled a cybercriminal is, OPSEC mistakes are bound to happen. Law enforcement agencies leverage OSINT, metadata analysis, undercover operations, and endpoint seizures to uncover the identities behind anonymous dark web operations.

Ross Ulbricht's case is a textbook example of how digital breadcrumbs and OPSEC missteps can lead to an arrest—a critical lesson for investigators tracking criminals on the dark web.

Final Thought: No anonymity system is foolproof. Patience, digital forensics, and strategic infiltration will always reveal weaknesses in a cybercriminal's security practices.

9. Investigating Ransomware & Extortion Groups

In this chapter, we will explore the world of ransomware and extortion groups operating on the Dark Web. These cybercriminal organizations are responsible for some of the most high-profile and financially damaging attacks, where they encrypt victims' data or threaten to release sensitive information unless a ransom is paid. We will examine the tactics and techniques used by these groups to distribute malware, communicate with victims, and launder ransom payments, often through cryptocurrencies. OSINT techniques will be discussed in detail, including how to trace ransom demands, analyze encrypted files, and uncover the identities of key players within these criminal networks. By understanding the operational structures and methods of ransomware and extortion groups, investigators can better predict their actions, track down perpetrators, and assist victims in mitigating further harm.

9.1 The Rise of Ransomware-as-a-Service (RaaS)

Over the past decade, ransomware has evolved from a scattered cybercriminal tactic into a highly organized, profit-driven enterprise. One of the most significant developments fueling this transformation is Ransomware-as-a-Service (RaaS)—a model where cybercriminals sell or lease ransomware tools to affiliates, enabling even low-skilled hackers to launch devastating attacks. RaaS has revolutionized cyber extortion, lowering the barrier to entry for cybercriminals while increasing the scale and frequency of ransomware incidents.

1. What is Ransomware-as-a-Service (RaaS)?

RaaS operates similarly to legitimate software-as-a-service (SaaS) businesses. Instead of developing their own ransomware from scratch, cybercriminals can simply subscribe to a ready-made ransomware toolkit from a RaaS provider. These services are often marketed on dark web forums and Telegram channels, with features such as:

◆ **Customizable payloads** – Attackers can modify the ransomware to target specific victims.

◆ **Automated infection & encryption** – Malware is designed to spread across networks and encrypt files efficiently.

◆ **Payment & negotiation services** – Some RaaS groups even provide customer support to facilitate ransom payments in cryptocurrency.

◆ **Affiliate programs** – RaaS developers take a percentage of the ransom payments in exchange for providing the malware and infrastructure.

This business-like approach has fueled a surge in ransomware attacks, as even non-technical criminals can now execute highly effective cyber extortion campaigns.

2. How RaaS Works: The Affiliate Model

The RaaS ecosystem is structured around affiliates—individual cybercriminals who use the provided ransomware tools to execute attacks. The model typically works as follows:

- **Developers create ransomware** – Cybercriminals with advanced coding skills design and maintain the malware.
- **RaaS platform is launched** – The ransomware is offered for rent or purchase on dark web markets.
- **Affiliates join the program** – Less-skilled criminals sign up as affiliates, gaining access to the ransomware kit.
- **Affiliates distribute the malware** – They infect victims using phishing emails, malicious ads, or exploiting software vulnerabilities.
- **Victims' files are encrypted** – A ransom note demands payment, usually in Bitcoin or Monero.
- **Profits are shared** – Developers take a percentage of the ransom (often 20-30%), while affiliates keep the rest.

This franchise-like structure allows cybercriminals to scale their operations rapidly while reducing risks for the developers.

3. Notorious RaaS Groups & Their Impact

Several high-profile RaaS groups have been responsible for major cyberattacks on corporations, hospitals, and government agencies:

✅ **REvil (Sodinokibi)** – One of the most prolific RaaS groups, responsible for attacks on JBS Foods, Kaseya, and Travelex.

✅ **DarkSide** – Infamous for the Colonial Pipeline attack, which disrupted fuel supply across the U.S.

✅ **Conti** – Targeted healthcare institutions, police departments, and large enterprises, with ransom demands reaching millions of dollars.

✅ **LockBit** – Continuously evolving, offering leak sites and double-extortion tactics to increase pressure on victims.

These RaaS groups operate like legitimate businesses, with customer support, affiliate recruitment, and even public relations efforts.

4. The Double-Extortion Trend: Ransomware 2.0

Traditional ransomware attacks involved encrypting files and demanding payment for decryption keys. However, modern RaaS groups employ double-extortion tactics:

◆ **Step 1: Encrypt Data** – Victims lose access to critical files and systems.
◆ **Step 2: Exfiltrate Data** – Attackers steal sensitive data before encryption.
◆ **Step 3: Threaten Public Release** – If victims refuse to pay, the stolen data is leaked on dark web leak sites or sold to competitors.

This tactic increases pressure on victims, as the damage extends beyond just downtime and operational disruptions.

5. Law Enforcement Crackdowns & Countermeasures

Governments and cybersecurity firms have stepped up efforts to dismantle RaaS networks:

✓ **Operation GoldDust (2021)** – Europol and the FBI arrested REvil affiliates and seized their infrastructure.
✓ **DarkSide Takedown (2021)** – U.S. authorities seized $2.3 million in Bitcoin paid to the Colonial Pipeline attackers.
✓ **Conti Leaks (2022)** – A disgruntled insider leaked Conti's internal communications, exposing their operations.

Despite these actions, RaaS groups continue to evolve, using bulletproof hosting, encrypted communication channels, and decentralized payment systems to evade law enforcement.

6. Conclusion: The Future of RaaS

RaaS has transformed ransomware from an elite hacker activity into a widespread criminal industry. With the rise of AI-powered malware, decentralized networks, and cryptocurrency mixers, tracking and disrupting these operations remains a challenge. However, improved threat intelligence, international cooperation, and stronger cybersecurity defenses are essential in combating the growing RaaS threat.

As ransomware attacks become more sophisticated, organizations must adopt proactive defense strategies—including threat hunting, employee training, and robust incident response plans—to mitigate the risks posed by this cybercrime-as-a-service model.

9.2 Tracking Ransomware Operators on the Dark Web

As ransomware attacks become increasingly sophisticated, tracking the threat actors behind these operations has become a priority for cybersecurity researchers, law enforcement agencies, and OSINT analysts. Many ransomware groups operate from the dark web, using Tor-hidden services, encrypted messaging platforms, and underground forums to recruit affiliates, communicate with victims, and negotiate ransom payments. However, despite their use of anonymity tools, ransomware operators leave digital footprints that can be analyzed and tracked using OSINT techniques, blockchain analysis, and infiltration strategies.

1. Where Ransomware Operators Operate on the Dark Web

Ransomware groups leverage various dark web platforms to conduct their activities, including:

◆ **Ransomware Leak Sites** – Many groups run dedicated leak sites on Tor where they publish stolen data if victims refuse to pay.
◆ **Cybercrime Forums** – Operators and affiliates use dark web forums to discuss attack methods, recruit new hackers, and advertise Ransomware-as-a-Service (RaaS) offerings.
◆ **Encrypted Messaging Platforms** – Many groups use Jabber/XMPP, TOX, or PGP-encrypted emails for internal communications.
◆ **Bitcoin & Monero Payment Trails** – Ransom demands are paid in cryptocurrency, leaving traces that can be tracked using blockchain analysis.

Despite these anonymity measures, OSINT and blockchain tracking tools can provide critical insights into their operations.

2. OSINT Techniques for Tracking Ransomware Operators

Investigators and cybersecurity researchers use multiple OSINT techniques to track ransomware operators, uncover their infrastructure, and identify their real-world identities.

2.1 Analyzing Dark Web Ransomware Leak Sites

Many ransomware gangs maintain leak sites on Tor, where they publish stolen data from victims who refuse to pay. Analysts can extract valuable intelligence by:

✓ Monitoring new leaks to identify recent victims and track emerging ransomware trends.

✓ Extracting metadata from leaked files, which may contain timestamps, usernames, or document properties linking to attackers.

✓ Checking site infrastructure using tools like OnionScan to find hidden vulnerabilities or mirror sites.

💡 **Example**: The Conti ransomware group maintained a dark web site where they publicly shamed non-paying victims and leaked sensitive data.

2.2 Tracking Ransomware Discussions on Cybercrime Forums

Ransomware operators and affiliates often communicate in dark web forums, where they:

◆ Advertise RaaS partnerships and recruit affiliates.
◆ Sell access to compromised networks (Initial Access Brokers).
◆ Discuss exploit techniques and target selection strategies.

Investigators can use forum infiltration techniques to gather intelligence, including:

✓ Identifying common usernames or aliases used by ransomware developers.

✓ Analyzing forum timestamps and writing styles to establish behavioral patterns.

✓ Cross-referencing usernames across different platforms to find real-world connections.

💡 **Example**: The LockBit ransomware group actively recruits affiliates on underground forums, offering high commissions to hackers who distribute their malware.

2.3 Blockchain Analysis: Following the Money Trail

Most ransomware gangs demand payments in Bitcoin (BTC) or Monero (XMR), but cryptocurrency transactions leave traces that can be analyzed using blockchain forensics.

Investigators can:

✅ Use blockchain explorers (e.g., Blockchair, BTCscan) to trace ransom payments.

✅ Identify wallets linked to ransomware operations and track fund movements.

✅ Monitor cryptocurrency mixers used to launder ransom payments.

✅ Correlate ransomware payments with exchange withdrawals to find potential real-world identities.

💡 **Example**: The FBI tracked Bitcoin transactions to seize $2.3 million in ransom payments from the Colonial Pipeline attack.

2.4 Identifying Ransomware Infrastructure & Hosting Services

Many ransomware gangs use bulletproof hosting services or compromised servers to host their dark web infrastructure. OSINT analysts can:

✅ Use DNS and WHOIS lookups to identify connections between domains.

✅ Scan Tor hidden services for vulnerabilities using tools like OnionScan.

✅ Analyze SSL certificate fingerprints to track ransomware-related domains.

💡 **Example**: Researchers discovered a connection between multiple ransomware leak sites using shared SSL certificates, exposing a network of affiliated operators.

2.5 Infiltrating Ransomware Affiliate Programs

Since many ransomware groups operate as a business, they recruit affiliates through underground forums and private channels. OSINT analysts and law enforcement agencies have successfully infiltrated these programs by:

✅ Creating fake hacker personas to gain access to ransomware operator networks.

✅ Engaging in controlled communications to extract intelligence on attack methods.

✅ Gathering insight on ransomware negotiation tactics used against victims.

💡 Example: Security researchers infiltrated the REvil ransomware group's affiliate program, uncovering their payout structures and attack strategies.

3. Law Enforcement Strategies to Track & Dismantle Ransomware Groups

Authorities worldwide use OSINT, blockchain analysis, and cyber operations to track and dismantle ransomware gangs. Some notable methods include:

✅ **Dark Web Marketplace Seizures** – Agencies like the FBI and Europol have taken down ransomware forums and leak sites.
✅ **Undercover Operations** – Law enforcement infiltrates ransomware affiliate programs to gather intelligence.
✅ **Cryptocurrency Seizures** – Governments have seized millions in ransom payments by tracking Bitcoin transactions.
✅ **Collaboration with Cybersecurity Firms** – Private firms provide intelligence on emerging ransomware threats.

💡 Example: In 2021, Operation GoldDust led to multiple arrests of REvil ransomware affiliates, thanks to coordinated efforts between Europol and law enforcement agencies.

4. Challenges in Tracking Ransomware Operators

Despite advancements in OSINT and cyber forensics, tracking ransomware operators presents several challenges:

◆ **Use of Privacy Coins** – Monero (XMR) transactions are nearly impossible to trace.
◆ **Decentralized Hosting** – Some ransomware groups use peer-to-peer infrastructure to avoid centralized takedowns.
◆ **Geopolitical Barriers** – Many ransomware operators operate from countries that do not cooperate with law enforcement (e.g., Russia).
◆ **Constantly Changing Infrastructure** – Ransomware groups frequently move their servers and rebrand to evade detection.

5. Conclusion: The Future of Ransomware Tracking

While ransomware operators take extreme measures to stay hidden, they are not invincible. OSINT analysts, law enforcement, and cybersecurity firms can leverage dark web monitoring, blockchain analysis, and undercover operations to track, expose, and disrupt ransomware networks.

As ransomware tactics evolve, so must investigative techniques—combining AI-driven threat intelligence, enhanced blockchain tracking, and global law enforcement cooperation to combat the growing ransomware threat.

Final Thought: The dark web may provide anonymity, but no cybercriminal is truly untraceable. With patience, advanced OSINT techniques, and international collaboration, ransomware operators can be identified and held accountable.

9.3 How Extortion Groups Use Leak Sites to Pressure Victims

In the evolving landscape of cybercrime, ransomware and extortion groups have adopted increasingly aggressive tactics to coerce victims into paying ransoms. One of the most effective methods used by these groups is the leak site, where stolen data is publicly exposed if the victim refuses to comply. These sites serve as both a pressure tool and a marketing strategy, showcasing the hackers' ability to carry out threats while warning future victims of the consequences of non-payment.

Leak sites have become a central part of modern ransomware operations, shifting the focus from simple encryption-based attacks to multi-layered extortion techniques. In this section, we will explore how ransomware groups use leak sites to pressure victims, how these sites operate on the dark web, and how investigators can track and analyze them.

1. What Are Ransomware Leak Sites?

Ransomware leak sites are dark web platforms where cybercriminals publish stolen data when victims refuse to pay a ransom. These sites serve several purposes:

✅ **Pressuring victims into paying** – By threatening public exposure, attackers force victims to reconsider non-payment.
✅ **Demonstrating credibility** – Successful leaks prove that the group has actual access to stolen data, enhancing their reputation.
✅ **Recruiting new affiliates** – Leak sites showcase successful attacks, attracting cybercriminal affiliates to join their ransomware program.
✅ **Selling stolen data** – Some groups auction off sensitive corporate or personal information to the highest bidder.

💡 **Example**: The Conti ransomware group operated a leak site where they published thousands of gigabytes of stolen corporate data, forcing companies into paying ransoms to prevent exposure.

2. The Evolution of Leak Sites in Ransomware Operations

2.1 From Data Encryption to Double Extortion

Initially, ransomware attacks focused solely on encrypting a victim's files and demanding payment for decryption. However, as businesses implemented backup strategies, attackers began using double extortion tactics:

1☐ **Encrypting files** – The victim loses access to critical data.

2☐ **Stealing sensitive information** – Attackers extract valuable data before encryption.

3☐ **Threatening to publish stolen data** – If the ransom is unpaid, the data is leaked.

2.2 Triple & Quadruple Extortion Tactics

Ransomware gangs have expanded their extortion tactics beyond just encryption and data leaks.

◆ **Triple Extortion**: Attackers also threaten to launch DDoS attacks on a victim's website if the ransom is unpaid.

◆ **Quadruple Extortion**: Criminals notify regulators, stockholders, or customers about the breach, increasing pressure on the company.

💡 **Example**: The REvil ransomware group would email customers of hacked companies, warning them that their personal data would be leaked unless a ransom was paid.

3. How Ransomware Groups Operate Leak Sites

3.1 Hosting & Infrastructure

Ransomware leak sites are typically hosted on Tor (The Onion Router) or I2P (Invisible Internet Project) to maintain anonymity. These hidden services allow attackers to:

◆ Evade law enforcement takedowns by frequently changing domains.
◆ Use bulletproof hosting providers that ignore abuse complaints.

◆ Mirror their sites across multiple locations to prevent downtime.

💡 **Example**: The DarkSide ransomware group hosted their leak site on Tor, using multiple mirrors to keep it online after law enforcement seizures.

3.2 Structure of a Leak Site

Most leak sites follow a similar structure:

📌 **Victim List**: A directory of companies that have been hacked.
📌 **Countdown Timer**: A deadline for the victim to pay before data is leaked.
📌 **Sample Data**: A small portion of leaked files as proof of breach.
📌 **Full Data Dump**: If the ransom is unpaid, the complete dataset is released.
📌 **Auction or Sale Option**: Some sites sell data to competitors or other criminals.

💡 **Example**: The Maze ransomware group pioneered structured leak sites, introducing the concept of auctioning stolen data to third parties.

4. Tracking and Analyzing Ransomware Leak Sites

4.1 OSINT Techniques for Monitoring Leak Sites

Investigators and cybersecurity analysts use OSINT (Open-Source Intelligence) techniques to track ransomware leak sites, including:

✅ Monitoring new victims to detect emerging ransomware campaigns.

✅ Extracting metadata from leaked files to uncover attacker infrastructure.

✅ Cross-referencing breach data with previous attacks to identify recurring threat actors.

4.2 Dark Web Crawling & Automation

Since ransomware groups frequently change their leak sites, analysts use dark web monitoring tools such as:

◆ **OnionScan** – Identifies vulnerabilities in hidden services.
◆ **Hunchly** – Captures and archives evidence from Tor sites.

◆ **Dark Web Search Engines (e.g., Ahmia, OnionLand)** – Index ransomware leak sites for analysis.

💡 **Example**: Security firms use web scrapers to track ransomware data leaks and alert affected companies before full leaks occur.

5. Case Study: The Conti Ransomware Leak Site

Conti, one of the most notorious ransomware groups, ran a highly organized leak site that functioned like a media platform for cyber extortion.

◆ **Tactics Used**: Conti attackers would release partial data leaks to pressure victims into paying.
◆ **Victims Targeted:** The group attacked hospitals, government agencies, and Fortune 500 companies.
◆ **Law Enforcement Action**: In 2022, a Ukrainian researcher leaked Conti's internal chat logs, exposing their operations.

💡 **Impact**: The leaked chat logs provided rare insight into Conti's hierarchy, payment structures, and technical methods, aiding future investigations.

6. Legal & Ethical Considerations in Monitoring Leak Sites

Tracking ransomware leak sites raises important legal and ethical questions:

◆ **Legality**: Accessing dark web leak sites may violate cybercrime laws in certain jurisdictions.
◆ **Ethical Dilemmas**: Viewing or downloading leaked data could expose analysts to privacy violations.
◆ **Law Enforcement vs. Research**: While security professionals aim to track criminals, law enforcement agencies must follow strict evidence collection rules.

💡 **Best Practice**: Researchers should use read-only access, avoid interacting with criminals, and ensure compliance with cyber laws.

7. Conclusion: The Future of Ransomware Leak Sites

As law enforcement intensifies efforts to dismantle ransomware groups, cybercriminals will continue evolving their extortion tactics.

◆ **Decentralization**: Future leak sites may adopt blockchain-based hosting to avoid takedowns.

◆ **AI-Assisted Attacks**: Machine learning could automate data theft and leak timing.

◆ **Global Crackdowns**: International cooperation will be key in seizing infrastructure and arresting operators.

💡 **Final Thought**: While ransomware groups rely on anonymity, their patterns, infrastructure, and financial transactions can be traced using OSINT and blockchain analysis. The fight against cyber extortion is far from over.

9.4 Investigating Crypto Wallets Linked to Ransomware Payments

The rise of cryptocurrency has played a crucial role in enabling ransomware operations, allowing cybercriminals to receive payments anonymously and launder illicit funds. However, despite the pseudonymous nature of cryptocurrencies like Bitcoin, blockchain analysis techniques have made it possible to trace ransomware-related transactions and identify crypto wallets linked to cybercriminals.

This section will explore how ransomware groups use cryptocurrency wallets, the methods law enforcement and researchers employ to track illicit transactions, and real-world case studies of successful crypto investigations.

1. How Ransomware Groups Use Crypto Wallets

Ransomware operators typically demand ransom payments in Bitcoin (BTC) or Monero (XMR) due to their ability to facilitate anonymous transactions. Their goal is to obfuscate the payment trail, making it difficult for authorities to track and seize funds.

1.1 Common Steps in a Ransomware Payment Process

1️⃣ **The Victim Receives a Payment Demand** – After a ransomware attack, the victim is instructed to send Bitcoin or Monero to a specified crypto wallet.

2️⃣ **The Payment is Transferred** – The victim purchases cryptocurrency from an exchange and transfers the required amount to the attacker's wallet.

3 **Funds Are Moved Through Multiple Wallets** – The ransom is split across multiple wallets (a process called "peeling") to make tracking difficult.

4 **Use of Mixing Services** – Criminals use cryptocurrency tumblers (mixers) to break the link between the original payment and the final withdrawal.

5 **Cashout via Exchanges or Gift Cards** – Laundered funds are eventually withdrawn through crypto-to-fiat exchanges, peer-to-peer (P2P) markets, or gift card purchases.

💡 **Example**: The DarkSide ransomware gang, responsible for the Colonial Pipeline attack, received over $4.4 million in Bitcoin, which was later tracked by blockchain analysts despite obfuscation attempts.

2. OSINT & Blockchain Tools for Tracking Ransomware Payments

Despite the anonymity that ransomware groups attempt to maintain, blockchain transactions are public and immutable, making it possible to follow the movement of funds.

2.1 OSINT Techniques for Identifying Ransomware Wallets

◆ **Monitoring Known Wallet Addresses** – Security researchers maintain databases of wallets linked to known ransomware groups.

◆ **Analyzing Ransom Notes & Dark Web Forums** – Many attackers reuse wallet addresses, making them traceable.

◆ **Tracking Bitcoin Heists & Large Transactions** – Suspicious movement of funds can reveal links between different ransomware campaigns.

2.2 Blockchain Analysis Tools

◆ **Chainalysis** – A widely used forensic tool for tracing cryptocurrency transactions across wallets and exchanges.

◆ **Elliptic** – AI-powered blockchain analytics for identifying illicit financial flows.

◆ **CipherTrace** – Helps law enforcement track transactions and identify suspicious patterns.

◆ **BitcoinWhosWho** – Allows users to check if a Bitcoin wallet has been linked to scams or criminal activity.

💡 **Example**: After the REvil ransomware attack on JBS Foods, investigators used Chainalysis to track the movement of Bitcoin ransom payments across multiple wallets, eventually leading to partial fund recovery.

3. Tracing Cryptocurrency Laundering Techniques

Ransomware operators use a variety of laundering techniques to obscure their financial trail and avoid detection.

3.1 Cryptocurrency Tumblers & Mixing Services

◆ Tumblers mix illicit funds with clean Bitcoin from various sources, making it harder to trace their origins.
◆ Wasabi Wallet & Samourai Wallet offer built-in mixing features that enhance privacy.
◆ Some mixing services operate as Tor-based hidden services to avoid takedown efforts.

💡 **Example**: The Bitcoin Fog mixing service laundered over $335 million before being shut down by law enforcement.

3.2 Privacy Coins Like Monero (XMR)

◆ Unlike Bitcoin, Monero transactions are fully private, concealing both sender and recipient addresses.
◆ Some ransomware gangs prefer Monero payments due to its untraceable nature.
◆ Despite this, authorities have developed techniques to analyze Monero transactions, using heuristic methods and exchange monitoring.

💡 **Example**: The Avaddon ransomware gang initially accepted Bitcoin but later switched to Monero due to increasing scrutiny of BTC transactions.

3.3 Crypto-to-Crypto Swaps & Exchange Hopping

◆ Criminals use decentralized exchanges (DEXs) like Uniswap to swap Bitcoin for privacy coins.
◆ They also use multiple exchanges in different countries to make detection harder.
◆ Some ransomware groups sell their Bitcoin for prepaid cards, gift cards, or NFTs to launder money further.

💡 **Example**: The Hydra dark web marketplace allowed criminals to cash out cryptocurrency through prepaid cards, making tracking more difficult.

4. Case Study: How Law Enforcement Tracked & Seized Ransomware Funds

Case: Colonial Pipeline Ransom Payment Recovery

In May 2021, the DarkSide ransomware group attacked the Colonial Pipeline, leading to fuel shortages across the U.S. The company paid $4.4 million in Bitcoin to regain access to its systems.

Investigation & Fund Recovery

✓ Blockchain analysts traced the ransom payment from the initial wallet through multiple transactions.

✓ The FBI obtained the private key of a wallet holding a portion of the funds.

✓ $2.3 million was recovered, marking a significant victory against ransomware operators.

💡 **Key Takeaway**: Even when criminals attempt to obscure transactions, blockchain forensics can still uncover illicit financial trails.

5. The Future of Crypto Investigations in Ransomware Cases

As ransomware gangs become more sophisticated, law enforcement and cybersecurity researchers must adapt by:

◆ Enhancing cross-border cooperation between crypto exchanges and financial regulators.
◆ Developing AI-driven blockchain analysis tools to detect laundering patterns.
◆ Imposing stricter regulations on crypto exchanges to prevent ransom payments.

💡 **Final Thought**: While cryptocurrency remains a critical tool for cybercriminals, OSINT and blockchain forensics provide investigators with the tools needed to follow the money and disrupt ransomware networks.

9.5 Case Study: A Deep Dive into a Ransomware Attack Investigation

Ransomware attacks have become one of the most lucrative and disruptive cybercrimes, with attackers extorting millions from businesses, governments, and individuals. In this case study, we will analyze a real-world ransomware attack, examining how the attackers gained access, executed the ransomware payload, demanded ransom, and attempted to launder illicit funds. We will also explore how OSINT (Open-Source Intelligence) and blockchain forensics played a role in investigating and tracking the criminals.

1. The Ransomware Attack: Overview

In early 2021, a large multinational corporation (we will call it "Company X") fell victim to a ransomware attack attributed to the REvil ransomware group. The attack resulted in the encryption of thousands of systems, disrupting operations and leading to financial losses in the tens of millions of dollars.

1.1 Attack Timeline

🗓 **Day 1: Initial Compromise** – Attackers gained access to Company X's network through a phishing email containing a malicious attachment.

🗓 **Day 3: Lateral Movement** – The ransomware operators used Cobalt Strike and stolen credentials to move laterally within the network.

🗓 **Day 5: Data Exfiltration** – Before encrypting files, attackers exfiltrated hundreds of gigabytes of sensitive company data.

🗓 **Day 7: Ransom Demand** – Attackers deployed the REvil ransomware payload, encrypting critical systems and displaying a $15 million ransom demand in Bitcoin.

🗓 **Day 10: Public Leak Threat** – When Company X refused to pay, the attackers threatened to leak stolen data on their dark web leak site.

2. Investigation Begins: Tracking the Ransomware Group

After the attack, Company X's security team and law enforcement agencies began their investigation, leveraging various OSINT techniques to track down the threat actors.

2.1 Analyzing the Ransom Note & Dark Web Communications

The ransom note left on encrypted systems contained a link to a Tor-based payment portal. Investigators used OSINT to analyze:

✓ The Tor hidden service address to check if it was linked to known ransomware groups.

✓ The ransomware gang's dark web blog, where they posted leaked victim data.

✓ Victim reports on cybersecurity forums, confirming similar attack patterns.

💡 **Key Insight**: Investigators identified that the ransom demand was hosted on REvil's infrastructure, linking the attack to the well-known cybercriminal gang.

2.2 Tracking the Ransom Payment on the Blockchain

Despite refusing to pay, Company X monitored Bitcoin ransom payments from other victims. Using blockchain analysis, investigators:

✓ Identified Bitcoin wallet addresses associated with the ransom demand.

✓ Tracked transactions linked to previous ransomware attacks.

✓ Discovered that the funds were split into multiple wallets before being laundered through crypto mixing services.

🔎 **Key Finding**: The same wallet addresses had been used in previous REvil attacks, strengthening attribution.

3. Following the Money: Cryptocurrency Laundering Tactics

Once ransom payments were received, the attackers moved funds through a series of obfuscation techniques:

◆ **Peeling Chains**: Breaking ransom payments into smaller amounts across multiple wallets.
◆ **Crypto Mixers**: Sending Bitcoin through mixing services to make tracing harder.
◆ **Monero Conversions**: Converting Bitcoin into Monero (XMR) to take advantage of its privacy features.
◆ **Cash-Out via Dark Web Markets**: Using peer-to-peer (P2P) exchanges to withdraw funds anonymously.

💡 Despite these tactics, investigators used blockchain forensics tools like Chainalysis and Elliptic to monitor suspicious transactions.

4. Unmasking the Threat Actors: OSINT & OPSEC Mistakes

Although ransomware groups take extreme precautions to remain anonymous, they often make operational security (OPSEC) mistakes.

4.1 Identifying Dark Web Forum Activity

Using OSINT techniques, researchers found:

✓ A forum post from months before the attack, where a user discussed ransomware deployment methods.

✓ The same alias was linked to other cybercrime forums, where the attacker accidentally posted with a personal email.

✓ That email was traced back to a known cybercriminal in Eastern Europe.

💡 **OPSEC Mistake**: The attacker reused their alias across multiple platforms, leading to their identification.

4.2 Domain & IP Correlations

✓ A Tor proxy server used in the attack was linked to a previous ransomware campaign.

✓ Investigators used passive DNS analysis to connect a domain used in phishing emails to a real-world hosting provider.

✓ The hosting provider logs revealed an IP address tied to a known cybercriminal group.

5. Law Enforcement & Arrests

With the collected intelligence, authorities were able to:

✓ Issue seizure warrants for cryptocurrency wallets linked to ransomware payments.

✓ Work with international agencies to shut down REvil's infrastructure.

✓ Conduct raids in multiple countries, leading to arrests of key operators.

5.1 Key Arrests & Takedowns

◈ **October 2021:** The REvil ransomware gang was dismantled after joint efforts by the FBI, Europol, and local authorities.

◈ **February 2022**: Several ransomware operators were arrested in Russia and Ukraine.

◈ **2023**: The U.S. Department of Justice recovered $6.1 million in Bitcoin from REvil-linked wallets.

💡 **Final Takeaway**: Even sophisticated ransomware groups can be unmasked through a combination of OSINT, blockchain forensics, and cybercrime intelligence gathering.

6. Lessons Learned & Future Ransomware Defenses

This case study highlights several important lessons for cybersecurity professionals, businesses, and investigators:

6.1 Defensive Strategies for Organizations

✓ **Implement Strong Email Security** – Most ransomware attacks begin with phishing emails.

✓ **Monitor for Dark Web Leaks** – Detect data breaches before attackers exploit them.

✓ **Use Network Segmentation** – Prevent ransomware from spreading across critical systems.

✓ **Regularly Back Up Data** – Having secure, offline backups can mitigate ransomware impact.

✓ **Train Employees on Security Awareness** – Educate staff on phishing tactics and social engineering threats.

6.2 OSINT & Blockchain Forensics for Investigators

✓ **Monitor Dark Web Forums** – Many ransomware actors advertise their services on underground forums.

✓ **Track Known Crypto Wallets** – Following ransom payments can reveal laundering patterns.

✓ **Correlate Alias Data Across Platforms** – Cybercriminals often reuse usernames or emails.

✓ **Work with Law Enforcement & Crypto Exchanges** – Collaborate to freeze illicit funds before they are laundered.

Final Thoughts

Ransomware attacks continue to be a significant threat, but the combination of OSINT, blockchain analysis, and international cooperation is making it increasingly difficult for cybercriminals to remain undetected. By studying real-world cases, investigators and cybersecurity professionals can refine their techniques and strengthen defenses against future attacks.

🔎 **Key Takeaway**: Even the most sophisticated ransomware groups make mistakes, and with the right investigative approach, they can be tracked, identified, and brought to justice.

9.6 Future Trends in Ransomware & Dark Web Extortion

Ransomware and dark web extortion tactics are evolving rapidly, with cybercriminals continuously adapting to new security measures and law enforcement actions. As organizations strengthen their defenses, threat actors refine their strategies to maximize their profits while minimizing detection risks. This section explores key trends that will shape the future of ransomware and extortion in the dark web, including emerging attack techniques, evolving monetization models, and the increasing role of artificial intelligence (AI) in cybercrime.

1. The Rise of AI-Driven Ransomware Attacks

1.1 AI-Powered Malware & Automation

Cybercriminals are beginning to leverage artificial intelligence and machine learning to improve the efficiency and effectiveness of ransomware attacks. AI can be used to:

- **Enhance Phishing Attacks**: AI-generated phishing emails can bypass spam filters and appear more convincing.
- **Automate Vulnerability Exploitation**: AI can scan networks for security weaknesses and launch attacks automatically.
- **Adaptive Malware**: Ransomware may soon be capable of self-learning to evade antivirus software and behavioral detection mechanisms.

Implication: Organizations will need AI-powered defense systems to counter AI-driven threats.

2. Double & Triple Extortion Models Will Dominate

2.1 Evolution of Ransomware Extortion Techniques

Ransomware operators are moving beyond simple data encryption and adopting multi-layered extortion tactics:

- **Double Extortion**: Attackers encrypt the victim's files and also threaten to leak stolen data if the ransom isn't paid.
- **Triple Extortion**: Beyond encryption and data leaks, attackers may launch DDoS attacks against victims or threaten customers, partners, or employees.
- **Quadruple Extortion (Emerging Trend):** Some ransomware gangs now report non-paying victims to regulators for failing to secure sensitive data, increasing the legal pressure to pay.

Implication: Future attacks will be more aggressive and financially devastating, forcing victims to consider reputational damage as well as financial loss.

3. Ransomware-as-a-Service (RaaS) & Affiliate Networks Expansion

3.1 The Increasing Popularity of RaaS

Ransomware is no longer limited to elite hacker groups—Ransomware-as-a-Service (RaaS) allows even low-skilled criminals to launch attacks by purchasing pre-built ransomware kits from dark web marketplaces.

- **Affiliates Handle the Attacks**: RaaS operators provide the malware, while affiliates carry out the attacks and share the profits.
- **Lower Barrier to Entry**: The availability of step-by-step attack guides and automated attack tools means more cybercriminals will join the ransomware ecosystem.
- **Customizable Ransomware Kits**: Dark web marketplaces now offer ransomware with custom branding, allowing criminals to personalize ransom notes and payment portals.

💡 **Implication**: More decentralized and diverse ransomware groups will emerge, making it harder for law enforcement to dismantle them completely.

4. The Shift to Privacy Coins & Decentralized Finance (DeFi) for Payments

4.1 Moving Away from Bitcoin

As law enforcement agencies become more proficient at tracking Bitcoin transactions, ransomware groups are shifting to more anonymous cryptocurrencies:

- **Monero (XMR):** Unlike Bitcoin, Monero transactions are untraceable, making it a preferred choice for ransom payments.
- **Zcash (ZEC):** Offers an option for fully private transactions, further complicating blockchain analysis.
- **Privacy Wallets & Mixers**: Criminals are using Wasabi Wallet, Samurai Wallet, and CoinJoin to obfuscate Bitcoin transactions.

💡 **Implication**: Tracking ransomware payments will become increasingly difficult, requiring advanced blockchain forensics and partnerships with crypto exchanges.

5. Ransomware Targeting Critical Infrastructure & Supply Chains

5.1 Nation-State Backed Ransomware Attacks

Governments are increasingly concerned about ransomware being used as a geopolitical weapon. Some ransomware groups operate with the backing or protection of nation-states, targeting:

- **Energy & Power Grids**: Attacks on oil pipelines (e.g., Colonial Pipeline attack) and power grids can cause massive disruptions.
- **Hospitals & Healthcare Systems**: Ransomware attacks on hospitals threaten lives by disrupting critical medical services.
- **Supply Chain Attacks**: Cybercriminals are exploiting vulnerabilities in software supply chains (e.g., Kaseya attack) to infect thousands of victims at once.

💡 **Implication**: Governments will increase cybersecurity regulations, but attackers will continue to exploit supply chain vulnerabilities.

6. The Rise of Cybercrime Cartels & Ransomware Alliances

6.1 Ransomware Gangs Are Collaborating

Instead of competing, cybercriminal groups are forming alliances to share resources and intelligence.

- **Cartel-Like Structures**: Groups like Conti, LockBit, and ALPHV are collaborating by sharing attack infrastructure and victim data.
- **Cross-Gang Partnerships**: Some threat actors outsource certain attack phases to specialists (e.g., hiring access brokers for initial compromises).
- **Data Exchange Marketplaces**: Ransomware gangs sell victim data to fraudsters who use it for identity theft and financial fraud.

💡 **Implication**: Investigating ransomware groups will become more complex due to their increasing interconnectivity and specialization.

7. Governments & Law Enforcement Response: New Countermeasures

7.1 Tougher Regulations & Bans on Ransom Payments

Governments worldwide are introducing new policies to fight ransomware, such as:

- **Banning Ransom Payments**: Some governments are exploring laws that prohibit organizations from paying ransoms, to remove criminals' financial incentives.
- **Sanctions Against Ransomware Groups**: The U.S. and EU have started sanctioning known cybercriminal groups, making it harder for them to use financial institutions.
- **Mandatory Ransomware Reporting**: New regulations require organizations to report ransomware attacks within hours of detection.

💡 **Implication**: While these measures increase pressure on cybercriminals, they may also push ransomware groups to target less-regulated industries and regions.

Final Thoughts: The Future of Ransomware Defense

As ransomware continues to evolve, organizations, cybersecurity professionals, and law enforcement agencies must stay ahead of emerging trends. Future ransomware attacks will be more sophisticated, financially devastating, and harder to trace, but advanced OSINT techniques, AI-driven threat detection, and stronger cybersecurity policies can help mitigate the threat.

Key Takeaways for the Future

✓ AI-powered ransomware will automate attacks and increase evasion techniques.

✓ Double, triple, and quadruple extortion will become the standard.

✓ Ransomware-as-a-Service (RaaS) will continue lowering the barrier to entry for cybercriminals.

✓ Privacy coins and DeFi will make ransom payments harder to trace.

✓ Critical infrastructure and supply chains will be prime ransomware targets.

✓ Cybercrime cartels and partnerships will increase operational efficiency for ransomware gangs.

✓ New government policies and regulations will attempt to curb ransomware but may create unintended consequences.

📌 **The Bottom Line**: Ransomware is not going away—it's evolving. Only proactive cybersecurity, AI-driven monitoring, and international law enforcement cooperation can slow its growth.

10. Dark Web Market Shutdowns & Law Enforcement Cases

In this chapter, we will investigate the key strategies and tactics used by law enforcement agencies to shut down Dark Web marketplaces and dismantle cybercriminal operations. Through case studies of high-profile market takedowns, such as Silk Road and AlphaBay, we will analyze the methods used to infiltrate and dismantle these illicit platforms. The chapter will explore the collaboration between international agencies, the challenges faced in gathering actionable intelligence from anonymous sources, and the impact of market shutdowns on criminal activity. Additionally, we will discuss how OSINT plays a crucial role in these investigations, from tracking digital footprints to monitoring the movement of goods and funds. By understanding the intricacies of Dark Web market shutdowns, investigators can gain valuable insights into the larger efforts of law enforcement to combat cybercrime and contribute to global security efforts.

10.1 The Fall of Silk Road & Other Major Dark Web Markets

Dark web marketplaces have long been the backbone of cybercriminal economies, facilitating the sale of illicit goods, stolen data, hacking tools, and even contract services. Among these, Silk Road was the first and most infamous, setting the stage for many successors. However, just as quickly as these markets rise, they often fall—either due to law enforcement crackdowns, internal conflicts, or exit scams.

This section explores the downfall of Silk Road and other major dark web markets, analyzing the tactics used by law enforcement to dismantle them, the impact on the underground economy, and how the dark web continuously adapts to such disruptions.

1. The Rise and Fall of Silk Road: The First Major Dark Web Market

1.1 What Was Silk Road?

Launched in 2011 by Ross Ulbricht (alias "Dread Pirate Roberts"), Silk Road was the first large-scale dark web marketplace that operated exclusively via Tor and Bitcoin payments. It was essentially the "Amazon of illicit goods," offering:

✓ Drugs (cannabis, cocaine, LSD, MDMA)

✓ Fake IDs and passports

✓ Stolen credit card information

✓ Hacking tools and malware

✓ Money laundering services

The marketplace grew rapidly, processing hundreds of millions of dollars in transactions, attracting media attention and law enforcement scrutiny.

1.2 Law Enforcement Investigation & Ulbricht's Arrest

Silk Road's downfall was a multi-agency operation, involving the FBI, DEA, IRS, and Homeland Security. Law enforcement:

🔍 Used blockchain analysis to trace Bitcoin transactions to real-world identities.
🔍 Identified server vulnerabilities in Silk Road's infrastructure.
🔍 Tracked Ross Ulbricht's online activity, linking him to forum posts promoting Silk Road.
🔍 Conducted an undercover sting operation to gather intelligence.

In October 2013, Ulbricht was arrested in San Francisco, caught red-handed with his laptop open, logged into Silk Road as an admin. He was later convicted and sentenced to two life terms plus 40 years without parole.

📌 **Impact**: The shutdown of Silk Road disrupted the dark web drug trade, but it did not eliminate it—instead, it inspired a wave of new dark web markets.

2. Other Major Dark Web Market Shutdowns

2.1 Silk Road 2.0 (2014 – 2015)

✓ Created by former Silk Road vendors after the original was taken down.

✓ Promised better security but was quickly infiltrated by law enforcement.

✓ Admin Blake Benthall (aka "Defcon") was arrested in November 2014.

2.2 AlphaBay (2014 – 2017)

✓ Became the largest dark web marketplace, surpassing Silk Road.

✓ Featured drugs, hacking services, weapons, and financial fraud tools.

✓ Taken down in July 2017 by a global law enforcement operation.

✓ Founder Alexandre Cazes was arrested in Thailand but died in custody.

2.3 Hansa Market (2015 – 2017)

✓ A leading dark web marketplace for drugs and cybercrime tools.

✓ Infiltrated and secretly operated by Dutch police for one month.

✓ 1,000+ buyers' details were collected before shutting down in July 2017.

2.4 Wall Street Market (2016 – 2019)

✓ One of the largest dark web markets in the post-AlphaBay era.

✓ Taken down by European law enforcement in 2019.

✓ Admins attempted an exit scam, stealing user funds before their arrest.

2.5 DarkMarket (2021)

✓ Shut down in a global law enforcement operation in early 2021.

✓ Over 500,000 users and 2,400 vendors were active before its seizure.

📌 **Pattern**: Every major marketplace takedown is followed by new markets emerging, but with stronger security measures and decentralized models.

3. How Law Enforcement Shuts Down Dark Web Markets

Despite the use of Tor, cryptocurrency, and operational security (OPSEC), dark web markets are vulnerable to:

◆ Human Errors: Admins or vendors reuse usernames, emails, or passwords.
◆ Undercover Operations: Law enforcement infiltrates forums and markets as buyers.
◆ Blockchain Tracing: Tracking Bitcoin transactions to exchanges and real identities.
◆ Hosting Vulnerabilities: Many dark web markets unknowingly leak server IPs.

◆ Cooperation Between Agencies: International agencies work together (FBI, Europol, Interpol).

💡 **Example**: Operation Bayonet (2017) saw law enforcement seize and operate Hansa Market, monitoring users before shutting it down, leading to multiple arrests.

4. The Dark Web's Response: Resilient & Adaptive

After each market takedown, the dark web adapts by:

✓ Moving to decentralized marketplaces that use blockchain-based hosting.

✓ Increasing security measures, including monero payments (harder to trace).

✓ Using end-to-end encrypted communication apps instead of forum messages.

✓ Implementing multi-signature escrow services to prevent exit scams.

✓ Adopting invite-only marketplaces to keep law enforcement out.

📌 **Future Trend**: Dark web markets may shift toward decentralized, peer-to-peer networks (e.g., OpenBazaar) to become harder to shut down.

5. Final Thoughts: The Ongoing War Between Law Enforcement & Dark Web Markets

✓ Silk Road's fall marked the beginning of law enforcement crackdowns on dark web markets.

✓ Each takedown leads to newer, more secure markets, creating a continuous cycle.

✓ Blockchain tracing, OPSEC mistakes, and international cooperation have led to major arrests.

✓ The future of dark web markets lies in decentralization and stronger encryption.

🔍 **Key Question**: Can law enforcement ever fully eliminate dark web markets, or will they continue to evolve and resurface indefinitely?

10.2 How Authorities Conduct Large-Scale Dark Web Takedowns

The dismantling of dark web marketplaces and cybercriminal networks is a complex, multi-agency effort that requires advanced digital forensics, blockchain analysis, and undercover operations. Authorities have developed sophisticated methods to infiltrate, track, and eventually take down these hidden services despite the use of Tor, encrypted communications, and cryptocurrencies.

This section explores how law enforcement agencies conduct large-scale dark web takedowns, from infiltrating marketplaces to seizing servers, identifying operators, and tracking illicit funds.

1. The Multi-Agency Approach to Dark Web Takedowns

Shutting down a dark web marketplace or criminal network is not a single-agency effort. It involves cooperation between:

✓ **National Law Enforcement**: FBI (U.S.), Europol, Interpol, DEA, Homeland Security, Secret Service.

✓ **Cybercrime Task Forces**: Dedicated units focused on cyber investigations, financial crimes, and counter-terrorism.

✓ **Blockchain Analysts & OSINT Specialists**: Agencies work with Chainalysis, Elliptic, and CipherTrace to track illicit cryptocurrency transactions.

✓ **Cybersecurity Firms & Ethical Hackers**: Organizations assist law enforcement by identifying vulnerabilities in dark web networks.

💡 **Example**: The takedown of AlphaBay in 2017 was a joint operation involving the FBI, DEA, Europol, Royal Thai Police, and Dutch National Police.

2. Key Tactics Used in Dark Web Takedowns

2.1 Undercover Operations & Market Infiltration

Law enforcement often infiltrates dark web forums and marketplaces by:

✓ Creating fake vendor accounts to gain trust.

✔ Buying illicit goods and services to track transactions.

✔ Collecting intelligence on market administrators, moderators, and frequent users.

✔ Analyzing forum conversations for potential OPSEC mistakes.

📌 **Example**: Operation Bayonet (2017) - Law enforcement secretly took over Hansa Market and monitored thousands of buyers before shutting it down.

2.2 Exploiting OPSEC Mistakes by Dark Web Admins

Despite strong anonymity practices, dark web operators often make mistakes that expose their identities. Common errors include:

✔ Reusing usernames and emails across different forums and websites.

✔ Logging into clear web accounts (e.g., Gmail, Reddit) using the same credentials.

✔ Accidentally revealing IP addresses when misconfiguring Tor or VPNs.

✔ Using identifiable metadata in uploaded files (e.g., images, documents).

📌 **Example**: Ross Ulbricht (Silk Road) was linked to forum posts on the clear web promoting Silk Road, allowing the FBI to trace his identity.

2.3 Blockchain & Cryptocurrency Tracing

Since most dark web transactions use Bitcoin, Monero, and other cryptocurrencies, authorities track these transactions through:

✔ Blockchain forensics tools (e.g., Chainalysis, Elliptic) to trace illicit funds.

✔ Identifying exchange platforms where criminals cash out their crypto.

✔ Monitoring "dusting attacks" where law enforcement sends tiny amounts of cryptocurrency to suspect wallets to track their movements.

✔ Subpoenaing crypto exchanges to reveal account information.

📌 **Example**: AlphaBay's downfall started with a tracked Bitcoin transaction that led to the marketplace admin Alexandre Cazes, who was arrested in Thailand.

2.4 Seizing Dark Web Servers & Hosting Infrastructure

Dark web sites are hosted on hidden services (.onion domains), but law enforcement can:

✔ Identify misconfigured Tor servers that reveal real-world IP addresses.

✔ Hack or compromise market admin devices to gain access to servers.

✔ Seize hosting services that support criminal operations.

✔ Exploit server-side vulnerabilities to take control of hidden services.

📌 **Example**: Wall Street Market (2019) was taken down after authorities seized its servers in Germany and arrested its operators.

2.5 Coordinated Global Raids & Arrests

Once enough evidence is gathered, law enforcement launches a coordinated operation that includes:

✔ Arresting market administrators, vendors, and key cybercriminals.

✔ Freezing cryptocurrency wallets and bank accounts linked to illicit transactions.

✔ Seizing server infrastructure and digital assets to prevent market resurrection.

✔ Informing the public by posting law enforcement messages on the seized dark web domains.

📌 **Example**: The takedown of DarkMarket (2021) led to arrests in multiple countries and the seizure of 20+ servers.

3. Case Study: Operation Bayonet & the Fall of AlphaBay & Hansa Market

One of the most successful dark web takedowns was Operation Bayonet (2017), which led to the shutdown of AlphaBay and Hansa Market, two of the largest dark web marketplaces at the time.

3.1 How AlphaBay Was Taken Down

✓ Authorities tracked Bitcoin transactions linked to AlphaBay's founder, Alexandre Cazes.

✓ Cazes used his real email address on early forum posts promoting AlphaBay.

✓ Law enforcement raided his home in Thailand, seizing his laptop while it was still logged into AlphaBay as an administrator.

✓ The site was shut down, and Cazes was arrested—but later found dead in his prison cell.

3.2 The Hansa Market Sting Operation

✓ At the same time, Dutch authorities secretly took over Hansa Market instead of shutting it down immediately.

✓ They monitored thousands of transactions and user activities, gathering intelligence.

✓ After collecting enough evidence, they shut down Hansa Market, leaving users exposed.

✓ Many AlphaBay users fled to Hansa Market, only to walk into law enforcement's trap.

📌 **Impact**: Thousands of dark web users were identified, and multiple arrests were made worldwide.

4. Challenges Faced in Dark Web Takedowns

Despite major successes, authorities still face significant challenges in dismantling dark web marketplaces, including:

◆ **Decentralization of Markets**: New platforms use peer-to-peer and decentralized networks that are harder to seize.

◆ **Use of Privacy Coins**: Cryptocurrencies like Monero provide stronger anonymity than Bitcoin, making financial tracking difficult.

◆ **Encrypted Communication**: Dark web users rely on PGP encryption, secure messaging apps, and private forums.

◆ **Fast Market Resurgence**: When one marketplace shuts down, new ones quickly emerge to replace it.

📌 **Example**: After AlphaBay was shut down, markets like Dream Market and Empire Market rose to take its place.

5. Future of Dark Web Takedowns: Can Authorities Keep Up?

Authorities continue to improve their techniques for targeting dark web marketplaces, but criminals also evolve their tactics. The future of dark web takedowns will likely involve:

✓ AI-driven blockchain analysis to track illicit crypto transactions more effectively.

✓ Machine learning-based OSINT tools for identifying cybercriminal patterns.

✓ Greater international cooperation to eliminate jurisdictional loopholes.

✓ Targeting decentralized dark web platforms before they become widespread.

The cat-and-mouse game between law enforcement and dark web criminals is far from over. While authorities have successfully taken down major marketplaces, new, more resilient platforms will continue to emerge, requiring ongoing innovation in digital forensics and cybersecurity.

10.3 Challenges in Prosecuting Dark Web Criminals

The prosecution of dark web criminals is one of the most complex legal challenges in cybercrime investigations. Despite successful takedowns of marketplaces, forums, and illicit service providers, bringing perpetrators to justice remains difficult due to issues such as jurisdictional conflicts, strong anonymity measures, encrypted communications, and lack of physical evidence.

This section explores the major legal, technical, and procedural obstacles that law enforcement and prosecutors face when attempting to convict cybercriminals operating in the dark web.

1. Jurisdictional Issues: Who Has Authority?

One of the biggest hurdles in prosecuting dark web criminals is jurisdiction—which country has the legal authority to investigate, arrest, and prosecute offenders?

✔ **Global Nature of Crimes**: Dark web operations often involve multiple countries—a marketplace may be hosted on a server in Germany, run by administrators in Russia, and serve customers in the United States.

✔ **Varying Cybercrime Laws**: Some countries have strict cybercrime laws, while others provide safe havens for cybercriminals due to lack of regulation or government inaction.

✔ **Extradition Challenges**: Even if a suspect is identified, they may reside in a country that refuses to extradite criminals to foreign authorities (e.g., Russia, North Korea).

✔ **Coordination Between Agencies**: International agencies like Europol, Interpol, and the FBI must work together, but legal differences slow down investigations.

📌 **Example**: Russian hacker Roman Seleznev, responsible for millions in credit card fraud, was arrested in Maldives and extradited to the U.S., despite Russia's protests.

2. Strong Anonymity & Encryption Make Attribution Difficult

Dark web criminals rely on advanced anonymity techniques, making it extremely difficult to prove their identity in court:

✔ **Tor & I2P Networks**: These technologies hide IP addresses, preventing law enforcement from easily tracing criminal activity back to a specific person.

✔ **PGP Encryption**: Cybercriminals use Pretty Good Privacy (PGP) encryption to secure communications, making it nearly impossible to intercept evidence.

✔ **Monero & Privacy Coins**: Unlike Bitcoin, privacy-focused cryptocurrencies like Monero are designed to be untraceable, making financial tracking difficult.

✔ **Multiple Aliases & Sock Puppets**: Dark web actors use several fake identities, making it hard to prove a connection between a real-world suspect and their dark web persona.

📌 **Example**: The FBI struggled to convict AlphaBay users due to lack of concrete evidence, as transactions were conducted in Monero and all communications were encrypted.

3. Lack of Physical Evidence & Digital Chain of Custody

✔ No Physical Crime Scene: Unlike traditional crimes, dark web crimes leave no physical trace, making forensic evidence difficult to obtain.

✔ Challenges in Proving Digital Ownership: Even if authorities seize a suspect's laptop, how do they prove the suspect controlled a dark web marketplace? Criminals often use encrypted drives, remote access, and hidden operating systems (e.g., Tails OS).

✔ Legal Admissibility of Digital Evidence: Prosecutors must prove that dark web evidence was obtained legally and that there was no tampering or chain of custody issues.

📌 **Example**: In the Silk Road case, Ross Ulbricht's conviction was secured only because his laptop was seized while logged into the marketplace as an admin—had it been locked or encrypted, proving his involvement would have been much harder.

4. Dark Web Marketplaces & Ransomware Gangs Are Highly Resilient

Even when law enforcement shuts down one dark web marketplace or ransomware gang, new ones emerge quickly, complicating prosecution efforts.

✔ **Decentralized Marketplaces**: Some dark web services now operate on blockchain-based, decentralized platforms, making takedowns much harder.

✔ **Resurgence of Cybercriminals**: Many arrested individuals are replaced by new actors, allowing operations to continue under different leadership.

✔ **Mirrors & Clones**: Once a market is seized, mirror sites and new versions often pop up, making it difficult to end operations permanently.

✔ **Cybercriminals Evading Arrest**: Many criminals use exit scams—shutting down their platforms, taking the money, and disappearing before authorities can catch them.

📌 **Example**: After AlphaBay was shut down, Dream Market and Empire Market quickly took its place, showing how difficult it is to eliminate these networks permanently.

5. Challenges in Holding Crypto Exchanges Accountable

✔ **Anonymous Crypto Transactions**: Unlike traditional banks, cryptocurrency exchanges often lack strict KYC (Know Your Customer) regulations, allowing criminals to cash out funds without revealing their real identity.

✓ **Unregulated Exchanges in Offshore Jurisdictions**: Some exchanges operate in countries with little or no regulation, making it nearly impossible for authorities to seize funds or obtain user records.

✓ **Mixers & Tumblers**: Criminals use cryptocurrency mixing services to launder money, making transactions untraceable.

📌 **Example**: BTC-e, a Russian crypto exchange, was linked to money laundering for dark web markets, but its founder Alexander Vinnik was only arrested after traveling to Greece, where he could be extradited.

6. Long & Complex Legal Processes

✓ **Multi-Year Investigations**: Cybercrime cases can take years to investigate before reaching court, making prosecutions difficult.

✓ **Legal Technicalities**: Defense lawyers often argue that law enforcement overstepped its bounds, challenging evidence collection methods.

✓ **Plea Bargains & Reduced Sentences**: Some dark web criminals cooperate with authorities, leading to lighter sentences in exchange for intelligence on bigger targets.

📌 **Example**: Hansa Market's takedown involved months of undercover operations, and only a handful of vendors were successfully prosecuted.

7. Case Study: The Trial of Ross Ulbricht (Silk Road)

✓ **The Arrest**: Ross Ulbricht (a.k.a. "Dread Pirate Roberts") was arrested in 2013 for operating Silk Road, a major dark web drug marketplace.

✓ **The Evidence**: The FBI seized his laptop while logged into Silk Road, giving prosecutors direct proof of his involvement.

✓ **The Conviction**: He was sentenced to two life terms in prison without parole in 2015.

✓ **Appeals & Controversy**: Many argue that his sentencing was too harsh, while others believe he was made an example to deter other cybercriminals.

💡 **Why This Case Was Successful:**

✓ Prosecutors had solid digital evidence linking Ulbricht to Silk Road.

✓ His laptop was seized while logged in, preventing him from using encryption to destroy evidence.

✓ The case set a legal precedent for prosecuting dark web criminals, but many other cases have failed due to lack of evidence.

Conclusion: Can Dark Web Criminals Ever Be Fully Prosecuted?

✓ Yes, but it remains difficult.

✓ The future of dark web prosecutions will depend on:

- Stronger international cooperation in cybercrime cases.
- Better blockchain forensics to track illicit funds.
- Improved legal frameworks for handling digital evidence.
- Stronger KYC regulations for cryptocurrency transactions.

The dark web is constantly evolving, and while law enforcement has had some major victories, the fight against cybercrime is far from over.

10.4 Lessons from AlphaBay, Hansa & Other Market Busts

The takedowns of major dark web marketplaces such as AlphaBay, Hansa, Silk Road, and Wall Street Market have provided critical insights into how law enforcement disrupts cybercriminal operations. These cases demonstrate effective investigative techniques, the resilience of cybercriminal networks, and the challenges of completely eradicating dark web markets. This section explores the key lessons learned from these high-profile market shutdowns.

1. AlphaBay: The Largest Dark Web Market Takedown

AlphaBay was the largest dark web marketplace at the time of its takedown in July 2017, surpassing even Silk Road in terms of scale and illegal transactions. It hosted hundreds of thousands of listings, including drugs, hacking tools, stolen data, and counterfeit goods.

How Law Enforcement Took Down AlphaBay

✓ **Operational Security Mistakes**: The site's administrator, Alexandre Cazes, used the same email address for AlphaBay-related services and his personal accounts, leading investigators to his real identity.

✓ **Coordinated International Effort**: The FBI, DEA, Europol, and law enforcement agencies in Thailand, Canada, and the Netherlands worked together to track and arrest Cazes.

✓ **Seizing Infrastructure**: Authorities seized AlphaBay's servers, gaining access to user data, transactions, and vendor information.

Lessons from the AlphaBay Case

✓ **OPSEC Mistakes Are Fatal** – Even highly sophisticated cybercriminals make small errors that can lead to their unmasking.

✓ **International Cooperation is Key** – The takedown succeeded because of cross-border collaboration among law enforcement agencies.

✓ **Seized Data Helps Further Investigations** – By accessing AlphaBay's servers, law enforcement obtained user data that led to subsequent arrests of vendors and buyers.

✦ **Case Outcome**: Cazes was arrested in Thailand, but he died in his jail cell under mysterious circumstances before he could be extradited to the U.S.

2. Hansa Market: A Brilliant Law Enforcement Sting Operation

Unlike AlphaBay, which was shut down immediately, Hansa Market was taken over and secretly operated by Dutch law enforcement for one month before being shut down.

How Law Enforcement Took Over Hansa

✓ Dutch authorities seized Hansa's servers and took full control of the marketplace without alerting users.

✓ While AlphaBay users fled to Hansa, law enforcement monitored every transaction, logging buyer and seller activity.

✓ **Tracked Cryptocurrency Payments**: Law enforcement gathered intelligence on Bitcoin wallets used for illegal transactions.

✔ **Analyzed Vendor Behavior**: Hansa operators tracked vendor PGP keys, messages, and operational security mistakes.

Lessons from the Hansa Case

✔ **Undercover Operations Yield Critical Intelligence** – Running Hansa covertly allowed law enforcement to monitor criminals in real time.

✔ **Market Shutdowns Can Be Used to Trap Users** – When AlphaBay was taken down, many of its users migrated to Hansa, unknowingly exposing themselves to law enforcement.

✔ **Cryptocurrency Tracking is Essential** – The operation helped develop better blockchain tracking techniques for cybercrime investigations.

📌 **Case Outcome**: Hansa was shut down in July 2017, alongside AlphaBay. The operation led to dozens of arrests and the seizure of user data for future investigations.

3. Silk Road: The First Major Dark Web Market Bust

Silk Road was the original dark web marketplace, founded by Ross Ulbricht (Dread Pirate Roberts) in 2011. It was taken down by the FBI in 2013, setting a precedent for future dark web prosecutions.

How Law Enforcement Took Down Silk Road

✔ Undercover FBI agents infiltrated the market, posing as vendors and buyers.

✔ Bitcoin transactions were traced, linking illegal payments to Ross Ulbricht's accounts.

✔ Ulbricht made a crucial mistake—he logged into the Silk Road admin panel without using Tor, exposing his real IP address.

✔ His laptop was seized while he was logged in, giving law enforcement direct access to his admin activities.

Lessons from the Silk Road Case

✔ **Bitcoin is Not Truly Anonymous** – Although Silk Road transactions used Bitcoin, investigators traced the funds to real-world accounts.

✓ **Seizing Devices While Logged In is Crucial** – Had Ulbricht's laptop been locked, proving his ownership of Silk Road would have been far more difficult.

✓ **Dark Web Marketplaces Are Not Invincible** – Even well-run markets with strong OPSEC can be infiltrated and dismantled.

📌 **Case Outcome**: Ulbricht was sentenced to two life terms in prison without parole in 2015.

4. Wall Street Market: An Exit Scam Gone Wrong

Wall Street Market was a major dark web marketplace that collapsed in 2019 after its administrators attempted an exit scam—stealing users' funds before shutting down the site.

How Law Enforcement Took Down Wall Street Market

✓ **Exit Scam Triggered Investigation**: As users complained about missing funds, law enforcement intensified monitoring of the site's administrators.

✓ **OPSEC Failures**: The admins made mistakes in their cryptocurrency transactions, revealing their real-world identities.

✓ **Server Seizure & Evidence Collection**: Authorities gained access to vendor transaction histories, user logs, and cryptocurrency wallets.

Lessons from the Wall Street Market Case

✓ **Exit Scams Can Backfire** – By attempting to steal funds, the admins drew more attention to themselves, leading to their arrest.

✓ **Tracking Crypto Transactions Remains a Key Law Enforcement Tactic** – Authorities followed the money trail to identify key suspects.

✓ **Market Admins Are the Most Vulnerable Targets** – While vendors and buyers can evade capture, market administrators are the easiest to prosecute.

📌 **Case Outcome**: The admins were arrested in Germany, and Wall Street Market was shut down.

5. Key Takeaways from Dark Web Market Busts

✅ Successful Takedown Strategies

✓ **Undercover Infiltration**: Law enforcement agencies have successfully posed as buyers and vendors to gather intelligence.

✓ **Server Seizures**: Gaining access to marketplace servers provides crucial evidence for prosecutions.

✓ **Crypto Tracking**: Following Bitcoin and Monero transactions helps identify key suspects.

✓ **Coordinated International Efforts:** The most successful busts involved agencies from multiple countries working together.

✘ Challenges That Remain

✓ **Markets Quickly Reappear**: When one market is shut down, new ones emerge almost immediately.

✓ **Stronger OPSEC Practices**: Criminals are learning from past mistakes, using better encryption, Monero, and decentralized hosting.

✓ **Jurisdictional Issues**: Many suspects escape justice by operating from countries that don't cooperate with international law enforcement.

6. Conclusion: The Future of Dark Web Market Busts

Law enforcement has made significant progress in dismantling dark web markets, but the cybercriminal ecosystem continues to evolve. Future takedowns will require:

✓ More advanced blockchain forensics to trace illicit transactions.

✓ AI-driven OSINT tools to monitor new dark web activity.

✓ Stronger international laws to prosecute cybercriminals across borders.

✓ Continuous undercover operations to infiltrate and monitor emerging marketplaces.

While AlphaBay, Hansa, and Silk Road were historic takedowns, the dark web remains a cat-and-mouse game—as soon as one market falls, another rises in its place.

10.5 What Happens After a Dark Web Market Shutdown?

The takedown of a major dark web marketplace creates a ripple effect across the cybercriminal ecosystem. Vendors, buyers, and law enforcement agencies each respond differently, shaping the future of illicit online trade. While some marketplaces vanish permanently, others reappear in new forms or migrate to alternative platforms. This section explores the immediate aftermath of a shutdown, the long-term impact on cybercriminal activity, and how law enforcement leverages these events for ongoing investigations.

1. Immediate Aftermath: Chaos, Panic & Migrations

1.1 Vendor & Buyer Reactions

When a dark web market goes offline—either due to law enforcement action or an exit scam—users typically respond in one of three ways:

✓ **Panic & Withdrawal**: Many buyers and vendors assume the worst and try to erase their tracks. Some abandon dark web activity altogether.

✓ **Market Migration**: Users seek alternative platforms, often moving to rival marketplaces or encrypted messaging services like Telegram and Discord.

✓ **Scam Surge**: Fraudsters take advantage of the chaos, creating fake "replacement" markets to steal Bitcoin deposits from desperate users.

1.2 Where Do Users Go?

After a shutdown, cybercriminals migrate to different platforms, including:

- **Competing Dark Web Markets** – Users move to alternative darknet marketplaces that are still operational.
- **Decentralized Marketplaces** – Some criminals turn to peer-to-peer trading networks that don't rely on central servers.
- **Encrypted Chat Apps** – Groups form on Telegram, Matrix, Signal, and Jabber to coordinate new operations.
- **Surface Web Forums** – Some discussions shift to Reddit, 4chan, or specialized clearnet forums before finding a new darknet home.

📌 **Example**: When AlphaBay was taken down, many users fled to Hansa Market, unknowingly stepping into a trap set by Dutch law enforcement.

2. Law Enforcement's Next Steps

2.1 Investigating Seized Data

When authorities shut down a marketplace, they often gain access to valuable intelligence, such as:

✓ **Transaction histories** (cryptocurrency records linking vendors to buyers).

✓ **User credentials** (email addresses, PGP keys, IP logs, and private messages).

✓ **Vendor listings & conversations** (used to track criminal operations).

This information helps law enforcement identify suspects, track money laundering operations, and build legal cases against cybercriminals.

📌 **Example**: The Silk Road seizure provided a roadmap of criminal activity, leading to multiple arrests in the years following its shutdown.

2.2 Targeting Vendors & High-Profile Criminals

✓ **Arrests & Indictments**: Key vendors and marketplace administrators are actively pursued after a shutdown.

✓ **Cooperation with Financial Institutions**: Law enforcement works with cryptocurrency exchanges to trace and freeze illicit funds.

✓ **Undercover Operations Continue**: Agents infiltrate new markets, posing as buyers or vendors to track illegal activity.

📌 **Example**: After AlphaBay's takedown, authorities used seized data to track dark web fentanyl vendors, leading to multiple arrests.

3. Evolution of Dark Web Marketplaces Post-Takedown

3.1 The "Hydra Effect" – Markets Keep Reappearing

Dark web markets operate like a hydra—cut off one head, and two more grow in its place. When a major market is shut down, criminals quickly adapt:

✓ **New Markets Emerge**: Fresh platforms rise to fill the vacuum, often run by different administrators.

✓ **Security Tightens**: New marketplaces enforce stronger OPSEC practices to prevent the mistakes that led to previous takedowns.

✓ **Trust Becomes a Problem**: After a takedown, users become suspicious of new markets, fearing law enforcement infiltration.

📌 **Example**: When Silk Road fell, it was quickly replaced by Silk Road 2.0, AlphaBay, and other markets, proving that demand for illicit goods remains constant.

3.2 The Shift Toward Decentralization

To reduce the risk of law enforcement action, criminals are increasingly turning to decentralized and encrypted solutions, including:

✓ **Blockchain-Based Marketplaces**: Some vendors explore smart contracts and decentralized platforms to avoid shutdowns.

✓ **Peer-to-Peer Transactions**: Direct, unmediated transactions via Tor-based escrow services are becoming more common.

✓ **Monero Over Bitcoin**: Privacy-focused cryptocurrencies like Monero (XMR) are replacing Bitcoin, making it harder for law enforcement to trace funds.

📌 **Example**: After the Wall Street Market shutdown, criminals migrated to decentralized dark web markets, making future takedowns more challenging.

4. How Dark Web Users Try to Evade Future Crackdowns

✓ **Improved OPSEC**: Vendors and buyers implement better anonymity practices, avoiding mistakes that led to past arrests.

✓ **Encrypted Messaging & Multi-Hop VPNs**: Criminals shift discussions to private chat groups and use multi-layered encryption.

✓ **Dead Man's Switch & Market "Failsafes"** – Some markets implement self-destruct mechanisms if law enforcement attempts a takeover.

✓ AI-Based Fraud Prevention – Newer marketplaces use AI-driven trust systems to detect and block law enforcement infiltration attempts.

📌 Example: Many AlphaBay vendors switched to invite-only platforms, reducing the risk of undercover agents joining.

5. Long-Term Impact on the Dark Web & Law Enforcement

5.1 Law Enforcement Successes

✓ Improved Crypto Forensics – Authorities have developed new blockchain tracking techniques, making it harder for criminals to launder funds.

✓ More Undercover Operations – Agents are embedding deeper into cybercriminal networks, making future takedowns easier.

✓ Cross-Border Cooperation Expands – More global task forces are being created to combat transnational cybercrime.

5.2 Ongoing Challenges

✓ Markets Keep Evolving – No matter how many shutdowns occur, new marketplaces always emerge.

✓ Better Privacy Tech for Criminals – Tools like Monero, decentralized hosting, and stronger encryption make investigations harder.

✓ Lack of Global Legal Frameworks – Some countries refuse to cooperate, allowing cybercriminals to operate freely.

📌 Example: The takedown of AlphaBay and Hansa led to a temporary drop in dark web activity, but within months, new markets filled the gap.

6. Conclusion: The Never-Ending Cat-and-Mouse Game

Dark web market shutdowns are critical victories for law enforcement, but they rarely end illicit activity altogether. Instead, they disrupt and reshape the cybercriminal ecosystem, forcing vendors and buyers to adapt, evolve, and migrate. As authorities refine crypto-tracing methods, undercover tactics, and OSINT strategies, criminals counter with decentralized markets, better OPSEC, and privacy-focused cryptocurrencies.

The cycle continues, but each takedown provides valuable intelligence, helping law enforcement track, arrest, and prosecute cybercriminals long after the marketplaces disappear.

10.6 Case Study: Law Enforcement Tactics in a Dark Web Operation

Dark web marketplaces and cybercriminal networks often operate under the illusion of complete anonymity. However, law enforcement agencies worldwide have successfully infiltrated, monitored, and dismantled some of the largest dark web operations using a combination of OSINT, blockchain forensics, undercover operations, and international collaboration. This case study examines a high-profile dark web takedown, detailing the methods used by authorities to track suspects, seize illicit assets, and bring criminals to justice.

1. Background: The Targeted Dark Web Market

One of the most significant dark web operations in history was the takedown of AlphaBay in July 2017. AlphaBay was the largest illicit marketplace at the time, far surpassing Silk Road in terms of transactions and user base. It hosted tens of thousands of vendors selling illegal drugs, stolen data, hacking tools, and firearms. The marketplace relied on Tor for anonymity and cryptocurrency for transactions, making it a prime target for global law enforcement agencies.

📌 **Key Facts about AlphaBay:**

✓ Operated from 2014 to 2017, handling over $1 billion in transactions.

✓ Used Bitcoin, Monero, and Ethereum to facilitate anonymous payments.

✓ Had over 400,000 users and 40,000 vendors globally.

✓ Administered by Alexandre Cazes, a Canadian national living in Thailand.

1.1 The Criminal Ecosystem Behind AlphaBay

AlphaBay functioned with strict rules for vendor reputation, escrow payments, and dispute resolution, mimicking a legitimate e-commerce platform. Law enforcement suspected that

AlphaBay's administrators were earning millions of dollars in commissions, fueling a cybercrime empire.

Given its global scale and sophistication, shutting down AlphaBay required a multi-agency operation involving the FBI, DEA, Europol, and law enforcement in Thailand, Canada, and France.

2. OSINT & Blockchain Forensics: Tracing the Digital Footprints

2.1 Identifying the Marketplace Administrator

Law enforcement analysts used OSINT techniques to track down AlphaBay's administrator. A critical mistake by Cazes provided the lead investigators needed:

✔ In early forum posts, Cazes used an email address (pimp_alex_91@hotmail.com) linked to his real identity.

✔ This email was found in past data breaches, allowing law enforcement to link it to personal accounts.

✔ Investigators cross-referenced his alias with financial transactions, domain registrations, and social media accounts, confirming his identity.

✦ **OSINT Takeaway**: Even skilled cybercriminals can make small mistakes that reveal their true identity.

2.2 Blockchain Analysis & Financial Tracing

✔ Authorities traced cryptocurrency payments flowing from AlphaBay's wallets to exchange platforms.

✔ Cazes converted millions of dollars in Bitcoin and Monero into fiat currency using regulated crypto exchanges.

✔ By subpoenaing exchange records, authorities identified real-world financial transactions linked to Cazes' accounts.

★ **Key Mistake**: Cazes deposited large amounts of money into his personal bank accounts, leaving a clear financial trail.

3. Undercover Operations & Marketplace Infiltration

Law enforcement used undercover identities to infiltrate AlphaBay, purchasing illicit goods and engaging with vendors. These operations allowed them to:

✓ Map vendor reputations and track trusted sellers.

✓ Gather transaction histories to connect dark web actors to real-world entities.

✓ Analyze encrypted messages and identify patterns in communication.

Undercover agents built trust with high-profile vendors, leading to further intelligence gathering and eventual arrests.

★ **Key Takeaway**: Long-term undercover engagements allow investigators to map criminal networks before executing takedowns.

4. The International Takedown Operation

4.1 Coordinated Raids & Server Seizures

On July 5, 2017, authorities executed a coordinated strike across multiple countries:

✓ **Thailand**: Thai police arrested Cazes at his residence in Bangkok.

✓ **Canada**: Authorities seized AlphaBay's main servers hosted in Quebec.

✓ **United States**: The FBI & DEA led the investigation, unsealing charges against AlphaBay's operators.

✓ **France & Europol**: Assisted in tracking AlphaBay's financial transactions.

4.2 Digital Seizure & Site Shutdown

✓ Authorities took control of AlphaBay's infrastructure, effectively shutting down the site.

✓ They seized transaction logs, user communications, and vendor listings, providing new leads for ongoing investigations.

✓ Users logging into AlphaBay after the seizure were met with a law enforcement banner, warning them that their activities were being investigated.

🔖 **Key Lesson**: Law enforcement doesn't just take down a site—they use seized data to track vendors and buyers for months or years afterward.

5. Aftermath & Law Enforcement Successes

5.1 Unraveling AlphaBay's Criminal Network

✓ Cazes' personal assets were seized, including luxury cars, real estate, and over $23 million in cryptocurrencies.
✓ Law enforcement gained a list of AlphaBay's top vendors, leading to dozens of arrests worldwide.
✓ Financial investigations traced additional dark web activity, helping to dismantle other cybercriminal groups.

5.2 The "Hydra Effect" – The Rise of New Marketplaces

Despite AlphaBay's takedown, the dark web community adapted:

✓ Some users migrated to Hansa Market, only to fall into another law enforcement trap (as Dutch police had taken over Hansa weeks before).
✓ Criminals improved their OPSEC, making future takedowns more difficult.
✓ Newer marketplaces began relying on Monero and decentralized platforms to reduce tracking risks.

🔖 **Key Challenge**: Every dark web takedown leads to the emergence of new, more secure criminal marketplaces.

6. Lessons from AlphaBay: Law Enforcement Strategies & Future Challenges

6.1 Law Enforcement Tactics That Worked

✓ **OSINT & Digital Profiling** – Identifying mistakes in online activity led to unmasking the marketplace administrator.

✓ **Blockchain Forensics** – Tracing cryptocurrency transactions revealed financial connections to real-world identities.

✓ **Covert Infiltration** – Undercover agents built vendor trust and gathered critical intelligence.

✓ **International Coordination** – A global task force ensured the simultaneous seizure of servers and arrests.

6.2 Ongoing Challenges for Future Dark Web Investigations

✓ **Decentralized Marketplaces** – Emerging blockchain-based dark markets are harder to shut down.

✓ **Improved OPSEC by Criminals** – Cybercriminals are learning from past takedowns and tightening security.

✓ **Increased Use of Privacy Coins** – Monero and other non-traceable cryptocurrencies make tracking harder.

📌 **Future of Dark Web Investigations**: Law enforcement is adapting to new encryption, anonymity tools, and decentralized platforms to keep pace with evolving cybercrime.

7. Conclusion: The Never-Ending War on the Dark Web

The AlphaBay takedown remains one of the most significant victories in the fight against dark web cybercrime. However, the constant cat-and-mouse game between law enforcement and criminals means newer, more secure markets will always emerge.

Despite these challenges, law enforcement agencies are continuously refining OSINT techniques, blockchain analytics, and undercover operations to dismantle the next generation of dark web threats.

11. Legal & Ethical Considerations for Dark Web OSINT

In this chapter, we will examine the legal and ethical challenges that OSINT analysts face when investigating the Dark Web. The anonymity that the Dark Web offers can complicate investigations, raising questions about privacy, consent, and the boundaries of legal surveillance. We will discuss the critical importance of understanding the laws surrounding data collection, digital forensics, and the use of intelligence gathered from hidden services, ensuring investigators stay within legal frameworks while maintaining effective analysis. Additionally, we will address the ethical considerations, including the potential harm of exposing sensitive information, entrapment risks, and the balance between protecting civil liberties and preventing cybercrime. By the end of this chapter, readers will have a clear understanding of the complexities involved in Dark Web investigations and the responsible practices required for conducting OSINT in compliance with legal and ethical standards.

11.1 The Legal Risks of Accessing & Investigating the Dark Web

The dark web is a valuable source of intelligence for law enforcement, cybersecurity professionals, and OSINT analysts, but accessing and investigating its hidden marketplaces, forums, and criminal networks comes with significant legal and ethical risks. Understanding the boundaries of the law, jurisdictional differences, and potential liabilities is crucial for anyone conducting dark web investigations. This section explores the legal challenges, potential criminal liabilities, and best practices for staying compliant while navigating the dark web.

1. Understanding the Legal Framework

Unlike the clear-cut legality of surface web investigations, dark web research exists in a legal gray area, where laws vary significantly between countries. Some key considerations include:

✓ Is accessing the dark web illegal?

- Simply using Tor, I2P, or other anonymity networks is legal in most democratic nations.
- However, in some countries (e.g., China, Russia, Iran, North Korea), using Tor or visiting dark web sites can lead to legal consequences.

✓ Are dark web investigations considered hacking?

- Accessing publicly available onion sites is generally legal.
- Attempting to breach security, bypass authentication, or access non-public data could violate cybercrime laws such as the U.S. Computer Fraud and Abuse Act (CFAA) or the UK's Computer Misuse Act (CMA).

✓ Are you committing a crime by viewing illegal content?

- Intent matters: If you knowingly access illicit materials (e.g., child exploitation, terrorism-related content), you may face legal repercussions.
- Automated scraping of dark web data could inadvertently expose investigators to illegal content, leading to liability concerns.

✓ What about purchasing or engaging with cybercriminals?

- Undercover operations by law enforcement require legal authorization.
- Private-sector investigators must avoid any actions that could be interpreted as aiding or abetting cybercrime.

📌 **Legal Takeaway**: Merely browsing the dark web is usually legal, but interacting with illicit marketplaces, engaging with criminals, or attempting to hack sites can lead to criminal charges.

2. Jurisdictional Issues: Laws Vary by Country

Dark web investigations often involve actors operating across multiple jurisdictions, complicating legal enforcement.

✓ United States:

- **CFAA (Computer Fraud and Abuse Act)** – Prohibits unauthorized access to computer systems.

- **Patriot Act** – Expands law enforcement powers for investigating cybercrime and terrorism.
- **Money Laundering Laws** – Criminalizes transactions involving illicit cryptocurrency.

✔ European Union (EU):

- **General Data Protection Regulation (GDPR)** – Restricts personal data collection, impacting OSINT research.
- **EU Cybercrime Laws** – Criminalizes hacking, identity theft, and the sale of illicit goods.

✔ United Kingdom:

- **Computer Misuse Act (CMA)** – Similar to the U.S. CFAA, prohibiting unauthorized access.
- **Terrorism Act 2000** – Criminalizes accessing or sharing terrorism-related materials.

✔ Russia & China:

- Strictly regulate anonymity tools like Tor and VPNs.
- Dark web investigations may be illegal for civilians and private organizations.

📌 **Key Takeaway**: What is legal in one country might be illegal in another, making cross-border investigations highly complex.

3. Privacy Laws & OSINT Investigations

Investigating individuals or groups on the dark web often involves gathering personally identifiable information (PII), which can raise privacy law concerns:

✔ GDPR (Europe):

- Restricts the collection and storage of PII.
- Requires explicit consent to process user data.

✔ CCPA (California, USA):

- Grants individuals the right to know and delete personal data collected about them.

✔ **ECPA (Electronic Communications Privacy Act, USA):**

- Prohibits intercepting private communications without legal authorization.

📌 **Legal Risk**: OSINT investigators must ensure they do not violate privacy laws when gathering intelligence on dark web actors.

4. Investigative Pitfalls: When Dark Web Research Becomes a Crime

Many dark web investigators accidentally cross legal lines due to common pitfalls, including:

✔ **Using personal or work devices**

- Accessing the dark web from corporate networks can violate IT security policies.
- **Solution**: Use a dedicated air-gapped device or virtual machine (VM) for investigations.

✔ **Downloading illicit data**

- Dark web markets often contain stolen data dumps (e.g., credit card numbers, passwords, leaked government documents).
- Possessing such data, even for research, may be illegal under anti-hacking laws.
- **Solution**: Work with legal counsel to obtain law enforcement exemptions before handling sensitive data.

✔ **Engaging with cybercriminals**

- Even posing as a buyer to gather intelligence can be construed as conspiracy.
- **Solution**: Private investigators should never interact directly—leave that to law enforcement.

✔ **Transacting with cryptocurrency for intelligence gathering**

- Buying illicit goods or services to gain intelligence could implicate investigators in money laundering.
- **Solution**: Avoid direct financial transactions on dark web markets.

📌 **Key Rule**: If an investigative action could be misinterpreted as criminal behavior, it's best to consult a legal expert before proceeding.

5. Best Practices for Conducting Legal & Ethical Dark Web Research

To minimize legal risks, OSINT analysts, cybersecurity researchers, and law enforcement must follow strict operational guidelines:

✓ **Obtain proper legal authorization**

- Government investigators should secure warrants or legal approvals before engaging in deep investigations.
- Private sector analysts should work within corporate legal and compliance guidelines.

✓ **Use anonymized & secure environments**

- Conduct research using dedicated, non-attributable systems.
- Use air-gapped machines or sandboxed virtual environments to protect against malware.

✓ **Consult legal & compliance teams**

- Before conducting dark web intelligence gathering, seek legal review of methods and targets.
- Stay updated on international cybersecurity laws that impact cross-border investigations.

✓ **Maintain detailed logs & ethical oversight**

- Document all investigative actions to demonstrate lawful intent.
- Ensure investigations align with ethical OSINT principles.

★ **Final Advice**: If uncertain about the legality of an investigative action, seek legal counsel first—the risks aren't worth it.

6. Conclusion: Navigating Legal Minefields in Dark Web Investigations

Dark web investigations offer critical intelligence on cybercriminal activity, but the legal risks are substantial. Investigators must understand their jurisdiction's laws, avoid common investigative pitfalls, and operate with ethical and legal safeguards in place. By following compliance best practices, professionals can effectively conduct dark web research without crossing legal boundaries.

11.2 Ethical Challenges in Monitoring Criminal Activities

Monitoring criminal activities on the dark web presents a complex ethical dilemma. While intelligence gathering is essential for disrupting cybercrime, it also raises concerns about privacy, entrapment, unintended consequences, and the fine line between investigation and complicity. Ethical considerations must guide law enforcement, cybersecurity professionals, and OSINT analysts to ensure that their work does not violate moral, legal, or human rights principles. This chapter explores the core ethical dilemmas, potential risks, and best practices for conducting dark web investigations responsibly.

1. The Privacy vs. Security Debate

One of the most fundamental ethical challenges in dark web monitoring is balancing privacy rights with the need for security.

✔ The Case for Privacy

- Many individuals use the dark web for legitimate purposes (e.g., whistleblowers, political dissidents, journalists).
- Overly aggressive surveillance can infringe on civil liberties and discourage free speech.

✔ The Case for Security

- Criminal networks exploit anonymity to sell drugs, weapons, stolen data, and child exploitation materials.

- Law enforcement must track, infiltrate, and dismantle these operations to prevent harm.

📌 **Ethical Question**: How can investigators ensure they target criminals without violating the rights of innocent users?

2. The Dangers of Entrapment & Ethical Investigative Techniques

Undercover operations are common in dark web investigations, but crossing the line into entrapment—where authorities induce someone to commit a crime—poses a serious ethical risk.

✓ Entrapment Concerns

- If law enforcement encourages illegal activities rather than merely observing, the operation may be unethical and legally questionable.
- Example: A cybercriminal forum may be infiltrated, but actively promoting cybercrime to catch criminals is problematic.

✓ Ethical Infiltration Best Practices

- Observing without actively engaging in illegal activity.
- Using intelligence gathering for preventive action, not provocation.
- Ensuring investigations target known criminal actors, not general users.

📌 **Key Ethical Principle**: Investigators should never initiate, facilitate, or escalate criminal behavior.

3. Collateral Damage: Unintended Consequences of Dark Web Investigations

Dark web monitoring can lead to unexpected ethical dilemmas, including:

✓ Risking Innocent Lives

- Investigations into ransomware groups or hitmen-for-hire sites could unintentionally expose innocent individuals.
- Example: If authorities shut down a forum where whistleblowers and criminals coexist, both groups lose anonymity protection.

✓ Driving Crime Further Underground

- Dark web market shutdowns often lead to new, harder-to-track platforms.
- **Example**: When Silk Road was shut down, markets like AlphaBay emerged with better security.

✓ Creating a False Sense of Security

- Law enforcement takedowns might deter crime temporarily but fail to address the root causes of cybercrime.
- Without preventive measures, criminals simply migrate to new platforms.

📌 **Ethical Concern**: Investigators must weigh short-term wins against long-term impacts on crime trends.

4. Ethical Use of Stolen Data & Intelligence

Investigating cybercrime often involves handling compromised or stolen data, raising ethical questions:

✓ Should law enforcement use leaked data?

- **Example**: If hackers expose a dark web drug cartel's internal communications, should investigators use that evidence?
- **Ethical stance**: If the data was obtained illegally, does using it legitimize cybercrime?

✓ The Ethics of Buying Intelligence from Criminals

- Some private firms purchase compromised data for threat intelligence.
- **Risk**: Buying stolen data funds cybercriminals and legitimizes illicit marketplaces.

📌 **Ethical Rule**: If intelligence gathering involves supporting cybercriminal enterprises, it is ethically unacceptable.

5. Transparency & Accountability in Dark Web Investigations

Without oversight, dark web investigations can easily become ethically questionable. Ethical OSINT investigations require:

✔ Clear Guidelines & Accountability

Investigators should operate under defined ethical codes, ensuring transparency and legal compliance.

✔ Regular Ethical Reviews

Law enforcement agencies and private cybersecurity firms should conduct routine ethical audits to review dark web investigation methods.

✔ Public Awareness & Debate

While some secrecy is necessary, governments and organizations should engage in public discussions on how dark web monitoring affects civil liberties.

📌 **Final Thought**: The best defense against ethically questionable practices is clear oversight and transparent policies.

6. Conclusion: Navigating the Ethical Minefield of Dark Web Investigations

Dark web investigations present serious ethical challenges, from privacy concerns to the risk of entrapment and unintended harm. Investigators must ensure that their work is legally sound, ethically justified, and free from practices that could inadvertently harm innocent individuals. The ultimate goal of ethical dark web monitoring should be to combat crime while upholding justice, privacy, and human rights.

11.3 How to Conduct Dark Web Research Without Breaking the Law

Investigating the dark web requires careful navigation of legal frameworks, ethical boundaries, and security measures to ensure that researchers, analysts, and law enforcement professionals do not violate laws or compromise their own safety. This chapter outlines the best practices for conducting dark web research legally and responsibly, while mitigating risks associated with accessing illicit content, handling compromised data, and interacting with cybercriminal communities.

1. Understanding the Legal Landscape

Before accessing the dark web, it is crucial to understand the laws governing online investigations. Legal frameworks vary by country, and some activities—even passive monitoring—may be considered illegal in certain jurisdictions.

✔ Key Legal Considerations:

- **Accessing vs. participating**: Viewing dark web content may be legal, but actively buying, selling, or facilitating illegal activities is not.
- **Possession of illicit materials**: Downloading certain files (e.g., stolen data, hacking tools, or explicit content) can lead to legal consequences.
- **Interacting with cybercriminals**: Engaging in discussions with criminals, even for intelligence-gathering, may be interpreted as aiding or abetting illegal activities.

✔ International Legal Differences:

- **The United States**: The Computer Fraud and Abuse Act (CFAA) criminalizes unauthorized access to networks.
- **The European Union**: The General Data Protection Regulation (GDPR) restricts the handling of personal data, including breached data found on the dark web.
- **The United Kingdom**: The Computer Misuse Act makes unauthorized access to computer systems illegal, including certain OSINT techniques.

📌 **Best Practice**: Consult legal experts or compliance teams before conducting dark web research, especially if working in law enforcement, cybersecurity, or OSINT analysis.

2. Safe & Legal Access to the Dark Web

To conduct legal research, researchers must follow strict operational security (OPSEC) measures to protect their identity, devices, and data.

✔ Recommended Steps for Secure & Legal Access:

- Use a Dedicated Research Machine
- Avoid accessing the dark web from personal or work devices.

- Use a virtual machine (VM) or isolated environment.

Connect Using Legal Privacy Tools

- Use the Tor browser for accessing onion services.
- Consider a Virtual Private Network (VPN) for additional anonymity.
- Avoid Interacting with Illegal Content
- Do not download, purchase, or engage in illegal transactions.

Keep Logs & Documentation

If conducting research for law enforcement or cybersecurity firms, maintain detailed records to demonstrate compliance with legal and ethical standards.

📌 **Warning**: Simply using Tor or accessing onion sites is not illegal, but engaging with illicit content, downloading illegal files, or attempting unauthorized access can result in criminal charges.

3. Ethical Guidelines for Dark Web Investigations

Even if certain activities are technically legal, they may still present ethical dilemmas. Researchers must follow ethical OSINT practices to avoid harming individuals or violating privacy laws.

✔ Ethical Research Principles:

- **Minimize harm**: Do not engage in activities that could expose individuals to risks (e.g., doxxing, hacking, or exposing informants).
- **Respect privacy laws**: Do not publish or share personal data collected from dark web sources unless legally permitted.
- **Avoid deception**: Using fake identities (sock puppets) can be useful for infiltration, but pretending to be a criminal or facilitating illegal activity crosses ethical lines.

📌 **Best Practice**: Follow industry-standard ethical frameworks, such as the Association of Internet Researchers' (AoIR) guidelines for ethical online research.

4. Monitoring Dark Web Marketplaces & Forums Legally

Many cybersecurity firms, law enforcement agencies, and journalists track dark web marketplaces to gather intelligence on data breaches, cybercrime trends, and threat actors. However, there are legal limitations to how this research can be conducted.

✓ **Legal Intelligence-Gathering Techniques:**

- **Passive Observation**: Viewing discussions without participating in illegal activity.
- **OSINT Tools**: Using legal intelligence tools to track leaked credentials, ransomware groups, and hacker activity.
- **Dark Web Search Engines**: Tools like Ahmia, OnionLand, and Dark.fail can help find indexed dark web sites legally.

🚫 **Illegal Activities to Avoid:**

- Attempting to purchase illicit goods (drugs, weapons, malware, stolen data).
- Accessing or downloading child exploitation materials (strictly illegal in all jurisdictions).
- Engaging in hacking, DDoS attacks, or unauthorized access to dark web sites.

📌 **Best Practice**: Stick to publicly available information and document research methods to avoid legal trouble.

5. Handling & Reporting Dark Web Intelligence

Once intelligence is gathered, researchers must handle and report findings responsibly to ensure they remain within legal and ethical boundaries.

✓ **If You Discover Stolen or Illegal Data:**

- Do not download or store the data on personal devices.
- Report findings to relevant law enforcement agencies or cybersecurity firms.
- Follow chain of custody procedures if data needs to be preserved for investigations.

✓ **Reporting Cyber Threats Responsibly:**

- If you find stolen corporate credentials, report them to the affected company or security teams.

- If you discover active cybercrime operations, report to organizations like Europol, the FBI's Internet Crime Complaint Center (IC3), or national cybercrime units.

📌 **Important**: Mishandling dark web intelligence can violate privacy laws, compromise investigations, or unintentionally aid criminals. Always ensure findings are reported through the proper channels.

6. Conclusion: Conducting Dark Web Research Responsibly

Investigating the dark web is a valuable but high-risk activity that must be conducted legally, ethically, and securely. By following strict OPSEC protocols, legal guidelines, and ethical research principles, analysts can gather critical intelligence without violating laws or endangering themselves.

✓ **Key Takeaways:**

- **Know the law**: Research the legal framework in your jurisdiction before accessing the dark web.
- **Use secure methods**: Always use a dedicated research machine, VPN, and Tor browser.
- **Avoid illegal activities**: Do not interact with or download illicit content.
- **Follow ethical guidelines**: Maintain privacy, transparency, and harm-minimization in all investigations.
- **Report findings responsibly**: Notify the appropriate authorities or organizations when uncovering cybercrime evidence.

By adhering to these best practices, researchers, cybersecurity professionals, and law enforcement can leverage dark web intelligence effectively—without breaking the law.

11.4 The Debate on Privacy vs. Surveillance in Dark Web Investigations

The dark web presents a paradox for governments, cybersecurity professionals, privacy advocates, and everyday internet users. On one hand, it is a refuge for whistleblowers, activists, and journalists who rely on anonymity to protect themselves from oppressive regimes. On the other, it is a hub for cybercriminals, terrorists, and illicit marketplaces, making it a prime target for law enforcement surveillance. This chapter explores the ongoing debate between privacy rights and government surveillance, the ethical implications of dark web monitoring, and the challenges of balancing security with civil liberties.

1. Privacy as a Fundamental Right

Privacy is a cornerstone of democratic societies and a fundamental human right. Many argue that access to anonymous communication and encryption technologies is essential for protecting personal freedoms in an era of increasing digital surveillance.

✓ **Why Privacy Matters on the Dark Web:**

- **Protection from authoritarian regimes**: Journalists, dissidents, and human rights activists use Tor and other anonymity networks to communicate securely.
- **Whistleblowing and corporate accountability**: Platforms like SecureDrop allow whistleblowers to report government or corporate misconduct.
- **Freedom from mass surveillance**: With widespread government tracking and data collection, some individuals seek refuge in privacy-enhancing technologies.

🏛 **The Counterargument**: Critics argue that absolute privacy can shield criminals, making law enforcement investigations nearly impossible.

📌 **Key Question**: Should privacy be absolute, or should exceptions be made to prevent crime and terrorism?

2. The Role of Government Surveillance in Dark Web Investigations

To combat cybercrime and national security threats, governments actively monitor dark web activities. Agencies like the FBI, Europol, and NSA deploy sophisticated surveillance techniques to track cybercriminals.

✓ Common Government Surveillance Methods:

- **Honeypots & undercover operations**: Law enforcement agencies create fake dark web markets and forums to track criminals (e.g., the Hansa Market sting operation).
- **Traffic analysis & exit node monitoring**: Agencies analyze Tor network traffic and compromise Tor exit nodes to monitor user activity.
- **Legal backdoors & subpoenas**: Governments pressure companies to provide access to encrypted communications and transaction records.

🔊 Privacy Concerns:

- **Mass surveillance risks**: Widespread monitoring can lead to false positives, targeting innocent individuals.
- **Overreach & abuse**: Governments have a history of using anti-terror laws to justify surveillance on activists and journalists.
- **Erosion of encryption**: Calls for backdoors in encryption protocols threaten the privacy of legitimate users.

📌 **Key Question**: How can law enforcement effectively investigate cybercrime without infringing on civil liberties?

3. Ethical Dilemmas in Dark Web Surveillance

The surveillance vs. privacy debate raises complex ethical questions about how far governments and corporations should go in monitoring online activities.

✔ **Ethical Questions in Dark Web Investigations:**

- Is it ethical to monitor private citizens under the guise of cybercrime prevention?
- Should law enforcement be allowed to break encryption to access criminal communications?
- Are mass data collection programs justifiable if they prevent cyberattacks and terrorism?

🔊 Case Study: The FBI's PlayPen Investigation

- The FBI seized and operated a child exploitation site on the dark web for several weeks, using it to identify and arrest users.
- Critics argued that law enforcement effectively distributed illegal content during the operation.
- Supporters claimed it was a necessary evil to capture offenders.

📌 **Key Question**: Where should the line be drawn between ethical policing and privacy invasion?

4. The Future of Privacy & Surveillance on the Dark Web

As governments and privacy advocates clash over encryption, anonymity, and surveillance, the future of dark web investigations remains uncertain.

✓ Emerging Trends & Challenges:

- **Stronger encryption technologies**: Decentralized and blockchain-based privacy networks may make surveillance more difficult.
- **AI-powered OSINT tools**: Law enforcement is leveraging AI-driven data analysis to track criminals without mass surveillance.
- **Legal & policy debates**: Countries are drafting new regulations on encryption, privacy rights, and cybercrime investigations.

📹 Potential Risks:

- Governments may use cybersecurity concerns as an excuse to push for extreme surveillance laws.
- Dark web users may migrate to even more anonymous, decentralized platforms.
- Ethical concerns over predictive policing and mass data collection will continue to grow.

📌 **Final Question**: Can society find a balance between security and privacy, or will surveillance always come at the cost of personal freedoms?

Conclusion: Striking a Balance

The debate over privacy vs. surveillance in dark web investigations is far from settled. While law enforcement needs effective tools to combat cybercrime, privacy advocates warn against the dangers of overreach, mass surveillance, and weakened encryption.

✓ Key Takeaways:

- Privacy is essential, but it can be exploited for criminal purposes.
- Law enforcement must operate within ethical and legal boundaries while investigating the dark web.
- Surveillance laws should balance security and civil liberties to prevent abuse.
- Emerging technologies will continue shaping the debate in the years to come.

Ultimately, the challenge lies in finding a middle ground—where governments can track criminal activity without violating the rights of innocent users. Whether that balance is achievable remains one of the most pressing questions in cybersecurity today.

11.5 Best Practices for Ethical OSINT in the Dark Web

Conducting Open-Source Intelligence (OSINT) investigations on the dark web requires a careful balance between ethical responsibility, legal compliance, and operational security (OPSEC). While law enforcement agencies, cybersecurity professionals, and threat intelligence analysts monitor illicit activities, they must adhere to strict ethical guidelines to prevent legal violations, entrapment, or unintended harm. This chapter outlines best practices for ethical OSINT in the dark web, ensuring investigations are conducted responsibly and lawfully.

1. Defining Ethical OSINT in the Dark Web

Ethical OSINT refers to the responsible collection, analysis, and use of publicly available information while respecting privacy, legal frameworks, and ethical standards. The dark web presents unique challenges, as anonymity networks (like Tor and I2P) enable both legitimate users and criminals to operate without direct attribution.

✓ **Ethical OSINT Principles:**

- **Legal Compliance**: Adhering to national and international laws while conducting investigations.
- **Non-Participation**: Avoiding any actions that could be construed as engagement in illegal activities (e.g., purchasing illicit goods).
- **Privacy Considerations**: Minimizing data collection on innocent individuals and focusing on criminal behavior.
- **Transparency & Accountability**: Maintaining clear justifications for OSINT activities and ensuring oversight.

🚨 **Ethical Pitfalls to Avoid:**

- Unintentional aiding of criminal activity (e.g., engaging with threat actors in a way that strengthens their operation).
- Data misinterpretation leading to false accusations.
- Exceeding legal boundaries, such as unauthorized hacking or surveillance.

📌 **Key Question**: How can OSINT professionals ethically monitor dark web threats without crossing legal or moral boundaries?

2. Legal Considerations & Compliance

Before conducting OSINT investigations on the dark web, analysts must understand jurisdictional laws regarding cybercrime, surveillance, and data collection.

✓ **Legal Compliance Checklist:**

- **Understand National Laws**: Each country has different regulations on cyber investigations and surveillance.
- **Know the Limits of OSINT**: Accessing publicly available data is legal, but using hacking techniques or violating platform terms may be illegal.
- **Obtain Proper Authorization**: Law enforcement agencies must often secure warrants or approvals before conducting dark web investigations.
- **Document Investigative Steps**: Keeping detailed logs of research activities ensures transparency and protects against legal repercussions.

🚨 **High-Risk Legal Issues:**

- Viewing or downloading illicit content (e.g., child exploitation material) can constitute a crime, even for research purposes.
- Engaging in conversations with cybercriminals may lead to legal complications if the analyst appears to be aiding or abetting an offense.
- Purchasing illicit goods or services for research could result in criminal liability.

📌 **Key Question**: How can OSINT investigators ensure they stay within the legal framework while gathering intelligence on the dark web?

3. Practicing Operational Security (OPSEC) & Anonymity

OSINT professionals must use strong OPSEC measures to protect their identity and prevent exposure to malicious actors.

✓ **Essential OPSEC Practices:**

- **Use Isolated & Secure Systems**: Conduct dark web investigations on a dedicated virtual machine (VM) or air-gapped system to prevent malware infections.
- **Employ VPNs & Tor Bridges**: Avoid IP address leaks by routing connections through VPNs, Tor, or I2P.
- **Create Compartmentalized Identities**: Use separate, non-traceable personas for different investigations to prevent linking activities.
- **Limit Digital Fingerprinting**: Disable JavaScript, WebRTC, and cookies to prevent sites from tracking investigative activities.

📸 OPSEC Mistakes to Avoid:

- Accessing the dark web from a personal or work device.
- Using real-world information (email, phone number) to create dark web accounts.
- Failing to encrypt sensitive data and logs.

📌 **Key Question**: How can investigators maintain anonymity while ensuring ethical and legal compliance?

4. Responsible Data Collection & Analysis

When gathering intelligence, OSINT professionals must prioritize accuracy, verification, and responsible data handling.

✔ Best Practices for Data Collection:

- **Verify sources before drawing conclusions**: Many dark web posts are disinformation, scams, or entrapment efforts.
- **Use automated tools responsibly**: Web scrapers and crawlers should respect ethical guidelines and platform terms of service.
- **Store and share intelligence securely**: Sensitive data should be encrypted and only shared with authorized parties.

📸 Data Ethics Concerns:

- Accidentally doxxing innocent individuals by misinterpreting dark web information.
- Spreading misinformation by citing unverified claims.
- Collecting more data than necessary, leading to ethical and legal risks.

★ Key Question: How can OSINT professionals filter credible intelligence from misinformation while protecting innocent individuals?

5. Engaging with Dark Web Communities Ethically

While OSINT investigations sometimes require monitoring or infiltrating dark web forums, analysts must avoid becoming active participants in criminal discussions.

✔ Ethical Engagement Guidelines:

- **Passive Monitoring**: Reading and analyzing discussions without engaging directly.
- **Avoiding Deception**: Using sock puppets without inciting illegal activities or entrapping users.
- **Respecting Privacy**: Avoiding the collection of personal data of non-criminal users.

⚠ Unethical Practices to Avoid:

- Encouraging criminal activity to gather intelligence.
- Manipulating dark web users into committing crimes.
- Sharing false identities or creating fake marketplaces to entrap users (unless law enforcement authorized).

★ Key Question: How can analysts ethically infiltrate criminal forums without crossing ethical or legal boundaries?

6. Ethical Use of OSINT Tools & Automation

While tools like blockchain explorers, web scrapers, and AI-powered analysis enhance OSINT investigations, they must be used responsibly and transparently.

✔ Best Practices for Using OSINT Tools:

- Ensure tools comply with ethical and legal standards.
- Avoid hacking, credential stuffing, or brute-force attacks when gathering intelligence.
- Use AI and automation responsibly to prevent false positives and bias.

🔔 Automation Risks:

- Over-collection of private data without consent.
- Automated tools engaging in illegal activity (e.g., scraping restricted content).
- AI misinterpreting context, leading to false accusations.

📌 **Key Question**: How can OSINT professionals use automation ethically while minimizing misuse or bias?

Conclusion: The Need for Ethical OSINT Standards

As dark web investigations grow in importance, OSINT professionals must follow clear ethical guidelines to ensure intelligence gathering remains legal, responsible, and fair.

✔ **Key Takeaways:**

- OSINT should never violate privacy laws or ethical boundaries.
- OPSEC measures protect both investigators and intelligence integrity.
- Passive monitoring is preferable to active engagement in criminal forums.
- Tools and automation must be used responsibly to avoid unethical data collection.

Ultimately, ethical OSINT is about striking the right balance—gathering intelligence without infringing on rights or engaging in illegal activity. By adhering to these best practices, investigators can enhance cybersecurity, support law enforcement, and protect civil liberties in the digital age.

11.6 Case Study: When OSINT Investigations Crossed Legal Boundaries

While OSINT investigations are crucial for cybersecurity, law enforcement, and threat intelligence, they can sometimes cross legal and ethical boundaries—intentionally or unintentionally. This case study explores instances where OSINT practitioners or organizations faced legal consequences for their investigative methods. By analyzing these cases, we can better understand the risks, mistakes, and lessons to ensure OSINT remains within legal and ethical limits.

Case 1: The Hacking Team Breach – When OSINT Became Cybercrime

Background

Hacking Team, an Italian cybersecurity firm, specialized in government surveillance tools, selling spyware to law enforcement and intelligence agencies worldwide. Their software, Remote Control System (RCS), was known for its stealth capabilities, often used to monitor journalists, activists, and dissidents in authoritarian regimes.

The OSINT Investigation

In 2015, independent security researchers and hacktivists began investigating Hacking Team's operations using OSINT techniques, including:

✓ Analyzing leaked documents and contracts with foreign governments.

✓ Tracking IP addresses and infrastructure linked to RCS deployments.

✓ Scraping online forums and LinkedIn profiles of employees for technical clues.

However, the investigation escalated when an anonymous hacker breached Hacking Team's servers and leaked 400GB of internal data, including:

- Source code for RCS spyware.
- Emails revealing questionable government clients.
- Financial records of software sales.
- Where It Crossed the Line

While traditional OSINT methods (public data analysis, monitoring social media, and document research) were ethical, the breach of private servers and data theft crossed into illegal hacking. Governments and security firms raised concerns that:

🔘 Exposing surveillance tools helped cybercriminals weaponize them.
🔘 Unauthorized access to private company data violated cybersecurity laws.
🔘 Leaked sensitive intelligence operations put lives at risk.

Legal & Ethical Consequences

- Hacking Team collapsed due to reputational damage and financial loss.
- Multiple researchers were investigated for potential collaboration with hackers.
- Governments lost covert surveillance capabilities, affecting intelligence operations.

📌 **Lesson Learned:**

While OSINT can uncover unethical activities, it must be conducted legally. Accessing private databases without permission turns OSINT into cybercrime.

Case 2: The Ashley Madison Breach – Privacy vs. Public Interest

Background

Ashley Madison, a website facilitating extramarital affairs, was breached in 2015 by a hacker group called The Impact Team. The hackers stole 32 million user records, including:

✓ Names, emails, and phone numbers.

✓ Credit card transaction details.

✓ Private messages exchanged between users.

After the breach, OSINT investigators and journalists began analyzing and publishing findings based on leaked data.

The OSINT Investigation

OSINT analysts used various methods to analyze and verify leaked information, including:

✓ Cross-referencing emails with government databases (e.g., officials using Ashley Madison accounts).

✓ Analyzing password reuse patterns to check for potential security risks.

✓ Using blockchain analysis to track payments made via Bitcoin.

Where It Crossed the Line

Initially, investigating the breach was legal—analyzing publicly available leaked data is a grey area. However, some OSINT researchers went further by:

🔍 **Doxxing individuals**—exposing real names and personal details.

💻 Publicly shaming government officials, military personnel, and corporate executives.

💻 **Forcing suicides**—multiple users took their lives after being exposed.

Legal & Ethical Consequences

- Ashley Madison faced lawsuits for failing to secure user data.
- Journalists and OSINT researchers were criticized for violating privacy laws.
- Some investigators faced legal threats for sharing personally identifiable information (PII).

📌 Lesson Learned:

Even when leaked data is already public, OSINT professionals must consider privacy laws and ethical implications. Investigating a data breach is not a license to expose or harm individuals.

Case 3: OSINT Investigators Impersonating Law Enforcement

Background

In an effort to track cybercriminals on the dark web, some independent OSINT researchers have posed as law enforcement officials to gain trust in illicit forums.

The OSINT Investigation

In multiple cases, analysts attempted to infiltrate hacker communities and criminal marketplaces by:

✓ Creating fake law enforcement personas to gather intelligence.

✓ Engaging with criminals under the guise of ongoing police operations.

✓ Threatening suspects with fake subpoenas or legal action to extract information.

Where It Crossed the Line

💻 Impersonating law enforcement is illegal in most countries and can lead to criminal charges.

💻 Entrapment concerns—posing as law enforcement can invalidate real investigations.

💻 OSINT analysts do not have the authority to conduct undercover operations like police.

Legal & Ethical Consequences

- Some OSINT researchers were arrested for impersonating federal agents.
- Real law enforcement investigations were compromised due to false identities creating confusion.
- Dark web criminals became more cautious, making infiltration harder for real intelligence agencies.

📌 **Lesson Learned:**

OSINT professionals must never pose as law enforcement or government officials. Doing so can disrupt real investigations and lead to criminal charges.

Key Takeaways: Staying Within Legal Boundaries in OSINT

These case studies highlight the fine line between ethical OSINT and illegal activity. To avoid legal consequences, investigators must follow these best practices:

✔ **Do Not Access or Share Stolen Data Illegally**

- Leaked data should be analyzed only if legally obtained.
- Do not download or store sensitive information from breaches.

✔ **Respect Privacy & Data Protection Laws**

- Avoid exposing personal details of innocent individuals.
- Do not engage in doxxing or shaming based on leaked data.

✔ **Never Impersonate Law Enforcement or Authorities**

- OSINT analysts should never claim to be police, federal agents, or intelligence officers.
- Infiltration tactics should not involve coercion or deception.

✔ **Avoid Hacking & Unauthorized System Access**

- Using hacking techniques even for research purposes is illegal.

- OSINT should rely on publicly available and legally accessible data.

✓ Ensure Investigations Have a Clear Ethical Justification

- Always weigh the public interest vs. potential harm before publishing findings.
- Seek legal guidance and approval when handling sensitive intelligence.

Conclusion: Ethical OSINT is Critical for Credibility

The integrity of OSINT investigations relies on adherence to legal and ethical standards. While the dark web and cybercrime investigations require deep research, investigators must avoid crossing legal lines.

By learning from past mistakes, OSINT analysts can conduct responsible investigations that contribute to cybersecurity, law enforcement, and public safety—without risking legal action, reputational damage, or ethical failures.

12. Case Study: A Dark Web Criminal Investigation

In this final chapter, we will walk through a real-world case study of a Dark Web criminal investigation, showcasing the OSINT techniques and strategies used to uncover and dismantle a cybercriminal network. From initial leads on underground forums to tracking financial transactions and analyzing encrypted communications, this case study highlights the practical application of the tools and methodologies discussed throughout the book. We will break down the investigative process step-by-step, illustrating how OSINT can be used to connect disparate pieces of evidence, identify key suspects, and build a case against those operating in the shadows of the internet. This chapter will provide a comprehensive, hands-on understanding of how OSINT can be effectively employed in a complex Dark Web investigation, reinforcing the skills necessary to tackle the evolving world of cybercrime.

12.1 The Background of the Criminal Operation

Dark web criminal operations have evolved into highly sophisticated enterprises, leveraging anonymity networks, encrypted communications, and cryptocurrency to evade detection. This chapter examines a real-world case study of a major criminal operation that thrived on the dark web, detailing its origins, structure, and eventual downfall.

Origins: The Rise of a Dark Web Empire

The criminal operation in focus was a large-scale dark web marketplace specializing in illegal narcotics, stolen data, hacking tools, and counterfeit documents. Emerging in the post-Silk Road era, it positioned itself as a "trustworthy" and "secure" platform for illicit transactions, quickly gaining popularity among cybercriminals and buyers worldwide.

Unlike earlier marketplaces that relied solely on Bitcoin, this operation integrated Monero (XMR), a privacy-focused cryptocurrency, to obscure financial transactions. Its administrators implemented advanced security measures, including:

✓ Multi-signature escrow systems to reduce scams.

✓ End-to-end encrypted messaging between buyers and sellers.

✓ Automatic tumbling and mixing services for cryptocurrency transactions.

Organizational Structure & Key Players

The marketplace was not run by a single individual but operated like a corporation, with designated roles, such as:

- **Administrators** – Controlled server infrastructure, security updates, and law enforcement countermeasures.
- **Moderators** – Enforced rules, resolved disputes, and prevented scams.
- **Vendors** – Independent sellers offering drugs, stolen data, malware, and forged documents.
- **Money Launderers** – Specialized in "cleaning" illicit profits through cryptocurrency mixing services and offshore exchanges.

Initial Success & Global Expansion

At its peak, the operation facilitated millions of dollars in weekly transactions, drawing attention from law enforcement agencies worldwide. It expanded its reach by:

✓ Establishing multiple mirror sites to prevent takedowns.

✓ Using invite-only access to screen new users and evade infiltration.

✓ Offering vendor verification systems to build trust within the criminal ecosystem.

However, as its reputation grew, so did the scrutiny from cybersecurity researchers, OSINT analysts, and law enforcement agencies—leading to its eventual downfall.

12.2 How OSINT Tools Were Used to Gather Intelligence

The takedown of the dark web criminal operation was not a result of a single breakthrough but a methodical OSINT-driven investigation that combined blockchain analysis, website fingerprinting, digital footprint tracking, and covert infiltration. This chapter explores how open-source intelligence (OSINT) tools and techniques were used to unmask the perpetrators and dismantle the illicit marketplace.

1. Identifying the Marketplace Infrastructure

Dark web marketplaces operate on Tor hidden services (.onion sites), which are designed to conceal their locations. However, OSINT analysts leveraged passive and active reconnaissance techniques to gather intelligence on the site's infrastructure.

Key OSINT Techniques Used:

✔ **Onion URL Enumeration** – Investigators used Ahmia, OnionScan, and specialized crawlers to identify alternative marketplace URLs, mirrors, and admin-controlled forums.

✔ **Metadata & Server Fingerprinting** – By analyzing SSL certificates, response headers, and hosting patterns, OSINT analysts found clues linking the marketplace to other illicit services.

✔ **Historical DNS Analysis** – Although the site was hosted on Tor, law enforcement uncovered previous clearnet infrastructure, mistakenly used during early testing phases.

✅ **Breakthrough**: The marketplace's early test version was briefly hosted on a clearnet VPS (Virtual Private Server), leaving behind a traceable hosting record.

2. Blockchain & Cryptocurrency Transaction Tracking

Since the marketplace primarily used Bitcoin and Monero (XMR) for payments, OSINT researchers and blockchain forensic teams followed the money trail to identify key financial connections.

Key OSINT Tools Used:

✔ **Blockchain Explorers (BTCscan, Blockchair, and Mempool)** – Tracked Bitcoin transactions from marketplace wallets to cryptocurrency exchanges.

✔ **CipherTrace & Chainalysis** – Used advanced blockchain forensics to identify patterns in money laundering activities.

✔ **Monero Analysis via Statistical Heuristics** – Although Monero transactions are highly obfuscated, investigators used timing analysis and exchange deposits to trace illicit funds.

✅ **Breakthrough**: Despite Monero's privacy features, some vendors converted funds into Bitcoin, which were later withdrawn through KYC (Know Your Customer) exchanges, revealing real-world identities.

3. Tracking Admin & Vendor Digital Footprints

Even the most security-conscious cybercriminals leave digital breadcrumbs—especially if they reuse usernames, PGP keys, or email accounts. OSINT analysts scoured multiple platforms to link marketplace operators to real-world identities.

Key OSINT Techniques Used:

✓ **PGP Key Reuse Analysis** – Some vendors reused their PGP keys on multiple forums, allowing law enforcement to correlate identities across platforms.

✓ **Username & Alias Cross-Referencing** – Investigators used DeHashed, Have I Been Pwned (HIBP), and social media lookup tools to find reused handles.

✓ **Forum & Pastebin Scraping** – Automated scrapers monitored dark web forums for leaked vendor information, including accidental OPSEC mistakes.

✅ **Breakthrough**: One administrator used the same alias on a now-defunct hacking forum, where he previously registered with a personal email address—leading to his identification.

4. Covert OSINT & Undercover Infiltration

To gather insider intelligence, investigators created sock puppet accounts to blend into the marketplace's ecosystem. They engaged in controlled transactions, interacting with vendors while extracting key intelligence.

Key OSINT Techniques Used:

✓ **Undercover Vendor Profiling** – Investigators posed as buyers to assess vendor activity and gather metadata from product listings.

✓ **Conversation Metadata Extraction** – By engaging with vendors via encrypted messaging apps, OSINT teams extracted server timestamps and behavioral clues.

✓ **Operational Security (OPSEC) Mistakes** – Vendors occasionally slipped up, revealing time zones, language preferences, or device information in chats.

✅ **Breakthrough**: A vendor accidentally revealed a time zone mismatch in a PGP-signed message, suggesting they were operating from a different country than they claimed.

5. Marketplace Shutdown & Final Takedown

Using OSINT-gathered intelligence, law enforcement orchestrated a coordinated takedown by:

✓ Seizing server infrastructure based on leaked hosting records.

✓ Arresting admins and vendors linked via blockchain trails and alias analysis.

✓ Poisoning vendor trust by spreading disinformation, leading to mass marketplace exit scams.

✅ **Final Outcome**: The marketplace was dismantled, millions in cryptocurrency were seized, and multiple arrests were made across international jurisdictions.

Key Takeaways: How OSINT Helped Crack the Case

◆ No anonymity network is perfect—small OPSEC mistakes can expose dark web criminals.
◆ Blockchain analysis can unmask illicit transactions, even with privacy coins.
◆ Alias and PGP key reuse are critical vulnerabilities in dark web operations.
◆ Undercover OSINT operations provide direct intelligence but require careful execution.

By leveraging OSINT tools and techniques, investigators transformed scattered digital breadcrumbs into actionable intelligence, ultimately leading to one of the biggest dark web takedowns in history.

12.3 Challenges Faced in Identifying the Threat Actors

The takedown of a dark web criminal operation is rarely a straightforward process. Threat actors leverage sophisticated anonymity techniques, advanced OPSEC practices, and decentralized communication methods to evade detection. Despite the extensive use of OSINT (Open-Source Intelligence) tools, blockchain analysis, and digital footprint tracking, investigators encountered significant challenges in identifying and prosecuting the individuals behind the illicit operation.

This chapter explores the major obstacles law enforcement and cybersecurity researchers faced in unmasking the threat actors involved in the case study.

1. The Challenge of True Anonymity on the Dark Web

Unlike the clearnet, where IP addresses, domain registrations, and social media activity can be easily traced, dark web operators hide behind Tor, I2P, and other anonymity networks.

Obstacles Encountered:

✓ **Tor's Onion Routing Encryption**: The multi-layered encryption of Tor made it nearly impossible to track traffic back to real-world IP addresses.

✓ **No Centralized Records**: Unlike traditional web hosting, onion services do not require domain name registrations, making ownership attribution difficult.

✓ **Use of Bulletproof Hosting**: Many criminals relied on offshore, no-logs VPS providers in jurisdictions resistant to law enforcement cooperation.

✓ **Workaround Used**: Investigators monitored OPSEC mistakes, such as misconfigured servers, leaking real-world metadata.

2. OPSEC Discipline Among Cybercriminals

Experienced dark web administrators and vendors follow strict Operational Security (OPSEC) protocols to avoid being unmasked.

Common OPSEC Practices Used by Threat Actors:

✓ No reuse of usernames, emails, or passwords across different platforms.

✓ Strict communication through encrypted channels (PGP, OTR, XMPP).

✓ Use of Monero (XMR) instead of Bitcoin to prevent blockchain tracking.

✓ Air-gapped devices and Tails OS to avoid forensic traces.

✓ **Breakthrough**: Some vendors accidentally reused usernames or PGP keys from older forums, which were linked to real-world identities.

3. The Complexity of Tracing Cryptocurrency Transactions

Cryptocurrencies power the dark web economy, and criminals leverage mixing, tumbling, and privacy coins to hide their financial trails.

Challenges Investigators Faced:

✓ **Bitcoin Tumbling Services**: These services obfuscated transaction histories, breaking traditional tracking methods.

✓ **Monero's Privacy Features**: Unlike Bitcoin, Monero (XMR) hides sender, receiver, and transaction amounts by default.

✓ **Decentralized Exchanges (DEXs)**: Criminals used peer-to-peer exchanges to cash out funds without KYC verification.

✓ **Breakthrough**: While Monero was largely untraceable, investigators identified Bitcoin conversion points where criminals mistakenly withdrew funds via KYC-compliant exchanges.

4. Dark Web Forums & Closed Marketplaces Are Hard to Infiltrate

Many criminal marketplaces and forums operate on an invite-only basis, restricting access to vetted members.

Roadblocks Faced by Investigators:

✓ **Strict Vetting Processes**: Many forums required existing vendor referrals before granting access.

✓ **Reputation Systems**: New users without verified transaction history were often flagged as suspicious.

✓ **Honey Pot Detection**: Cybercriminals actively monitored for law enforcement infiltration attempts.

✓ **Successful Infiltration Method**: Investigators built long-term sock puppet accounts, slowly gaining trust by conducting small, controlled transactions.

5. The Global Jurisdictional & Legal Challenges

Dark web operations often involve actors from multiple countries, creating jurisdictional hurdles for law enforcement.

Legal Barriers Encountered:

✔ **Non-Cooperative Jurisdictions**: Many cybercriminals operated in countries with weak extradition laws, delaying investigations.

✔ **Privacy Laws Protecting Hosting Services**: Some bulletproof hosting providers legally refused to turn over data.

✔ **Different Legal Standards for Cryptocurrency Investigations**: Some countries lacked clear regulations on whether blockchain analysis was admissible in court.

✅ **Workaround**: Law enforcement used international task forces (Europol, FBI, Interpol) to coordinate multi-jurisdictional investigations.

6. The Challenge of Verifying Digital Identities

Even when investigators collected IP addresses, blockchain transactions, and forum aliases, linking them to real-world identities was difficult.

Hurdles Faced in Identity Attribution:

✔ **Use of VPNs & Proxy Chains**: Threat actors frequently switched IP addresses to prevent tracking.

✔ **False Flags & Misdirection**: Some cybercriminals planted misleading information to divert investigators.

✔ **Use of Multiple Dark Web Personas**: A single person often maintained multiple vendor accounts under different identities.

✅ **Breakthrough**: Investigators correlated behavioral patterns, writing styles, and time zone inconsistencies across multiple accounts to establish real identities.

Final Takeaways: Lessons from the Investigation

◆ **Even skilled cybercriminals make mistakes**—a single OPSEC slip can lead to their downfall.

◆ Blockchain analysis remains a key investigative tool, despite mixing and privacy coins.

◆ **Undercover infiltration requires patience**—long-term credibility-building is essential.

✦ International collaboration is crucial, as no single agency can combat dark web crime alone.

By overcoming these challenges, OSINT analysts and law enforcement agencies successfully unmasked the key threat actors behind the dark web operation, leading to their eventual arrests and prosecution.

12.4 The Role of Blockchain Analysis in Tracing Payments

Cryptocurrency is the lifeblood of dark web transactions, facilitating illicit trade while providing users with a degree of anonymity. However, blockchain analysis has emerged as a powerful tool for investigators, enabling them to track and trace payments despite the efforts of cybercriminals to obfuscate their transactions. This chapter explores how blockchain analysis played a crucial role in unraveling financial flows within a dark web criminal operation.

1. Understanding Blockchain's Role in Dark Web Transactions

Unlike traditional banking systems, cryptocurrencies like Bitcoin (BTC), Monero (XMR), and Ethereum (ETH) operate on decentralized ledgers, meaning transactions are publicly recorded. While blockchain networks do not inherently reveal personal identities, transactions leave behind a permanent and traceable record that can be analyzed using OSINT and forensic tools.

◆ **Why Criminals Use Cryptocurrency on the Dark Web:**

✓ **Decentralization**: No central authority controls transactions.

✓ **Anonymity Features**: Users don't need to provide real-world identity details.

✓ **Global Accessibility**: Cryptocurrencies can be sent anywhere in seconds.

✓ **No Reversals**: Transactions are irreversible, reducing fraud risks for sellers.

However, blockchain transactions are not entirely anonymous, and sophisticated tracking techniques can reveal patterns, wallets, and, ultimately, real-world identities.

2. Key Blockchain Analysis Techniques Used in the Investigation

A. Transaction Chain Analysis

Investigators leveraged blockchain explorers to trace cryptocurrency flows across multiple wallets and identify suspicious transactions.

✓ **Tracking Bitcoin Transactions**: Since Bitcoin operates on a transparent ledger, every transaction can be followed from sender to receiver using blockchain explorers like Blockchair, BTCScan, and Chainalysis Reactor.

✓ **Identifying Wallet Clusters**: Investigators used heuristics and clustering algorithms to determine which wallets belonged to the same individual or organization.

✓ **Analyzing Time Stamps & Spending Patterns**: Repeated transaction patterns helped connect dark web vendors to their known withdrawal points.

✅ **Breakthrough**: By analyzing withdrawal patterns, investigators identified a vendor who cashed out Bitcoin through a centralized exchange, leading to a real-world identity match.

B. Unmasking Mixing & Tumbling Services

To evade tracking, criminals often use mixers (tumblers) to shuffle their funds with other users, making it difficult to trace transactions.

How Mixers Work:

✓ The user sends BTC to the mixer → The mixer pools it with other users' BTC.

✓ The mixer sends back 'cleaned' BTC to a different address, breaking the transaction link.

✓ No direct connection exists between the sender and receiver.

◆ **Investigation Challenge**: Mixers break the direct traceability of funds, complicating OSINT efforts.

✅ **Workaround**: Investigators used statistical analysis and transaction volume matching to detect mixing patterns. Some mixers also had logs compromised, providing insight into illicit transactions.

C. Tracing Monero (XMR) & Privacy Coins

Unlike Bitcoin, Monero (XMR) transactions are fully anonymous—sender, receiver, and transaction amounts are hidden using:

✓ **Ring Signatures** (masking sender identity)

✓ **Stealth Addresses** (one-time recipient addresses)

✓ **Confidential Transactions** (hiding transaction amounts)

◆ **Challenge: Monero's privacy features prevent direct tracking.**

✅ **Workaround**: Investigators tracked Monero-Bitcoin exchange points, where criminals converted Monero into BTC before cashing out.

✅ **Breakthrough**: A suspect was identified when they exchanged large amounts of Monero for Bitcoin on a regulated exchange, requiring identity verification.

D. Identifying Cash-Out Points: The Weak Link

Criminals need to convert their cryptocurrency into fiat currency (USD, EUR, etc.), creating opportunities for identification.

✓ **KYC (Know Your Customer) Regulations:** Many exchanges require identity verification before withdrawal.

✓ **Peer-to-Peer (P2P) Marketplaces**: Some criminals avoid KYC by using Paxful, LocalBitcoins, or gift card trading.

✓ **ATM Withdrawals**: Bitcoin ATMs require a phone number and may have security cameras.

✅ **Breakthrough**: A suspect used a KYC-compliant exchange to withdraw funds, allowing law enforcement to subpoena their account details.

3. Case Study: How Blockchain Analysis Led to an Arrest

A dark web vendor selling stolen credit card data was suspected of laundering millions in Bitcoin through a complex network of wallets, mixers, and exchanges.

Step 1: Identifying the Vendor's Wallet

Investigators scraped dark web forums and linked the vendor's advertised Bitcoin address to multiple transactions on blockchain explorers.

Step 2: Analyzing Transactions & Mixing Patterns

Using blockchain forensics tools, they observed large BTC deposits moving through mixers and privacy wallets before eventually landing in a suspected cash-out exchange.

Step 3: Tracking Fiat Conversions & KYC Breakthrough

The suspect converted BTC into Monero, hoping to erase the trail. However, when they later converted Monero back into BTC and withdrew via a regulated exchange, the exchange's KYC verification linked the transaction to a real-world identity.

Step 4: Law Enforcement Intervention

A subpoena was issued to the exchange, and the suspect was arrested when they attempted to withdraw funds at a Bitcoin ATM.

4. Lessons Learned: Strengths & Weaknesses of Blockchain Analysis

◆ **Strengths of Blockchain Analysis in Dark Web Investigations:**

✓ **Public Ledger**: Bitcoin transactions are permanently recorded and cannot be erased.

✓ **Wallet Clustering**: Investigators can group related addresses to identify criminal networks.

✓ **Transaction Patterns** Reveal Behaviors: Repeated patterns can expose money laundering, ransomware payments, or illicit sales.

✓ **Fiat Conversion is the Weakest Link**: Most criminals eventually cash out, creating an opportunity for identification.

◆ **Challenges & Limitations:**

✓ **Privacy Coins (Monero, Zcash) Limit Visibility** – Making direct tracking difficult.

✓ **Mixing Services Obfuscate Transaction Trails** – Increasing investigative complexity.

✓ P2P Trading & Gift Cards Bypass KYC – Allowing some criminals to remain anonymous.

5. Final Takeaways: The Future of Blockchain OSINT

The case study highlights how blockchain analysis is a critical OSINT tool for dark web investigations. While criminals continue to develop new obfuscation techniques, law enforcement and researchers are constantly innovating to unmask illicit transactions.

◆ Emerging Trends in Blockchain OSINT:

✓ AI & Machine Learning for Transaction Analysis – Automating wallet clustering.

✓ Government Regulation of Cryptocurrency Exchanges – Strengthening KYC requirements.

✓ Enhanced Privacy Coin Tracking – Research into forensic techniques for Monero.

Despite its challenges, blockchain analysis remains one of the most effective methods for tracking dark web financial activity, helping investigators follow the money and dismantle cybercriminal networks.

12.5 How Law Enforcement & OSINT Analysts Collaborated

The fight against cybercrime on the dark web requires a joint effort between law enforcement agencies and OSINT (Open-Source Intelligence) analysts. Criminals operating in the hidden corners of the internet use sophisticated anonymity tools, but by combining investigative tactics with OSINT methodologies, authorities can track, identify, and apprehend perpetrators. This chapter explores how law enforcement and OSINT analysts worked together in a real-world case, highlighting the strategies, tools, and intelligence-sharing processes that led to a successful operation.

1. The Need for Collaboration in Dark Web Investigations

Why Law Enforcement Needs OSINT Analysts

Traditional law enforcement methods alone are often insufficient for investigating cybercriminals on the dark web. OSINT analysts bring specialized skills in:

✓ Data mining and intelligence gathering from open sources

✓ Blockchain analysis to track cryptocurrency transactions

✓ Social media and forum infiltration to engage with cybercriminals

✓ Metadata analysis to connect anonymous users to real-world identities

While law enforcement agencies have legal authority, including the ability to issue subpoenas and execute arrests, OSINT analysts provide the technical expertise needed to uncover key intelligence that law enforcement can act on.

Why OSINT Analysts Need Law Enforcement

OSINT analysts, whether working independently or in private firms, lack the legal power to take action against criminals. Even if they identify a dark web vendor or track cryptocurrency flows, they cannot execute arrests or obtain court orders. By partnering with law enforcement, OSINT intelligence can be transformed into actionable evidence in criminal cases.

2. Division of Responsibilities in the Investigation

In the case study of a dark web criminal operation, law enforcement and OSINT analysts divided their roles:

◆ **OSINT Analysts: Gathering Intelligence**

✓ **Scraping Dark Web Marketplaces & Forums** – Analysts used automated tools to monitor vendor activity, product listings, and transaction histories.

✓ **Tracking Cryptocurrency Transactions** – Blockchain explorers helped follow illicit funds from buyers to vendors and through laundering services.

✓ **Identifying Patterns & Threat Actors** – Analysts studied behavioral patterns, writing styles, and online aliases to link multiple accounts to the same individuals.

✓ **Leveraging Social Media & Surface Web Intelligence** – Cross-referencing leaked databases and social media profiles helped connect anonymous users to real identities.

◆ **Law Enforcement: Legal Action & Arrests**

✓ **Obtaining Subpoenas & Warrants** – Law enforcement secured court orders to access transaction records from cryptocurrency exchanges.

✓ **Deploying Undercover Agents** – Officers posed as buyers to gather evidence and interact with suspects.

✓ **Coordinating with International Authorities** – Many dark web criminals operate across borders, requiring global cooperation with agencies like Europol and Interpol.

✓ **Executing Search Warrants & Arrests** – Once enough evidence was gathered, law enforcement raided locations, seized servers, and arrested suspects.

✅ **Collaboration Success**: OSINT analysts uncovered key digital breadcrumbs, and law enforcement converted the intelligence into evidence for prosecution.

3. OSINT Tools & Techniques Used in the Investigation

A. Dark Web Monitoring & Intelligence Gathering

✓ Tools Used:

- **Ahmia, OnionSearch, and DarkOwl** – Search engines for dark web content
- **Hunchly & Maltego** – Link analysis and data visualization tools
- **SpiderFoot** – Automated OSINT reconnaissance

✓ **Outcome**: Analysts monitored dark web forums where criminals discussed illicit activities and identified key players in the network.

B. Cryptocurrency & Blockchain Analysis

✓ Tools Used:

- **Chainalysis & CipherTrace** – For tracking Bitcoin and Monero transactions
- **Blockchair & BTCScan** – Identifying wallets linked to dark web vendors
- **Elliptic Forensics** – Analyzing cryptocurrency laundering techniques

✓ **Outcome**: Blockchain analysis traced illicit transactions to a KYC-compliant exchange, where law enforcement obtained real-world identities.

C. Social Media & Surface Web Cross-Referencing

✓ Tools Used:

- **Pipl & Skopenow** – People search engines for identifying real identities
- **Have I Been Pwned** – Checking leaked credentials
- **OSINT Framework** – A collection of intelligence-gathering tools

✓ **Outcome**: An OSINT analyst matched a suspect's alias on a dark web forum to an email address found in a past data breach, leading to further identification.

D. Undercover Law Enforcement Operations

✓ Tactics Used:

- Officers posed as buyers on a dark web marketplace.
- They ordered illicit goods to track shipping routes and supplier networks.
- Surveillance teams monitored cash-out locations, where suspects withdrew cryptocurrency funds.

✓ **Outcome**: Undercover agents infiltrated the vendor's trust network, gaining access to private forums that revealed operational details.

4. Overcoming Challenges in the Investigation

◆ **1. Anonymity Barriers**

✓ **Challenge**: Dark web criminals used Tor, VPNs, and privacy coins to hide their identities.

✓ **Solution**: OSINT analysts identified weak OPSEC practices, such as reuse of usernames and email accounts across multiple platforms.

◆ **2. Legal & Jurisdictional Issues**

✓ **Challenge**: Many suspects operated in countries with weak cybercrime laws.

✓ **Solution**: Law enforcement coordinated internationally to extradite criminals to jurisdictions where they could be prosecuted.

◆ 3. Encryption & Secure Communications

✓ **Challenge**: Criminals used PGP encryption and private chat apps like Signal and Tox.

✓ **Solution**: Investigators captured unencrypted data through undercover interactions and subpoenaed metadata from communication platforms.

5. Case Study: The Arrest of a Dark Web Drug Vendor

One high-profile case saw law enforcement and OSINT analysts collaborate to dismantle a multi-million-dollar drug trafficking operation.

◆ Step 1: OSINT Analysts Tracked the Vendor

- Analysts monitored dark web listings and identified a vendor selling fentanyl.
- They extracted Bitcoin addresses and used blockchain analysis to follow the money.

◆ Step 2: Law Enforcement Conducted Undercover Operations

- Agents ordered drugs from the vendor, tracking shipments and identifying a distribution hub.
- Surveillance teams monitored package drop-offs, linking them to real-world suspects.

◆ Step 3: Digital Clues Led to a Breakthrough

- The vendor accidentally reused an alias from an old social media account.
- Analysts cross-referenced usernames and found a matching email in a past breach.

◆ Step 4: Arrest & Seizure

- Law enforcement executed a search warrant, seizing cryptocurrency wallets, servers, and illicit substances.
- The vendor was arrested and sentenced to 15 years in prison.

✓ **Result**: The operation led to over $5 million in asset seizures and shut down a major drug supply chain.

6. Final Takeaways: The Power of Collaboration

This case study demonstrates how OSINT analysts and law enforcement can effectively work together to combat dark web crime.

◆ **Key Lessons Learned:**

✓ Combining technical OSINT expertise with legal enforcement powers is critical for success.

✓ Cybercriminals often make small OPSEC mistakes that can be exploited.

✓ Following the money trail remains one of the best ways to track dark web activity.

✓ International cooperation is essential in cases involving cross-border cybercrime.

As dark web threats evolve, law enforcement and OSINT collaboration will continue to be a cornerstone of modern cyber investigations.

12.6 Lessons Learned & Future Strategies for Dark Web Investigations

The ever-evolving nature of cybercrime on the dark web presents constant challenges for law enforcement, intelligence agencies, and OSINT analysts. Despite successful operations against darknet markets, ransomware groups, and fraud rings, cybercriminals continuously adapt, leveraging new technologies and improved OPSEC (Operational Security) practices. This chapter reflects on key lessons learned from past dark web investigations and explores future strategies for staying ahead in this digital arms race.

1. Key Lessons Learned from Dark Web Investigations

◆ **1.1 Cybercriminals Are Not Perfect – OPSEC Mistakes Lead to Breakthroughs**

One of the most significant takeaways from past investigations is that even the most sophisticated criminals make mistakes. These errors, often small, can be exploited by OSINT analysts and law enforcement.

Common OPSEC Failures by Criminals:

✓ Reusing usernames and email addresses across different platforms

✓ Accidentally exposing metadata (e.g., image EXIF data, PDF author names)

✓ Connecting cryptocurrency wallets to regulated exchanges requiring KYC (Know Your Customer)

✓ Sloppy operational security in darknet forums (e.g., using personal language quirks or posting at consistent time zones)

Example: In the Silk Road case, law enforcement traced Ross Ulbricht by connecting an old pseudonym he used in Bitcoin forums to a Gmail account linked to his real identity.

◆ **1.2 Following the Money Trail is Still One of the Best Tactics**

Despite cybercriminals attempting to obfuscate their cryptocurrency transactions, blockchain forensics remains one of the most effective tools in dark web investigations.

Key Strategies Used:

✓ Blockchain analysis tools (e.g., Chainalysis, CipherTrace) to track Bitcoin, Monero, and other cryptocurrencies

✓ Identifying mixing and tumbling services used to launder funds

✓ Tracing cash-out points at crypto exchanges and subpoenaing account records

✓ Monitoring darknet escrow services for payment flows

✓ **Lesson Learned**: Most criminals eventually need to convert crypto to fiat, and those conversion points create vulnerabilities.

◆ **1.3 Dark Web Market Takedowns Do Not Eliminate Cybercrime – They Displace It**

While shutting down major marketplaces (e.g., Silk Road, AlphaBay, Wall Street Market) has disrupted illegal trade, history shows that new markets quickly emerge to replace them.

✔ **Post-market takedown trends:**

- Vendors and buyers migrate to alternative platforms (e.g., decentralized markets, encrypted messaging apps)
- Market operators increase security (e.g., Monero-only transactions, multi-signature wallets)
- Criminals turn to smaller, invite-only forums instead of large public markets

✔ **Lesson Learned**: Instead of focusing solely on takedowns, investigators must monitor migration trends and adapt to new criminal tactics.

◆ **1.4 International Collaboration is Critical for Success**

Since dark web criminals operate across multiple jurisdictions, no single country can tackle the problem alone. Successful operations have required coordinated efforts between:

✔ Europol, Interpol, and the FBI

✔ Local cybercrime units and intelligence agencies

✔ Financial institutions and cryptocurrency exchanges

✔ Private-sector OSINT firms and cybersecurity companies

✔ **Lesson Learned**: Global cooperation accelerates investigations, ensuring cybercriminals cannot escape prosecution by hiding in countries with weak cybercrime laws.

◆ **1.5 Monitoring Encrypted Communication Channels is Essential**

With the shutdown of large darknet markets, many criminals have moved to encrypted messaging apps (e.g., Telegram, Signal, Tox) and decentralized forums.

✔ **Challenges:**

- PGP encryption prevents easy access to message contents
- End-to-end encryption means law enforcement must rely on metadata rather than direct message access
- Some messaging apps do not cooperate with authorities

✓ Solutions:

- Undercover infiltration of cybercriminal groups
- Analyzing metadata and communication patterns
- Using AI-powered language analysis tools to detect suspicious conversations

✓ **Lesson Learned**: OSINT analysts must track migration patterns and develop strategies for intelligence gathering beyond traditional forums and markets.

2. Future Strategies for Dark Web Investigations

◆ 2.1 Leveraging AI & Machine Learning for OSINT

As cybercriminal tactics evolve, AI-powered tools will be essential for automating intelligence collection and pattern recognition.

✓ Potential AI Use Cases:

- Automated dark web crawling to detect new marketplaces and forums
- Language and sentiment analysis to identify threats in real-time
- Deepfake detection to counter disinformation and fraudulent identities
- Anomaly detection in blockchain transactions to flag potential laundering schemes

✓ **Future Strategy**: Develop AI-driven OSINT tools to scale investigations and reduce manual workload.

◆ 2.2 Improving Blockchain Analysis to Track Privacy Coins

Bitcoin tracking has been highly successful, but criminals are increasingly using privacy-focused cryptocurrencies like Monero, Zcash, and Dash.

✓ Solutions Being Explored:

- Combining OSINT techniques with on-chain analysis (e.g., linking Monero transactions to off-chain behaviors)
- Targeting fiat conversion points (most exchanges still require KYC)
- Exploiting weaknesses in coin-mixing services (some have been compromised in the past)

✅ **Future Strategy**: Invest in advanced blockchain forensics and focus on points of vulnerability, such as crypto exchanges and illicit cash-out operations.

◆ 2.3 Decentralized Dark Web Intelligence Networks

Cybercriminals increasingly use decentralized tools (e.g., ZeroNet, IPFS, blockchain-based forums) to avoid detection.

✓ New Approaches Needed:

- Developing OSINT tools that can map decentralized sites
- Infiltrating blockchain-based markets
- Using smart contract analysis to track illicit transactions

✅ **Future Strategy**: Expand OSINT methodologies to cover decentralized platforms, which are becoming harder to monitor.

◆ 2.4 Strengthening Private-Public Partnerships in Cybercrime Investigations

Cybersecurity firms, financial institutions, and law enforcement must work more closely to share intelligence on cybercriminals.

✓ Proposed Initiatives:

- Dark web intelligence sharing hubs between public and private sectors
- Real-time collaboration on major cybercrime threats
- Training programs for OSINT analysts and law enforcement on emerging threats

✅ **Future Strategy**: Encourage stronger private-public partnerships to enhance intelligence gathering and enforcement actions.

3. Final Thoughts: Staying Ahead in the Dark Web Arms Race

Dark web investigations are a constant battle of adaptation. As law enforcement and OSINT analysts develop new investigative techniques, cybercriminals refine their methods to evade detection.

◆ **Key Takeaways for the Future:**

✓ Cybercriminal OPSEC mistakes will always be a weak point—exploiting them remains a top strategy.

✓ Cryptocurrency tracking must evolve to counter new privacy-focused coins.

✓ AI and automation will be essential for monitoring dark web activity at scale.

✓ International cooperation and intelligence-sharing are critical for tackling cybercrime effectively.

✓ Law enforcement and OSINT professionals must continuously adapt to new platforms and technologies.

As new threats emerge, staying proactive, innovative, and collaborative will be the key to maintaining the upper hand in dark web investigations.

The Deep and Dark Web remain some of the most misunderstood yet vital areas for cyber investigations. While the surface web is easily accessible, a vast amount of intelligence lies beneath, hidden from conventional search engines. Criminal activities, illicit marketplaces, hacking forums, and confidential leaks often exist in these hidden layers, making them crucial for Open-Source Intelligence (OSINT) investigations.

OSINT for Deep & Dark Web: Techniques for Cybercrime Investigations is your comprehensive guide to navigating these hidden areas of the internet safely and ethically. Whether you're an investigator, law enforcement professional, journalist, or cybersecurity analyst, this book equips you with the tools and methodologies needed to uncover digital threats, track cybercriminals, and investigate cybercrime on the deep and dark web.

What You'll Learn in This Book

- **Understanding the Deep & Dark Web**: Learn the differences between the surface web, deep web, and dark web, and how they impact OSINT investigations.
- **Tor, I2P, and Other Anonymity Networks**: Explore how these networks operate and how investigators can safely access them.
- **Dark Web Marketplaces & Criminal Activities**: Gain insights into illegal trade, data breaches, ransomware operations, and underground forums.
- **Searching the Deep & Dark Web Effectively**: Use specialized tools and search engines like Ahmia, DarkSearch, and Onion.link to uncover hidden information.
- **Tracking Threat Actors & Cybercriminals**: Learn how to monitor hacker groups, cybercriminal forums, and ransomware gangs.
- **Investigating Leaked Data & Breaches**: Discover how to find and analyze leaked credentials, confidential corporate data, and compromised databases.
- **Using Cryptocurrency OSINT**: Trace Bitcoin and other cryptocurrency transactions to follow the money trail in cybercrime investigations.
- **Operational Security (OpSec) for Dark Web Investigations**: Protect your identity and secure your investigations while exploring hidden networks.
- **Legal & Ethical Considerations in Dark Web Investigations**: Understand the boundaries of ethical cyber investigations and how to operate within legal frameworks.

With real-world case studies, practical exercises, and expert methodologies, OSINT for Deep & Dark Web provides you with the knowledge to conduct deep cyber investigations safely and effectively. Whether you're tracking cyber threats, uncovering illegal activities, or analyzing digital intelligence, this book will be an essential tool in your OSINT arsenal.

Thank you for reading **OSINT for Deep & Dark Web: Techniques for Cybercrime Investigations**. The deep and dark web hold vast amounts of intelligence, both for legitimate privacy-focused users and those engaged in illicit activities. Understanding these networks is essential for tracking cyber threats, investigating criminal activities, and uncovering critical intelligence.

We encourage you to use these techniques responsibly and ethically. Investigating the dark web requires caution, awareness, and respect for legal boundaries. As an OSINT investigator, your role is to gather intelligence, protect digital communities, and contribute to a safer internet.

Your curiosity and dedication to learning are what make the OSINT community stronger. If you found this book valuable, we'd love to hear your feedback! Your insights help us refine future editions and create even more in-depth resources.

Stay safe, stay ethical, and keep investigating.

Continue Your OSINT Journey

Expand your skills with the rest of **The OSINT Analyst Series**:

- **OSINT Foundations**: The Beginner's Guide to Open-Source Intelligence
- **The OSINT Search Mastery**: Hacking Search Engines for Intelligence
- **OSINT People Finder**: Advanced Techniques for Online Investigations
- **Social Media OSINT**: Tracking Digital Footprints
- **Image & Geolocation Intelligence**: Reverse Searching and Mapping
- **Domain, Website & Cyber Investigations with OSINT**
- **Email & Dark Web Investigations**: Tracking Leaks & Breaches
- **OSINT Threat Intel**: Investigating Hackers, Breaches, and Cyber Risks
- **Corporate OSINT**: Business Intelligence & Competitive Analysis
- **Investigating Disinformation & Fake News with OSINT**
- **OSINT Automation**: Python & APIs for Intelligence Gathering
- **OSINT Detective**: Digital Tools & Techniques for Criminal Investigations
- **Advanced OSINT Case Studies**: Real-World Investigations
- **The Ethical OSINT Investigator**: Privacy, Legal Risks & Best Practices

We look forward to seeing you in the next book!

Happy investigating!